TREKKING IN THE ALPS

Tiny Lac Flégère may not be as well known as Lac Blanc, but views from its shore are no less impressive (photo: Kev Reynolds)

TREKKING IN THE ALPS

edited by Kev Reynolds

Contributors

Alan Castle, Allan Hartley, Gillian Price,
Hilary Sharp, Kev Reynolds,
Paddy Dillon, Justi Carey and Roy Clark

2 POLICE SQUARE, MILNTHORPE, CUMBRIA LA7 7PY
www.cicerone.co.uk

First edition 2011
ISBN 978 1 85284 600 8

© in the compilation: Kev Reynolds, 2011
© in each chapter remains with the author, 2011
© in the photographs remains with the photographer, 2011
Photographs are by the authors of the chapters in which they appear, unless otherwise credited.

Maps © OpenStreetMap contributors, CC-BY-SA
ASTER GDEM is a product of METI and NASA
Cartography by Lovell Johns www.lovelljohns.com

FFRandonnée 🏃 The routes of the GR®, PR® and GRP® paths in this guide
www.ffrandonnee.fr have been reproduced with the permission of the Fédération
Française de la Randonnée Pédestre holder of the exclusive rights of the routes.
The names GR®, PR® and GRP® are registered trademarks.

© FFRP 2011 for all GR®, PR® and GRP® paths appearing in this work.

Printed by KHL Printing, Singapore
A catalogue record for this book is available from the British Library.

Front cover: Below the Augstbordpass the Dom suddenly reveals itself (Walker's Haute Route) (photo: Kev Reynolds) *Back cover:* The higher slopes of the Cheval Blanc (Tour of Mont Ruan) (photo: Hilary Sharp)

Acknowledgements

Sincere thanks to Jonathan Williams at Cicerone with whom this book was planned at a time when financial institutions across the globe faced meltdown. Recalling joyful days in the Alps, and dreaming more for the future, gave perspective to the daily crises trumpeted from radio, TV and newspapers. How good it is to have a publisher with vision!

I am also indebted to each of my fellow authors who so enthusiastically agreed to take part in this project, and who regularly lifted my spirits by producing such inspiring text and photographs. It's been a real privilege to work with them.

As ever, I wish to record my gratitude to all the team at Cicerone who work wonders in transforming a disc full of words and another of photographs into the attractive volume you hold in your hands. My fellow authors and I have the pleasure of walking the trails and reliving them through our work; the production team in Milnthorpe weaves the magic.

My thanks, then, to everyone involved in *Trekking in the Alps* – and to you for buying a copy. May it inspire you to follow some of these treks and give you as much pleasure as we gained while walking and reliving them.

Kev Reynolds

Map Key

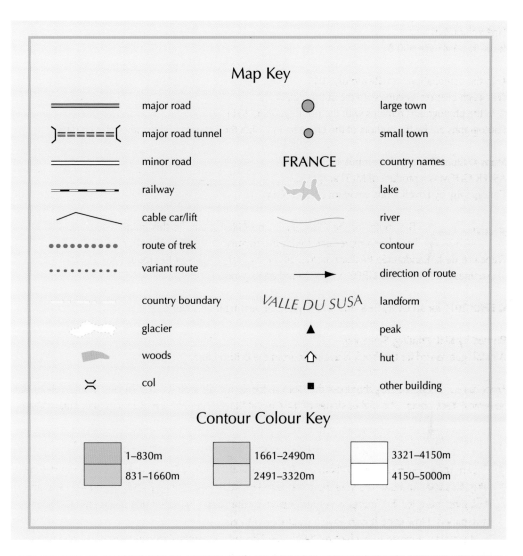

══════	major road	⦿	large town	
)══════(	major road tunnel	○	small town	
════	minor road	FRANCE	country names	
─ ▬ ─ ▬ ─	railway	✈	lake	
╱╲	cable car/lift	～～～	river	
••••••••••	route of trek		contour	
• • • • • •	variant route	⟶	direction of route	
	country boundary	*VALLE DU SUSA*	landform	
	glacier	▲	peak	
	woods	⌂	hut	
⋊	col	▪	other building	

Contour Colour Key

	1–830m		1661–2490m		3321–4150m
	831–1660m		2491–3320m		4150–5000m

Lac Combal in Vallon di Lex Blanche (Trek 5) (photo: Gillian Price)

CONTENTS

The Treks

ABOUT THE AUTHORS

Alan Castle has trekked and travelled in over 50 countries within Europe, Asia, Australasia and North, Central and South America, and for 17 years led organised walking holidays in several European countries. A member of the Outdoor Writers and Photographers Guild, he has written 18 walking guidebooks, several on long-distance mountain routes in France, and one on mountain biking, and has published articles for a number of magazines, particularly for *Strider*, the magazine of the Long Distance Walkers' Association (LDWA). His longest solo walks include a Grand Traverse of the European Alps between Nice and Vienna (2430km), the E2 across Europe from Holland to the Mediterranean (2253km), the Pilgrim's Trail from Le Puy via Santiago de Compostela to Finisterre (1545km) and a Coast to Coast across the French Pyrenees (870km). A mountain walker for over 40 years, he completed the Munros in 2000. Erstwhile National Secretary and Long Distance Information Officer of the LDWA, Alan founded the successful Hillwalkers Register for the LDWA in 1994, and the National Trail Walkers Register in 2009. A keen cyclist and one-time marathon runner, he lives among the hills of the Southern Uplands of Scotland.

Roy Clark and **Justi Carey** started visiting the British mountains in their teens, a discovery which has shaped their whole lives. Rock climbing and walking in North Wales and the Lake District eventually prompted a move to the Scottish Highlands, with its remoter hills and potential for winter climbing. Their passion for the outdoors has led to travels across the world, including Iceland, North America, Jordan and New Zealand, and their continuing interest in being 'out there' has resulted in an enthusiasm for downhill and cross-country skiing, canoeing, cycle-touring, as well as mountaineering. Since moving to Slovenia in 2002, Justi has worked as an English teacher while Roy has developed his skills in and passion for landscape photography, and their exploration of the local mountain environment has resulted in two Cicerone guidebooks, *The Julian Alps of Slovenia* and *Trekking in Slovenia*, with a further work in progress on the Karavanke Mountains, which form the natural border between Slovenia and Austria. See www.rivercottageslovenia.com.

Paddy Dillon is a prolific outdoor writer, with over 40 guidebooks to his name and contributions to 20 more. He is an indefatigable long-distance walker, who has walked all the National Trails in Britain, as well as several European trails, stretching from the sub-tropical Canary Islands and Mediterranean northwards beyond the Arctic Circle. Further afield he has walked in Nepal, Tibet and the Rocky Mountains of Canada and the United States. What he enjoys most in his travels is variety, climbing mountains and following coastlines, crossing semi-deserts and penetrating evergreen 'cloud forests', enjoying the simple pleasures of an easy nature trail as much as a challenging long-distance trail. Paddy aims for a quick turnaround with his guidebooks, partly to present the most up-to-date information to readers, but also because he is always eager to start the next project, wherever it might be. Next destination – everywhere! His website is: www.paddydillon.co.uk

Allan Hartley has been passionate about mountains and photography since his early teens. He has climbed extensively throughout the Alps, discovering Austria by chance in the early 1970s while trying to avoid atrocious weather conditions in the higher mountains of the Western Alps. He maintains that Austria and

the Dolomites of neighbouring Italy remain among mountaineering's best kept secrets, with their heady mix of super scenery and good huts with excellent food, and are better suited to the average mountaineer than the higher mountains to the west. In addition to Austria and the Alps, Allan has climbed from East Africa to the Falkland Islands, the Greater Ranges of Nepal and Pakistan, the lesser known Zagros mountains of Iran, and the Al Hajr mountains of the Arabian Peninsular. Not surprisingly, he is a long-term member of the Austrian Alpine Club, a member of the Outdoor Writers and Photographers Guild, an Associate of the Royal Photographic Society and a holder of the International Mountain Leaders Award. His home is on the edge of the Yorkshire Dales. See www.allanhartley.co.uk

Gillian Price was born in England but moved to Australia when young. After taking a degree in anthropology and working in adult education, she set off to travel through Asia and trek in the Himalaya. The culmination of her journey was Venice where, her enthusiasm fired for mountains, the next logical step was towards the Dolomites, only hours away. Starting there, Gillian is steadily exploring the mountain ranges and flatter bits of Italy and bringing them to life for visitors in a series of outstanding guides for Cicerone. When not out walking and taking photos with Nicola, her Venetian cartographer husband, Gillian works as a freelance journalist and translator. An adamant promoter of public transport to minimise impact in Alpine areas, she is an active member of the CAI (the Italian Alpine Club) and the Outdoor Writers and Photographers Guild. See www.gillianprice.eu

Kev Reynolds, the contributing editor for this book, first visited the Alps in the 1960s and has returned almost every year since to walk, trek or climb. He has produced brochures and other publicity material for various tourist authorities of Alpine countries, and for many years organised and led walking holidays there, as well as in other European mountain regions and the Himalaya. A member of the Alpine Club, Austrian Alpine Club and the Outdoor Writers and Photographers Guild, Kev has written more than a dozen guides to different Alpine regions and individual treks, including *Tour of the Vanoise, Tour of the Oisans, Tour of Mont Blanc, Tour of the Jungfrau Region, Alpine Pass Route* and *Chamonix to Zermatt: the Walker's Haute Route*, all of which are published by Cicerone Press. He is also author of the authoritative *Walking in the Alps* which covers the whole range. Check him out on www.kevreynolds.co.uk

Hilary Sharp is British, a qualified Accompagnateur en Montagne (International Trekking Guide) based permanently in the village of Vallorcine, near Chamonix Mont Blanc in the French Alps where she runs her own trekking business, Trekking in the Alps, offering guided walks and hiker's summits in winter (where she specialises in snowshoeing), and in spring and summer. Her love of walking and climbing has taken her to many parts of Europe and further afield. Hilary has been a contributor to several British walking magazines, and is the author of *Trekking in the Western Alps* (published by New Holland in 2002), and *Snowshoeing: Mont Blanc and the Western Alps, Tour of Monte Rosa, Tour of the Matterhorn*, and *Mont Blanc Walks* – all published by Cicerone Press. For Hilary's guided summer hikes and winter snowshoeing in the Alps, Corsica, Dolomites and beyond, go to: Trekking in the Alps, info@trekkinginthealps.com, www.trekkinginthealps.com

Locations of the treks

GERMANY

SWITZERLAND

LIECHTENSTEIN

15

Schesaplan ▲

10

▲ Tödi

14

▲ Piz Bu

BERN ●

11 GRINDELWALD ●

Jungfrau

▲ Cristallina

ST MORITZ ●

Or

GENEVA ●

7

8

9

13

ZERMATT ●

Matterhorn

Piz Bernina ▲

CHAMONIX

12

●

Ad.

LYON ●

6

Mont Blanc ▲

FRANCE

AOSTA ●

4

Grande Casse ▲

5

Gran Paradiso ▲

GRENOBLE ●

MILAN ●

3

Pelvoux ▲

TURIN ●

2

▲ Monviso

▲ Argentera

1

NICE ●

MEDITERRANEAN SEA

N

0   100km

MÜNICH

VIENNA

AUSTRIA

SALZBURG

▲ Watzmann

Ellmauer Halt

▲ Dachstein

INNSBRUCK

Zuckerhütl Dreiherrenspitze

▲ [17] ▲ Grossglockner

Hochfeiler

itze

[19]

BOLZANO Marmolada [18]

▲

ENTO

[20] Triglav

▲

LJUBLJANA

SLOVENIA

ITALY

TRIESTE

VENICE ADRIATIC
         SEA

1	Grande Traversata delle Alpi: GTA	11	Tour of the Jungfrau Region
2	Tour of the Queyras	12	Tour of the Matterhorn
3	Tour of the Oisans	13	Tour of Monte Rosa
4	Tour of the Vanoise	14	Tour of the Rätikon
5	Gran Paradiso Alta Via 2	15	Across the Eastern Alps: E5
6	Tour of Mont Blanc	16	Stubai High-Level Route
7	GR5: Through the French Alps	17	Zillertal High-Level Route
8	Tour of Mont Ruan	18	Dolomites Alta Via 1
9	The Walker's Haute Route	19	Dolomites Alta Via 2
10	Alpine Pass Route	20	Julian Alps Traverse

OVERVIEW OF ROUTES

TREKKING GRADES

Each of the treks has been rated according to difficulty within the following guidelines:

- moderate: 6–12 days of trekking, with some reasonably demanding ascents/descents, but on mostly good paths.
- strenuous: 7–14 days with some high or steep passes to cross – could involve exposed sections.
- demanding: 10+ days with a succession of high or steep passes, occasional difficult and exposed terrain and/or glacier crossing.

Where a trek's classification falls between these categories either a + sign is given to indicate a higher level of difficulty, or two grades have been amalgamated. The table below lists all 20 treks showing their total distances, ascents, average daily ascents and estimated completion times.

Trek	Distance	Duration	Total Ascent	Average Daily Ascent	Grade
Tour of the Rätikon	56km	6 days	3000m	500m	Moderate
Tour of the Vanoise	154km	10–12 days	7500m	650m	Moderate
Tour of the Queyras	186km	12 days	14,000m	1150m	Moderate
Tour of the Jungfrau Region	111–135km	9–11 days	6500m	650m	Moderate +
Eastern Alps E5	495km	29 days	21,000m	750m	Moderate +
Dolomites AV1	120km	11 days	7000m	650m	Moderate/Strenuous
Stubai High-Level Route	80km	9–10 days	10,000m	1000m	Strenuous
Tour of Mont Blanc	168km	10–12 days	10,500m	900m	Strenuous
Grande Traversata delle Alpi	633km	47 days	44,000m	950m	Strenuous
Zillertal High-Level Route	70km	9–10 days	6500m	650m	Strenuous +
Tour of Mont Ruan	67km	5–6 days	4000m	700m	Strenuous/Demanding
Gran Paradiso AV2	143km	12 days	9500m	800m	Strenuous/Demanding
Tour of Monte Rosa	134km	8–10 days	9500m	950m	Demanding
Tour of the Matterhorn	145km	8–10 days	10,000m	1000m	Demanding
Tour of the Oisans	176km	10–12 days	12,000m	1000m	Demanding
Dolomites AV2	150km	13 days	12,000m	950m	Demanding
Julian Alps Traverse	122km	14–15 days	10,000m	700m	Demanding
Walker's Haute Route	180+km	12–14 days	12,000m	900m	Demanding
Alpine Pass Route	326km	15+ days	18,000m	1200m	Demanding
GR5: Through the French Alps	645–725km	30+ days	34,000m	1150m	Demanding

At Pian dei Cantoni (Dolomites Alta Via 2) (photo: Gillian Price)

Torrents cascade down the hillside below Refuge des Bans (Tour of the Oisans) (photo: Kev Reynolds)

INTRODUCTION

The breathtaking sight of Mont Blanc on the final stage of the Gran Paradiso Alta Via (photo: Gillian Price)

Trekking in the Alps is immensely satisfying. The physical challenge is part of it, but so too is the sense of achievement on gaining a lofty pass that may have taken several hours to reach. Then there are the views, the ever-changing panoramas, the distant horizon of peaks and ridges that lure you on day after day. Not just mountains, but all the essential features that build a mountain landscape – individual rocks, boulders and screes, the glaciers and snowfields and torrents of snowmelt. There are lakes and waterfalls, meadows full of flowers; marmots that fill the silences with their shrill calls, chamois roaming the high places, ibex too, and the noisy choughs that haunt passes and summits alike.

They may be the world's best-known, most comprehensively mapped, catalogued and photographed mountains of all, but the Alps still have the power to excite and surprise with every visit.

Although trekking may seem a fairly modern concept, in truth it's centuries old, for in 1767 the Genevese scientist Horace Bénédict de Saussure made the first of three circular tours of Mont Blanc; in 1837 James David Forbes from Edinburgh wandered across the Dolomites, and two years later made a complete circuit of Monte Viso and followed in Saussure's footsteps around Mont Blanc. Both were men of science, but a good part of the inspiration for their travels was not just scientific enquiry, but a love of mountains and the joy of wandering among them. 'The scenery is stupendous,' wrote Forbes in his account of the mountains of Dauphiné.

When our Victorian forefathers were lay-
ing the foundations of mountaineering, they
were divided into two types: 'centrists', who
based themselves in Chamonix, Zermatt or
Grindelwald, for example, and set out to climb
neighbouring peaks, returning after each ascent to
the comfort of their valley hotel; and 'ex-centrists'
– men like Edward Whymper (who made the first
ascent of the Matterhorn), AW Moore, John Ball
and Francis Fox Tuckett – who strode across the
Alps from region to region, crossing peaks, passes
and glaciers with astonishing vigour. Whymper's
restless energy is seldom mentioned, but his classic *Scrambles Amongst the Alps* is far more than
an account of winning summits, for it describes
the travails and triumphs of finding a way from
one district to the next, from which we discover
that in order to get from Briançon to Grenoble in
1860 it was necessary to 'set out at 2pm … for
a seventy-five mile walk', which he achieved in
a day and a half. As for Tuckett, between 1856
and 1874 he crossed no less than 376 passes and
climbed 165 peaks. And all this before a chain of
mountain huts provided accommodation, and the
few hotels or inns that did exist outside the main
centres offered little comfort.

Sometimes these Alpine pioneers sought refuge in the home of a local priest, but the accommodation on offer was not always what they
might have hoped for, as Alfred Wills discovered
when he arrived in Valtournanche in the summer
of 1852. 'In each of the side rooms,' he explained,
'were a bed, a chair, a table made of an unshaped
block of wood on three legs, and a pie dish. The
floors were so thick with dirt, that your boots left
foot-marks as you walked across the room; and
everything you touched soiled your hands. We
could get scarcely anything to eat – a serious evil
after eleven hours' walk … and we went to bed
hungry and tired.'

Simple alp chalets provided an alternative.
Used by dairymen during the summer months,
an overnight could sometimes be found in remote
locations. On their way to attempt a crossing of

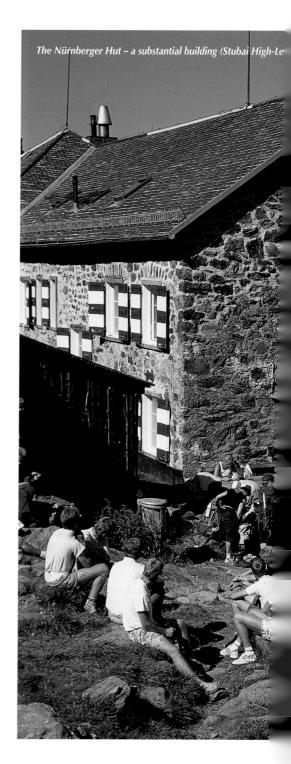
The Nürnberger Hut – a substantial building (Stubai High-Le

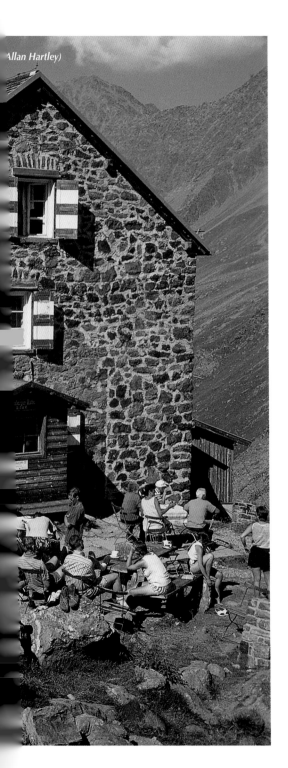

Allan Hartley)

the Moming Pass in 1864, Whymper and Moore took advantage of a cheesemaker's hut in the magnificent Ar Pitetta cirque above Zinal. 'It was a hovel,' wrote Whymper in Scrambles, 'growing, as it were, out of the hillside; roofed with rough slabs of slaty stone; without a door or window; surrounded by quagmires of ordure, and dirt of every description.'

It is no surprise then, that early Baedeker guides warned against sleeping in chalets unless absolutely necessary: 'Whatever poetry there may be theoretically in a "fragrant bed of hay", the cold night air piercing abundant apertures, the ringing of the cow bells, the grunting of the pigs, and the undiscarded garments, hardly conduce to refreshing slumber.'

Being eminently 'clubbable' men, the Victorians got together to found the Alpine Club in 1857. Following their lead, the Austrian Alpine Club was formed in 1862, and a year later the Swiss, whose members built their first mountain hut on the Tödi in order to shorten the time needed to make an ascent of the peak. In 1868 another was erected on the Matterhorn, partly financed by Alexander Seiler of Zermatt. In its first 25 years the Swiss Alpine Club built almost 40 such huts, and by 1890 the French Alpine Club had 33 of their own. Meanwhile, the Austrian, German and Italian clubs were also busy providing overnight shelters for the growing number of visitors to their mountains.

The majority of these huts were small and spartan and, in some instances consisted of little more than a cave with a door. Others could be described as wooden sheds whose roofs were held in place with rocks, although some were soundly constructed of timber and stone and contained a stove, an axe and a supply of firewood. A few blankets or sheepskins might be provided, plus a saucepan or two, but little more.

But in the century or so since then, there has been a marked improvement in standards of accommodation throughout the Alpine chain. In Austria and the Italian Dolomites many of these

1   *Large-flowered leopardsbane grows among
    rocks and meadows (photo: Kev Reynolds)*
2   *Young ibex shedding its coat (photo: Hilary
    Sharp)*
3   *Houseleeks spread their rosettes among the
    rocks (photo: Hilary Sharp)*
4   *The willow gentian is a showy flower, often
    found in great clumps (photo: Kev Reynolds)*
5   *In summer the marmot is seen in almost every
    district of the Alps (photo: Hilary Sharp)*

huts are now inn-like buildings capable of sleeping a hundred visitors each night. Most have large
communal dormitories, although it's not unusual
to find smaller two- or four-bedded rooms available. The majority are staffed in summer, meals and
drinks are available, hot showers and drying rooms
are not uncommon, and fresh provisions are often
helicoptered in several times during the season.

While huts have been built in just about every Alpine district, there are also *gîtes d'étape*, *gasthofs* and rustic mountain inns scattered among the valleys and hillsides, often in the most idyllic of locations. Austria, for one, has numerous charming gasthofs in its valleys, but boasts more than 1000 actual *hütten*, about half of which have been built by members of the Austrian or German Alpine Clubs; the rest are privately owned but open to all. The Swiss have in excess of 300, while the French, Italian and Slovenian Alpine Clubs have plenty more. Given sufficient time, energy and money, it would be possible to trek virtually from one end of the Alps to the other staying in a different mountain hut each night, unencumbered by a heavy pack and carrying just the basic essentials.

But since few of us are able to commit ourselves to such an epic dream journey, numerous hut-to-hut tours of varying length have been developed that are immensely satisfying to contemplate and complete. Enticing the trekker along trails and crossing passes they reveal the Alps' rich diversity, providing challenge and reward in equal measure, and as the huts themselves are invariably built in spectacular locations, night-times can be as memorable as the days.

So whether you have a week to spare, a two-week holiday to fill, or a whole summer free to wander, this book describes some of the very best treks in Europe's premier mountain range. But newcomers beware: trekking is addictive.

ABOUT THIS BOOK

The 20 treks described are listed in a clockwise arc, starting at the southwestern end of the Alpine chain where the GTA (Grande Traversata delle

Rifugio Cinque Torri dwarfed by a rock tower (Dolomites Alta Via 1) (photo: Gillian Price)

Cabane d'Ar Pitetta, not far from the 'hovel' in which Whymper spent a night in 1864

Alpi) begins in the Ligurian Alps just 40km from the Mediterranean, and working north and north-east to end with a traverse of the beautiful Julian Alps of Slovenia.

All the well-known classics are included, such as the Tour of Mont Blanc, the Walker's Haute Route from Chamonix to Zermatt, and the terrific Stubai High-Level Route in Austria. But you will find a number of little-known treks too; treks like the Tour of Mont Ruan, Tour of the Queyras and Tour of the Vanoise. Apart from the GTA already mentioned, Italy is well represented, with routes in the Gran Paradiso and two in the bewitching Dolomites, and Gillian Price also offers a description of the 495km European route, the E5 across the Eastern Alps from Lake Constance on the German–Austrian–Swiss border to Verona in Italy. If it's ultra-long treks that appeal, Paddy Dillon entices with the GR5 from Lac Léman to Nice (725km), while at the other end of the scale we have a six-day tour of the Rätikon mountains, straying from Switzerland into Austria and back again.

The Tours of the Matterhorn and of Monte Rosa are also cross-border treks that give cultural as well as scenic variety, while Allan Hartley concentrates on Austrian treks, including the Zillertal circuit. Switzerland is crossed from east to west by the Alpine Pass Route, the famous Bernese Oberland is explored on the Tour of the Jungfrau Region, and in addition to several other great treks, France rewards in the Écrins with the challenging Tour of the Oisans.

While this book is intended to be an introduction to some of the most exciting and rewarding of multi-day treks, it would be impractical to include precise route descriptions for each one. Details of available guidebooks, along with a summary of basic route information, map and profile, are given alongside a broad overview of the trek intended to whet your appetite. These guidebooks provide travel details, map information, the location of huts and their facilities and, of course, all the in-depth route descriptions necessary to make your trek a success.

HUT CONVENTIONS

- To book a place in a mountain hut, telephone in advance. Numbers are usually listed in the individual guidebooks; otherwise check with the nearest tourist office. Hut wardens will often telephone ahead for you.
- On arrival leave your boots and trekking poles in the boot room or porch, and select a pair of hut shoes or clogs usually provided for indoor wear.
- Locate the warden to announce your arrival, and book whatever meals are required.
- Once a room has been allocated, make your bed using a sheet sleeping bag (sleeping bag liner) carried for the occasion. Have a torch handy, as the room may not be lit when you need to go there after dark.
- Snacks and drinks are usually available during the day, but meals are served at set times. Food for lunch is often available to carry away.
- It is customary to pay for all services (in cash only) the night before departure. Note that reductions (up to 50%) on overnight fees are given to members of other European Alpine Clubs, and to BMC members who have purchased a reciprocal rights card (www.thebmc.co.uk). Consider joining the UK branch of the Austrian Alpine Club (www.aacuk.org.uk) before making a hut-to-hut tour; as well as discounted overnight fees, membership benefits include free mountain rescue insurance.

ADVICE FOR TREKKERS

As this book clearly illustrates, the European Alps are not the sole preserve of the experienced mountain climber. Those who regularly walk the trails and sometimes pathless terrain of the English Lake District or Scottish Highlands should find that trekking in the Alps is well within their capabilities. But should you be nervous about making your first trek,

1   *Old-style hut accommodation*
2   *Dormitory in a traditional mountain hut, where duvets have replaced heavy blankets*
3   *Hut shoes – photos don't impart the odour!*
4   *Breakfast in a remote gasthof*
(Photos 1 and 3: Hilary Sharp; photos 2 and 4: Kev Reynolds)

consider booking with an adventure travel company, a number of whom advertise group holidays along some of the routes described here. Several of the authors who have contributed chapters to this book have guided treks in the past, and one of them, Hilary Sharp, has her own company with the same name as this book, based in Vallorcine near Chamonix (www.trekkinginthealps.com).

Trekking implies walking day after day, so you need to be fit from the outset. Don't wait until you arrive in the Alps before you think about it – take regular exercise to prepare for those times when the trail climbs remorselessly for hundreds of metres to gain a distant pass. Although technical mountaineering skills are not required to achieve any of these routes (apart from glacier crossing on two of the treks), almost all routes will have stages where the trail is narrow or exposed, or perhaps safeguarded with a length of cable or chain; in some places a section of steel ladder or a few metal rungs may have been bolted to a rockface as an aid. Great care should be exercised when using these – it certainly helps if you have a 'head for heights'.

1   *Alta Via 2 has clear, distinct waymarking (photo: Gillian Price)*
2   *Encouraging signs at a trail junction near Obersteinberg (Trek 11) (photo: Kev Reynolds)*
3   *Waymarks painted on rocks, trees and the sides of buildings ensure you stay on route (photo: Kev Reynolds)*

The vast majority of trails are clearly defined, well maintained and signed at major junctions. Waymarks are usually adequate on most routes, with lines of cairns directing the way where the terrain is such that no footpath could be made. But you should always remain alert, for even the most undemanding of paths can become hazardous when transformed by rain, snowmelt or a glaze of ice, and every trek will at some time cross rough and remote country where even a minor accident could have serious consequences.

Before setting out each morning, study the guidebook's description of that day's trek and make a mental note of any potential hazards, changes of direction or landmarks that need to be watched for. Keep the map handy and make sure you can identify your correct position at any time; should visibility become impaired by mist, your chance of becoming lost is greatly reduced. Unless the weather is threatening, or you're running short of time, allow yourself a few minutes every hour or so to sit on a rock and contemplate the peace and natural beauty that are among the souvenirs you will take home with you. You'll not regret it.

The frequency of accommodation and provision of meals makes backpacking unnecessary. A light daypack is all that's required to contain the essentials for a two-week walking tour, but ensure it has a waterproof cover, and take a large polythene bag in which to pack your gear.

- Comfortable, lightweight boots are of prime importance.
- Make sure the socks you choose meet your needs, and change them daily to avoid discomfort or blisters.
- Waterproofs are essential; not only for rain protection, but also to double as windproofs. Lightweight jacket and overtrousers made from 'breathable' fabric are recommended, as is a small collapsible umbrella (indispensable for those who wear glasses).
- A fleece or pile jacket ought to be included, plus a warm hat and gloves – for even in midsummer wintry conditions may be experienced.
- Sunglasses, a brimmed hat and high-factor suncream should be carried – the intensity of UV rays increases by ten per cent with every 1000m of altitude gained.
- Carry a first aid kit, water bottle (1 litre minimum capacity), map, guidebook, whistle, compass (or GPS) and a headtorch with a spare bulb. Also a small penknife and emergency food.
- Take a lightweight towel and basic personal toiletries (plus toilet paper and a lighter to burn it in case of being caught short during the day), and a sheet sleeping bag for use in huts and gîtes.
- Telescopic trekking poles give assistance when crossing streams, help maintain balance over rough ground, and ease the strain on legs during steep descents.

Other items you may consider taking include a camera (essential to some), an altimeter and a mobile phone and charger – but note that it may not always be possible to get a signal, and you may have difficulty recharging it.

WHEN TO GO

As a general rule the midsummer months of late June to mid-September offer the best and safest opportunities for trekking in the Alps, although in some years snow remains on the highest passes well into July. Of course, there are occasions when snow falls even in July or August, so be prepared for the worst but hope for the best. Typical summer conditions enable you to walk in T-shirt, shorts and sunhat, but long periods of mist, rain or storm should never be discounted. At altitude even a mild breeze can lower the temperature by several degrees. The moral is clear – keep warm, weather-proof clothing handy.

Depending on altitude, wild flowers are at their best from June until late July, and huts are usually staffed from mid-June until late September, with the busiest period running from mid-July until late August.

SAFETY IN THE MOUNTAINS

Trekking should be a safe and healthy pursuit, but all mountain regions contain a variety of objective dangers for the unwary. Without overstating the risk factor, it should be borne in mind that with narrow and exposed paths, stream crossings, high passes, and steep ascents and descents to negotiate, a high degree of

SAFETY DOS AND DON'TS

- Ensure you are both physically and mentally prepared for the challenge of your chosen route.
- Plan each stage carefully; study the route outline, the amount of height gain and loss, and the estimated time it will take to reach your destination.
- Phone ahead to book your next night's accommodation.
- Check the weather forecast before setting out.
- Carry liquid refreshment, a few emergency rations and a first aid kit.
- Watch for signs of deteriorating weather, and never be too proud to turn back should it be safer to do so than continue in the face of an oncoming storm, or on a trail that has become unjustifiably dangerous.
- If your plans change and you decide against continuing to the hut where you've booked accommodation, telephone at the earliest opportunity to inform them.
- Do not venture onto exposed ridges if a storm is imminent. In the event of being caught by one, avoid isolated trees, prominent rocks or metallic objects (temporarily discard trekking poles), and refrain from taking shelter in caves, beneath overhanging rocks or in gullies. Instead, kneel or squat on your rucksack with head down and hands on knees.
- In the unhappy event of an accident, stay calm. Move yourself and, if possible, the injured person (taking care not to aggravate the injury) away from any imminent danger and apply first aid. Keep the victim warm, using any spare clothing available. Make a written note of the precise location where the victim can be found, and either telephone for assistance using a mobile phone (emergency numbers are given in the individual guidebooks), or if you cannot get a signal, send for help. If a mountain hut is nearby seek assistance there. Failing this, give the international mountain distress signal: six blasts on a whistle (and flashes with a torch after dark) spaced evenly for one minute, followed by a minute's pause. Repeat for as long as is necessary. The response is three signals per minute followed by a minute's pause.

concentration will be called for, even under good conditions. A moment's carelessness could have serious repercussions.

Remember: although mountain rescue in the Alps is highly efficient, it is not a free service. The cost of rescue and subsequent hospital treatment can be extremely high; it is therefore essential to be adequately insured. Specialist companies offering insurance for trekking in the Alps include the BMC (www.thebmc.co.uk) – members only – and Snowcard Insurance Services (www.snowcard.co.uk). As mentioned earlier, membership of the Austrian Alpine Club (UK branch) gives automatic mountain rescue cover.

WORDS OF GREETING

Trekking in the Alps is a sociable activity. Whether you trek alone, with friends or with a group, you'll find that meeting or passing others on the trail will inevitably inspire a word or two of greeting – a recognition of shared experience. So, what do you say in response? It depends where you are:

France	bonjour
Italy	buon giorno
Switzerland	grüetzi
Austria & Germany	grüss Gott
Slovenia	dober dan

The unmistakable Matterhorn (Tour of the Matterhorn) (photo: Hilary Sharp)

Trek 1

Grande Traversata delle Alpi: GTA

by Gillian Price

For many who go trekking in the mountains, the Italian Alps mean the Gran Paradiso, the Pennines crowned by Monte Rosa, or perhaps the exotic Dolomites. But there's so much more than these justifiably popular districts, and on the GTA the Ligurian, Maritime and Cottian Alps will surprise and reward with scenes as unforgettable as those further north. This epic trek climbs and descends around 44,000 metres on its way from the Mediterranean to Monte Rosa, which gives a clue to the nature of the journey. Day after day arduous passes have to be crossed that reveal horizons of rugged rock and gleaming snowscapes and, in the opening stages, more than a hint of the sea. Marguareis, Monte Gelàs, Argentera, Monviso, Rocciamelone – each one becomes a milestone on the way north. Then there's the Gran Paradiso at last, and Mont Blanc, the Matterhorn and Monte Rosa to underscore the route's pedigree.

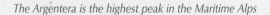

The Argentera is the highest peak in the Maritime Alps

Route summary

Location	Western Alps, Piemonte, Italy
Start	Viozene near Ormea
Finish	Molini di Calasca in Val Anzasca near Monte Rosa
Distance	633km
Duration	47 days
Maximum altitude	2804m
Accommodation	Walkers' hostels, village guesthouses and mountain huts
Grade	Strenuous
Guidebook	*Through the Italian Alps: GTA* by Gillian Price (Cicerone Press, 2005)

This route had been hovering at the back of my mind for a long time. It just wouldn't go away. I'd read in an Italian Alpine Club magazine about a long-distance trail in Piemonte stretching over the arc of valleys and mountains that lay beyond the grand regional capital of Torino. But it was a hint from my publisher, Cicerone Press, that prompted me to set out. I found the idea of travelling across the Alps on foot hugely attractive, and spent hours poring over large-scale maps tracing the route and dreaming of the panoramas that my eyes would be treated to. The Grande Traversata delle Alpi – what an inspiring title! The distance was not to be underrated: a mere 200km as the crow flies but a huge 633km on the ground, in terms of paths and actual walking, accounting for a mind-boggling third (yes, a third!) of the immense Alpine curve.

It was a terribly exciting prospect that would take me across the Western Alps on the very far side of Italy from my home in Venice. It also meant navigating across five of Italy's Alpine regions – the Ligurian, Maritime, Cottian, Graian and Pennine Alps

Lovely Piano di Valasco in the Maritime Alps

– past a procession of legendary stone giants from the Argentera, Monviso (Monte Viso) and Gran Paradiso, before the final crowning queen Monte Rosa. Brand new Alpine landscapes were to be revealed, along with captivating tales of the life of men and animals on the mountain slopes.

The first year I managed to slip in a quick trip late September when the huts were beginning to shutter up as the season drew to an end. Contacts in the regional capital Cuneo suggested that I'd find comforting similarities with my beloved Dolomites in the limestone landscapes of the Ligurian Alps. This definitely proved true, but they omitted to warn me of the marvels of the adjoining Maritimes that took my breath away. That winter I found myself counting the months until I could go back, and the following summer ranks as one of the most memorable in the whole of my Alpine life as I wandered on for 36 blissful days, only a single short interruption due to inclement weather – zero visibility caused by dense fog and blinding rain.

All I needed was on my back in my rucksack, and by

my side in the shape of my companions, whose importance I never underrated. A motley crew of friends swept up by my enthusiasm joined me on holiday windows of opportunity, meeting up at strategic railway stations and bus stops along the way. I dubbed them my 'shift walkers'.

The GTA became something of a cheese trail for me. Piemonte is a prime producer for Italy, much credit going to the tiny mountain communities that cling on, specialising in unique flavours. The fact is that each valley has different conditions, exposure of pasture slopes, variety of fodder, and individual time-tested techniques for concocting cheeses from cow, sheep and goat milk. For storage, rudimentary sheds half-excavated, half-built into the mountainside are lined with shelves of rounds laid down for ageing. In the Gran Paradiso area I even discovered dwarf fridges – tiny stone cabinets set over running streams which keep the temperature at a constant low. Who needs electricity! When farms close up at the end of summer and herds and herders return to the valley, the treasure is packed in straw and loaded onto horseback, but not before gourmet walkers have appreciated the likes of Brüs and Maccagno.

The Ligurian Alps:
from Viozene to Limonetto
Low profile yet splendid, the Ligurian Alps host the opening section of the trek. Modest limestone reliefs that launch the eastward sweep of the mighty Alpine arc, they lie a mere 40km from the Mediterranean; not surprising then that hints of the sea can be perceived, first and foremost in the vegetation with aromatic herbs and even lavender and broom that drench the air with their perfume.

From the tiny hamlet of **Viozene**, which comes to life in summer, an easy path transits at the foot of splendid Mongioie. By way of Passo delle Saline, a reminder of the long-gone salt trade, it touches on friendly Rifugio Mondovì, where the risk of being waylaid by a mouth-watering lunch is elevated. But it is crucial to push on to see 2651m Marguareis, the highest mountain in the Ligurian Alps. Here

beautiful sweeps of limestone landscape include tell-tale signs of karstification – sink holes, dolina basins and extensive underground caves. An old paved military track winds unhurriedly upwards to the exhilarating grassy ridge separating France and Italy, where a remarkable string of six monumental forts from the late 1800s still stand guard. Showcase Fort Central overlooks Colle di Tenda, where views now embrace the Maritime Alps, pale and very promising.

The Maritime Alps:
from Limonetto to Pontebernardo
A morning's walk from Limonetto, Passo Ciotto Mieu acts as the gateway to the wonderful Maritimes. A short detour is rewarded with a brilliant lookout over the vast Po plain to the unmistakable pyramid of Monviso, succeeded by glittering

Tiny lakes at Colle di Fenestrelle

Grande traversata delle alpi: GTA

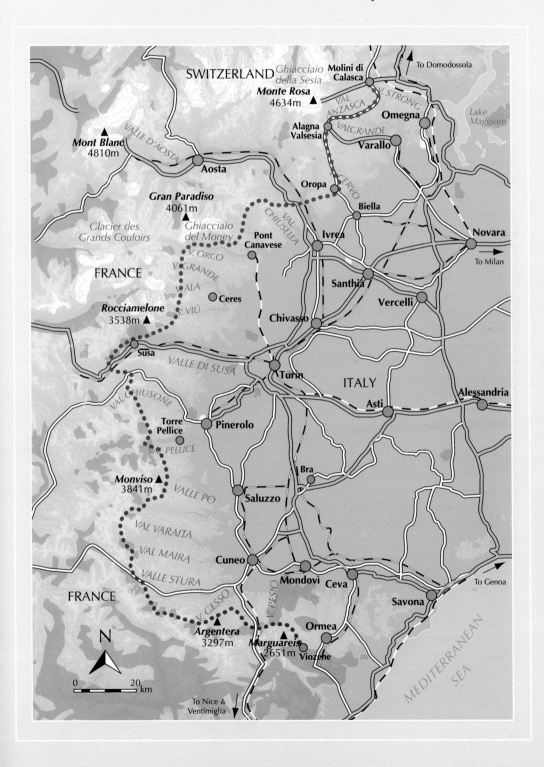

if distant glaciated Monte Rosa, where the GTA will come to its grandiose finale many weeks on.

Down Vallone degli Alberghi with its pretty tarns, the steep path passes through beautiful beech wood, glorious colours highlighted by filtered sunlight. The day comes to a satisfying if tiring end at the peaceful hamlet of **Palanfré**, home to an excellent dairy and walker's hostel.

Grassy slopes precede broad-ridged Costa di Planard. It's hard to know which way to look here. In late summer the best direction is up for the airborne procession of birds of prey migrating south – golden eagles, black kites and sparrowhawks. Volunteers spend days on end monitoring their progress and keeping a tally of numbers and species. The birds' flight takes them over the wild heart of the Maritimes, a multitude of sharp, toothy grey-green points. What a sight!

Over in wooded Valle Gesso a steep track emerges at the foot of neck-cricking 3142m Monte Gelàs, dubbed the 'Mont Blanc of the Maritimes'. Here Rifugio Soria-Ellena at 1840m is a good place to overnight and fraternise with the French *randonneurs* who come via Col di Fenestre, a pass that has seen centuries of pilgrims, traders and even hapless refugees in 1943 fleeing occupied France.

A crazily zigzagging path concludes at 2463m **Colle di Fenestrelle** and an unworldly corridor where ibex hang out on vertical perches, keeping a watchful eye on the two-legged intruders. Just a few steps on comes the breathtaking vision of the Argentera, the queen of the Maritimes, and what a beauty! A huge clump of interlinked mountains rather than a single peak, reminiscent of an awesome impenetrable fortress. A roller-coaster route across rock-strewn slopes in the company of chamois and vast spreads of wild flowers leads along its northern flanks and Canale di Lourousa, a vertiginous ice-bound gully. A tiny red bivouac hut can be spotted up there, essential shelter for climbers.

The contrast with the day's destination couldn't be more striking; nestled in beechwood hundreds of metres below in Vallone Gesso della Valletta is the old-style spa resort of **Terme di Valdieri** (1368m), all the rage in the 1800s thanks to scorching hot mineral springs used for therapeutic purposes. The ageing Grand Hotel and Swiss-style chalets offer a hint of erstwhile charm and elegance. At the time this beautiful valley was at the heart of a game reserve owned by Italy's royal family, and paved tracks designed for horse-ridden parties still venture high onto Piano di Valasco, popular these days with picnicking Italian families taking a day out from the summer heat on the plains. Streams cascade through the pasture basin carpeted with a riot of wild flowers and crowned by a majestic line-up of soaring grey

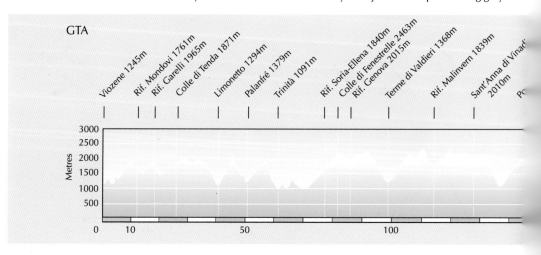

jagged ridges. Past a hunting pavilion converted into a refuge, the path gains height beneath Testa di Claus. A highly recommended detour branches off to Rifugio Questa, a spartan hut with an outdoor loo that doubles as a superb belvedere.

An intact section of hunting track leads via pretty tarns on a section to be savoured slowly for its beauty. Further ahead comes Vallone di Riofreddo, a clearly recognisable U-shape created by an ancient glacier. Soaring at its head is superb Testa di Malinvern, which can be admired at length thanks to the modern refuge on the valley floor.

The following stage visits the historic sanctuary of **Sant'Anna di Vinadio**, the highest of its kind in the whole of the Alps. It has provided a roof and victuals to pilgrims and travellers since the Middle Ages, and modern-day visitors can enjoy comfortable lodgings. The tiny porticoed

Laghi della Valletta en route to Passo di Orgials

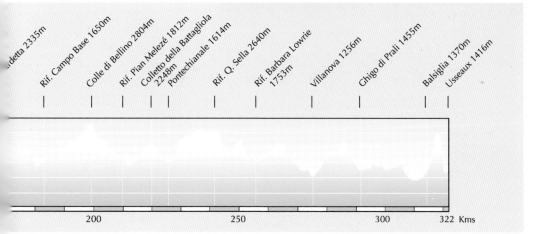

church is a masterpiece of popular art, its walls plastered with *ex voto* plaques to thank the Virgin Mary's mother for her mercy. Further down, Vinadio and its hot baths are touched on as the GTA transits via the traffic artery of Valle Stura.

The Cottian Alps:
from Pontebernardo to Susa

The incontestable star and a highlight of the Cottian Alps is the Monviso. The GTA's approach to the stone giant takes place over a full four stages, with an excited build-up of anticipation. In the meantime there are stunning locations to be enjoyed. A 1300m uphill slog on old military tracks leads into the beautiful high-altitude plateau, Piano della Gardetta, and a lively refuge. Here the focus is the elegant soaring form of Rocca La Meja, its unusual pale aspect due to the dolomite rock that is its main constituent.

More treats are in store with the crossing of upper Val Maira in the company of twin quartzite needles Rocca Provenzale and Castello, the antics of acrobatic climbers providing a good excuse for a rest stop. Splendid waterfalls form the backdrop for concentrations of divine blue mountain cornflowers that stain the grass, while the scent from pinks is all-pervading. All the while the path

The village of Chiappera with Rocca Provenzale

ascends unremittingly to the isolated 2804m pass of **Colle di Bellino**.

Below is Valle Varaita di Bellino, a wonderland of slate-roofed houses with overhanging

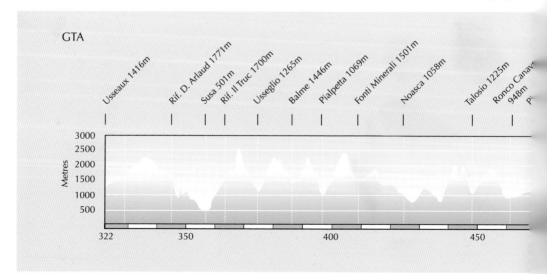

eaves sustained by graceful round stone columns. It would be a great shame to rush through here and miss a stroll through the quiet atmospheric villages; time seems to have passed them by, and

the traditional farming lifestyle persists. Artistic sundials grace the walls as do wise sayings, many in the curious medieval language of the Occitan population, which has strong links to faraway Provence. Passers-by are reminded that *Lou soulei nais per tuchi*, 'the sun rises for everyone'.

On the neighbouring ridge is 2248m **Colletto della Battagliola**, a breathtaking lookout to the Monviso, which entirely fills your field of vision with its massive pyramidal bulk. An inspiring sight. Now two very special full days can be looked forward to, with an exhilarating climb to rugged heights where desolation reigns amidst clutters of tarns and snow patches. It's quite a haul to where the vertiginous southeastern face of the Monviso rises a jaw-dropping 1200m from its base to peak at 3841m. And what better place to drink in this magnificence than at **Rifugio Quintino Sella**, a landmark Italian mountain hut named in honour of one of the founders of the Italian Alpine Club in 1863.

Several valleys on, as the path emerges from the cover of wood, walkers are treated to the extraordinary sight of the 18th-century fortress of Fenestrelle crawling up the flanks of Val Chisone opposite, with a 3km wall that rises an incredible 600m in height. A full day is needed to explore this

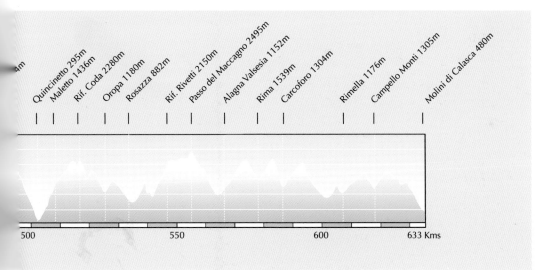

spectacular place, but the cosy hostel at **Usseaux** makes a lovely base. Then it's a mere wander via **Rifugio Arlaud** nestling in the Salbertrand wood to reach the Valle di Susa, where the Cottians come to an end.

The Graian Alps:
from Susa to Quincinetto

The township of Susa is quickly left behind for high-altitude pasture slopes that make up the billowing skirt of 3538m Rocciamelone that holds sway here, marking the French border with a cascading spill of snow and ice. An amble is enjoyed across Valle di Viù, then the GTA embarks on a tough crossing that sets the tone for many days to come. Desolate cirques, tiny tarns reflecting magnificent little-known mountains, and birds of prey or chamois as companions in lieu of humans. Accommodation is on the valley floors so this means mornings are spent tramping uphill to cols around the 2400–2500m range, before the inevitable plummet

through successive bands of vegetation, bushes and conifers giving way to deciduous trees.

At the lovely village of **Balme** in Valle di Ala, it's well worth taking time out to explore upper Pian della Mussa, which boasts inspiring glacial scenery, comfortable huts and herds of docile ibex – all dominated by the stately Uia di Bessanese.

The main route presses on over arduous passes to be rewarded by the exciting sight of the Gran Paradiso peak soaring over the Valle dell'Orco, where the following days are spent. Close to Ceresole Reale, another former royal resort village, walkers stay at **Fonti Minerali**, the source of therapeutic hot water with a distinct iron flavour.

A pleasant take-it-easy stage follows on, with a memorable meander down Vallon del Roc dotted with tiny mountainside hamlets, their stone-roofed houses in varying states of abandon. Farming communities lived here until the 1950s with their own school and church, not to mention folk art in the form of decorated images of

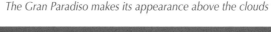

The Gran Paradiso makes its appearance above the clouds

The GTA follows Valchiusella with its lovely stone bridges

saints. These days only a shepherd or two are left, reserved folk to a T.

After **Noasca**, a string of strenuous traverses reaches Val Soana, the eastern border of the Gran Paradiso National Park. Stopovers are enjoyed in the villages of **Ronco Canavese** and tiny **Piamprato** near the valley head beneath the striated bulk of Rosa dei Banchi. Here walkers are put up in a 'doll's house', the old school erected by the magnanimous king for his subjects, only a handful of whom still call this home.

Neighbouring Valchiusella is a showcase for seven elegant stone footbridges, leftovers from the 1700s. Another point in its favour are the dairy farms dotted along its flanks. Local families at Alpe Chiaromonte, for instance, turn out delicious goat and sheep cheeses. The proximity of the key traffic artery Valle d'Aosta is soon felt; this is a bilingual French–Italian language region, the heritage of the Savoy dynasty. The GTA touches on **Quincinetto**, a handy place for joining or leaving the trek.

The Pennine Alps:
from Quincinetto to Molini Calasca

Parallel to the road is the mighty Dora Baltea river, its waters milky grey from the melted snow and ice that flow from Mont Blanc upstream. It irrigates the traditional vineyards, supported on pergolas and stone columns, which produce niche wines. A paved way through chestnut wood winds up to **Maletto** and its welcoming village inn. Next comes a long ridge, where views are dominated by the adjoining Colma di Mombarone, an austere triangle of grey rock. A tad of scrambling is encountered, aided stretches dictated by the degree of exposure. This day's conclusion is **Rifugio Coda** at 2280m, with a breathtaking outlook over the spread of the Western Alps with Mont Blanc, the Matterhorn and Monte Rosa.

Around a couple of rocky corners is an 800m drop to the 'St Peter's of the Alps', the mammoth sanctuary of Oropa. This sports a huge domed church and cavernous premises catering for the thousands of pilgrims attracted by its reputation for miracles, but is rather too busy a place for walkers to linger at length.

The peaceful Valle Cervo which follows has Alpine attraction in the shape of pretty villages. It was put on the map by an ambitious well-intentioned senator in the mid-1800s, who gave his name to Rosazza, a model village with ornate turreted palaces, mock villas and fountains, once a popular mountain resort for the well-off.

An aided stretch after leaving Rifugio Coda in the Pennine Alps

At the head of this charming valley and lively Piedicavallo, a stiff climb of 1050m leads relentlessly to **Rifugio Rivetti** (2150m), an eyrie back up in the clouds again. Meals are provided by an energetic team who race each other up the access path (the one you've just slaved up!) bearing loaded rucksacks. Just above is Punta Tre Vescovi, where a lot more was at stake during the culinary competitions held by the 'three bishops' who would spread out their feasts of cheese and wine on the rock slabs on the top! The outlook's not bad either, though a short way along, at 2495m **Passo del Maccagno**, things open up superbly to the awe-inspiring icy sprawl of Monte Rosa.

However, not only is the vicinity of the landmark massif exciting, but the GTA is also about to enter Valsesia, homeland of the ancient Walsers who migrated to here from the North with their distinctive language and culture. Their picture-postcard timber houses have survived the ravages of time, with a little restoration, their shaded terraces and window boxes draped with bright red geraniums.

Alagna Valsesia is a perfect place for forays onto the immense southeastern flanks of Monte Rosa dotted with all manner of mechanised lifts and refuges. As a destination 3153m Punta Indren is hard to beat, set amidst green-tinged tarns and glaciers and a jumping-off point for Capanna Margherita, the highest manned hut in the whole of Europe. At 4554m, it stands on renowned Punta Gnifetti, named in honour of the parish priest who first 'conquered' it in 1842 in order to dispel the long-standing myths depicting it as the abode of wandering spirits.

Back on the trail, spreads of raspberries and bilberries make a tasty distraction from the fatigue of continual ups and downs en route to the peaceful traditional villages of **Rima**, **Carcoforo**, **Rimella** then **Campello Monti**, where walkers are put up in the spotless old school house, where bunks have replaced the desks. On these five final days, the GTA edges its way around the easternmost fringes of Monte Rosa to its conclusion in Valle Anzasca. Here a bus can be caught to the Alpine village of Macugnaga for close-ups of dramatic icy landscapes beneath the southeastern face of majestic Monte Rosa.

Near the trek's conclusion, this view from Bocchetta dell'Usciolo overlooks the Ossola valley through to Switzerland

Trek 2

Tour of the Queyras

by Alan Castle

*C*ontained within a fortnight's holiday, this tour would make a splendid introduction to the Alps – and to the joys of Alpine trekking – for the keen hillwalker. Isolated and unspoilt, villages and valleys of the Queyras region will be as memorable as peaks and passes as the route weaves a meandering course, nudging against the Italian border in the French département of Hautes-Alpes. Of the many tantalising peaks on show, spectacular Monte Viso (Monviso to the Italians) entices the trekker across the border to give an optional diversion, while several summits accessible to walkers add further excuses to stray from the basic tour. But it is the fine scenery and unique cultural heritage of this comparatively remote area that makes the Queyras truly special and worthy of its status as a Regional Nature Park, and this multi-day tour unearths its essence.

The view from Col de l'Eychassier

The 7 Degrés Est gîte d'étape at l'Echalp

Route summary

Location	French and Italian Alps between Briançon and Turin
Start/Finish	Montdauphin-Guillestre in the Durance Valley, 34km south of Briançon
Distance	186km
Duration	12 days (a shortened version of about 8 days is also easily possible)
Maximum altitude	2921m (3208m optional ascents)
Accommodation	Gîtes d'étape and mountain refuges, with occasional optional hotels
Grade	Moderate
Guidebook	*Tour of the Queyras* by Alan Castle (Cicerone Press, 2009)

Where to go for a first Alpine trek?

If you are unsure of your abilities you wouldn't want to plunge in at the deep end by choosing a very demanding and exposed trail. But several areas of the Alps would fit the bill, and I always advise first-timers to look seriously at an area of the French Alps that lies adjacent to the Italian border – the Queyras. Although in sight of Monte Viso, one of the most dramatic and iconic giants of the Alps, the quiet, unassuming, seductive Queyras, despite being very popular with the French, is largely unknown to outsiders, and is one of the Alps' best kept secrets. Sheltered to the west by the high peaks of the Écrins, it is one of the sunniest areas of the Alps, with a mass of Alpine flowers early in the season. And what a thrill it would be to explore this magical

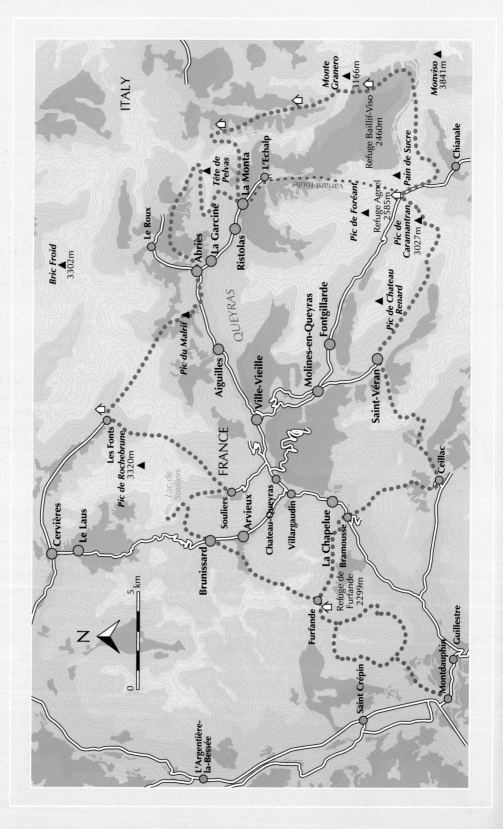

Tour of the Queyras

wonderland for the very first time! The Tour of the Queyras requires little or no scrambling ability, and no more exposure than might be expected on an average walk in the mountains of Britain, although some of the route is over areas of schist which can be rather loose and slippery, particularly in bad weather conditions.

Not only is the Queyras a good area for an Alpine walking novice to explore, but as there are no glaciers and most of its summits are at a relatively low altitude, it's a great place for competent hillwalkers and non-technical peak baggers who want to climb a summit or three without the necessary climbing equipment, experience or guides.

I've known the Queyras for well over 20 years, visiting it many times, but rarely have I seen other British walkers, for they flock to the popular regions further north and west, and miss out on one of the true gems of the Alps. The great beauty and allure of the Queyras, the friendliness of her people, the abundance of her charming hamlets, villages, gîtes and refuges, make it an extremely special area, and I feel a deep love for this land which, as a foreigner, I am quite at a loss to explain.

I hope you will choose the Queyras for your next walking holiday, and embark on a special journey through an enchanting region, over high cols, up remote summits, through scented pine forests, along lush Alpine valleys, across high pastures and flower-strewn meadows. To see the region at its best there's nothing to beat a refuge-to-refuge, or gîte-to-gîte, walking tour. On such an adventure you will be sleeping each night high up in the mountains, where gorgeous sunsets can be enjoyed, or in one of the many tranquil, age-old hamlets and villages in the Alpine glens of the Queyras.

The main Grande Randonnée trail here is the circular GR58, and for the most part our trek follows this, although on the first and last day we make use of the excellent GR541, which offers two alternatives to reach the high ranges of the Queyras from the deep trench of the Durance valley to the west. To visit three of the most dramatic of the nearby Italian valleys, the Tour takes a two-day excursion over the border, allowing a close-up view of the mighty Monte Viso. But there are several alternative routes to explore on the way around this spectacular region, depending on your whim, whether you want to climb a mountain peak or visit a particular gîte d'étape renowned for its cuisine and homely welcome. The Tour of the Queyras offers high-level, but generally moderate-grade mountain walking, and includes the crossing of the highest point reached on any GR trail in France. In all, 24 cols above 2000m are crossed, with options to climb up to 17 summits of varying difficulty, five of which are above the magic 3000m altitude.

The Durance Valley to Furfande

The start of the Tour is easily reached by mainline train from Nice or Marseilles on the Mediterranean, from Geneva or Lyons, or even from London via Eurostar to Paris and TGV from there. It is therefore quite feasible to reach **Montdauphin-Guillestre** within a day from the UK, and enjoy a night in a comfortable hotel before setting out refreshed for the mountains on the following day.

All forms of transport are left way behind on the long, slow but gradual climb out of the Durance valley, following a variant of the GR541. Those who haven't kept in shape before the trip may realise their folly on this first day, but take heart, for with perseverance the first col of the trip will be reached. The world is different on the other side of Col de Moussière, as the scenery changes abruptly from woodland and grassy hillsides to austere rocky ridges and rough scree slopes.

The serene Lac du Lauzet is a good spot for lunch, before the short pull up to the second col of the day, the 2458m **Col Saint-Antoine**. The descent from here leads to the verdant summer pastures of Furfande where, at the Granges de Furfande, a number of buildings are now used as holiday homes. The trail wanders amongst these to arrive at the first mountain hut of the Tour. Refuge de Furfande is situated in a magnificent spot below the Col de Furfande, with widespread views of the surrounding high mountains. On my first visit decades ago, the hut was rather basic; all I was presented with for food were some burnt sausages, and an extremely thin mattress poked through the hard, unforgiving springs of my iron bed! But refurbishment and a greatly improved cuisine nowadays ensure a pleasant and memorable stay.

The view from Saint-Véran

Furfande to Ceillac and on to Saint-Véran

The GR58 is encountered at Furfande, and is then followed in an anti-clockwise circuit around the region. Those who have stiffened after the exertions of the first day will be relieved to learn that the trail south to Ceillac is a relatively easy one, climbing to the lowest col of the Tour, the 2251m Col de Bramousse. But this is not tackled until the delightful hamlet of Les Escoyères, with its fine church and refreshing water fountain, is passed, and certainly not before a stop at the café-restaurant of the splendid gîte in **Bramousse**.

Ceillac is the first of two places where the GR58 and the GR5 meet and cross (the other being Brunissard later in our Tour), and is situated on a level plain where two valley systems merge, the Mélezet from the south and the Cristillan, a steep glacial hanging valley running

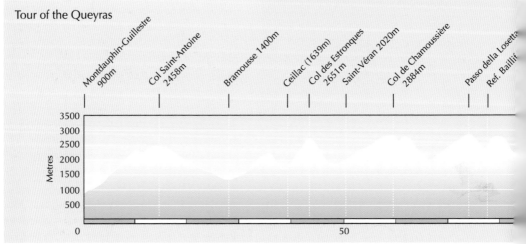

Tour of the Queyras

east-west. During the late 20th century, the village expanded considerably to accommodate the growing ski trade, the speciality of the region being *ski de fond*, which uses long, narrow skis. Ceillac is the main centre for this. Despite expansion, the village retains its original character as a small farming community; there are many fine old buildings, and the 19th-century church of Saint Sébastien makes a perfect setting for the music recitals that are occasionally held there. Ceillac is a major centre for traditional and modern wood carving, and two large carved 'carpenter's crosses' will be found there. A Queyras speciality, these crosses are adorned with articles relating to the life and death of Christ (carpenter's tools, the Roman soldier's spear and the crown of thorns).

The village is a very good centre for Alpine walking, as there are no less than four high cols accessible on foot, and it is interesting to try to locate their position from the high street. Two are crossed on this Tour of the Queyras, namely Col de Bramousse and Col des Estronques. The other two, Col Fromage to the north and Col Giradin to the south, are both situated on the GR5.

The trek east to Saint-Véran offers the opportunity to climb a small peak, the 2757m Tête de Jacquette, from **Col des Estronques**. From the summit, sightings of some of the 3000m giants of the

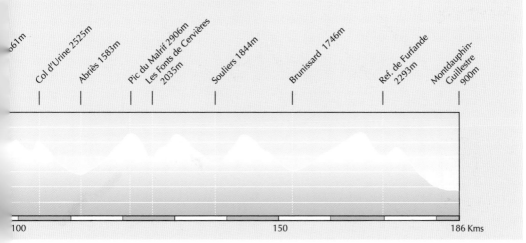

region will be made in clear conditions: Monte Viso (Monviso in Italian) (3841m), Visolotto (3348m) and Le Grand Queyras (3114m), all superb mountains that will be seen at closer quarters in a few days' time. The next objective, the village of Saint-Véran, is also visible on the opposite side of the valley below.

Saint-Véran, at 2020m, has the distinction of being the highest continuously inhabited community in Europe. The population in 2000 was 271, but at its peak in the early 19th century it stood at 865 souls. The village today depends largely on tourism, and the ski trade in particular, for its survival. Nevertheless, it has resisted the more garish developments that mar so many French ski resorts, and still retains the air of a simple mountain village. Much of the building is in wood, and the houses are constructed in such a way as to avoid being in each other's shade. This makes full use of the warmth from the sun, so important at this altitude. The church is an interesting, ornate

building containing several gilded figures of the saints. Opposite the main entrance is another finely decorated 'carpenter's cross'.

The Queyras is well known for its sundials (*cadrans solaires*), several of which will be found in Saint-Véran, painted on the south-facing walls of a number of buildings. Perhaps the finest is that on the wall of the church. Notice that the time indicated is nearly always an hour or more 'slow'. Perhaps the local time, when these sundials were painted several centuries ago, was different from modern French summer time?

Refuge Agnel and Le Pain de Sucre

The next day penetrates into the heart of the Queyras along the 'Grand Canal' route, which follows the course of an old, but now dry canal used in the days of copper and silver mining in the valley in earlier centuries. For the first time this Tour exceeds 3000m, if you choose to ascend Pic de Caramantran. The route also has the distinction of

Walkers at the Col de Saint-Véran

The Grand Queyras, seen from the path between Col de Chamoussière and Col de Saint-Véran

reaching the highest col on any standard GR trail in France, the **Col de Chamoussière** at 2884m, although this will be of little concern to the wayfarer, who will be far more interested in the area's magnificent rock scenery. One of the most striking mountains in the whole region, the 3175m Tête de Toillies is on view for much of today's ascent. This imposing Matterhorn-like peak, which sits on the Franco-Italian border, provides challenging sport for rock climbers from all over the world.

After four days carrying a pack over steep mountain passes, it's a good idea to give the shoulders and back a rest and have a day off in the high mountains. Refuge Agnel is perfect for such a day as it is situated at high altitude, in stunning surroundings, with some of the best peaks easily accessible, and there is a variety of walking excursions available in the area. Moreover, if not too crowded the refuge is a pleasant place to stay awhile; sunsets can be spectacular. Having a complete rest day would be pleasant enough, but for the more energetic and adventurous an ascent of Le Pain de Sucre (3208m), the French 'Sugar Loaf', can be made. This is the highest point reached by any of the ascents on whole tour and, if you do it, will be the first time that you get to over 10,000ft. Although the peak appears quite formidable, under good conditions the practised hillwalker used to scrambling and a little exposure should experience few problems, provided the waymarked route is followed to the top. It's a fairly easy, albeit steep scramble to the summit, although the inexperienced are better advised to admire the peak from afar.

Into Italy

From Refuge Agnel the border is soon reached at Col Agnel, thought by scholars to be one of the possible crossing places used by Hannibal and his elephants on their journey over the Alps into Italy. After a long descent to the south down the Vallone dell'Agnello, the route changes direction to climb, gradually at first, up the isolated and lovely Soustra valley. After a stiff climb to an Italian ridge at the **Passo della Losetta**, there's an optional ascent of Pointe Joanne, another stunning high viewpoint.

The highlight of this part of the journey is the close-up view of the northwest face of Monte Viso, almost 1000m of very steep rock. This really is an impressive mountain that deserves to be better known outside the region, for it ranks amongst the most spectacular of Alpine peaks. Standing alone, wholly in Italy, it towers above all other peaks in the vicinity. Monte Viso (Monviso) is seen to best advantage from the balcony path between Passo della Losetta and Col de Valante. France is re-entered at this col, with a night spent at the **Refuge Baillif-Viso**, from whose balcony spectacular views of Monte Viso are again on offer. From the refuge, Italy is re-entered at Col Sellière for an excursion in the Pellice valley beneath another giant of the region, the 3166m Monte Granero.

For those with less time there's a shorter option – wholly within France – from Refuge Agnel, via picturesque Lac Egourgéou, with an opportunity to reach the summit of Pic de Foréant, another giant of more than 3000m, much less climbed than the neighbouring Pain de Sucre, but an equally fine viewpoint. The trail leads down to the small village of L'Echalp, where the food in the Seven Degrees East gîte d'étape is to die for (be sure to ask for their blueberry pie). The Italian and French routes eventually reunite in the pretty hamlet of **La Monta**, from where once again there are two alternative routes, a high-level or low-level option. Those wanting a demanding high-level traverse choose the Sommet de la Lauzière route, again with peakbagging opportunities;

those with scrambling ability can tackle the towering 2929m Tête du Pelvas above the **Col d'Urine** – yes, it means the same in French! But equally good is a gentle stroll down the attractive Guil valley from La Monta via the village of Ristolas to the veritable metropolis of **Abriès**.

Abriès via Malrif and Souliers back to the Durance Valley

The Tour continually offers alternative routes, and it is often difficult to choose as most are so delectable. Another major decision has to be made on leaving Abriès. Either take the direct standard route via Lac de Grand Laus, a high Alpine lake hemmed in by an impressive cirque of mountains, or the longer and more demanding variant via Col de Thures and Col de Rasis, the latter at 2921m being the highest col on the entire Tour, less than 80m below the magic 3000m mark. Both routes come together at **Pic du Malrif**, the highlight of the day's itinerary, a fine perch from which to admire the snow-capped giants of the Écrins National Park to the west: Mont Pelvoux, Barre des Écrins and La Meije. There's only one place to spend the night, the gîte d'étape in the upland summer pasture of Les Fonts de Cervières. But if the Ritz itself were on offer, it could not compare with this engaging hamlet; and the food … oh, the food!

Strong walkers could manage the next stage to **Brunissard** in one long day, but to do so would rather miss the point of the Tour of the Queyras, which is the opportunity to explore the many side valleys and peaks of this delightful region. Instead, the stage can easily be broken at **Souliers**, where another feast awaits the guest at the village gîte, after which a day can be enjoyed picnicking at the picturesque Lac de Souliers. From here peakbaggers have the opportunity to climb Pic Quest, from whose 2844m summit the magnificence of the view is almost beyond description.

A penultimate day completes the circuit of GR58 for a second night back at the **Refuge de Furfande**, where your last night in the mountains will be a time of reflection, reliving the joys of the

Queyras and, if you lucky enough, enjoying one of the magnificent sunsets that delight so many visitors to this region. The next day you bid a fond farewell to the mountains on the mainly descending trail of the standard route of GR541, back to the Durance valley, no doubt with a strong resolve to return one day. Those wanting to climb one last peak can do so by making the ascent of Garnier, above the col of the same name ... but take care!

Before returning home, be sure to allow time to visit nearby Briançon, at 1290m the highest city of its size in all France, an ancient settlement with a rich and varied history, and a good place to buy souvenirs and presents.

By now you will realize that the Queyras is a land of superlatives. Its popularity among French walkers and those from several other European countries, notably the Netherlands and Germany, has increased considerably since the 1980s, and facilities to accommodate them have improved in terms of enlarged and upgraded gîtes d'étape and refuges. There is now also a well-established, inexpensive 'sherpa' service to transport luggage (and even weary walkers) from gîte to gîte. But, judging by the entries in the hut and gîte books, relatively few of my fellow countrymen have discovered the area. While it is the responsibility of a guidebook writer to ensure that his work does not result in a mass assault on a previously unspoilt area that will change its character forever, the Queyras could well cope with a doubling, trebling or even quadrupling of the number of British walkers to its high mountains and valleys. Eager to share this wonderland with other Brits, and perhaps tired of giving gentle encouragement to visit the region, I now want to shout from the highest summits: 'Go, go, go to the Queyras!' You will not be disappointed, and perhaps just a few of you will fall deeply and everlastingly under the spell of this remarkable and enchanted land.

Trekkers on GR58 about an hour out of Abriès

Le Bourg-
d'Oisans
La Grave
Valsenestre
La Chapelle Vallouise
FRANCE

Trek 3
Tour of the Oisans

by Kev Reynolds

The renowned French military engineer Vauban once described the region covered by this route as having 'mountains reaching for the sky, and valleys sinking to incredible depths', which perhaps helps explain why the Tour of the Oisans is reckoned by some seasoned hillwalkers to be one of the toughest of all Alpine treks. Not that every stage is particularly demanding, for some days are fairly relaxing, with streams and pools to laze beside, gentle passes to cross and meadows to amble through. But on the second half of the circuit, where cols and ridges are high, steep, remote and challenging, sections of brutal severity and sudden exposure can spark a rush of adrenalin and call for a clear head and steady feet. That being said, it's a tour of rugged beauty that should appeal to all experienced trekkers with a good head for heights.

The rugged country of the Cirque d'Arsine, an hour's hike from the Villar d'Arêne refuge

Route summary

Location	The Massif des Écrins, Haut Dauphiné, France
Start/Finish	Bourg d'Oisans
Distance	176km
Duration	10–12 days
Maximum altitude	2761m
Accommodation	Mountain refuges, gîtes d'étape and hotels
Grade	Demanding
Guidebook	*Tour of the Oisans: the GR54* by Kev Reynolds (Cicerone Press, 2008)

Southeast of Grenoble, the Massif des Écrins is celebrated as the highest block of mountains in France outside of the Mont Blanc range. It's a dramatic region of abrupt rocky peaks and small glaciers, cols of black shale, precipitous screes and wild hanging valleys whose silences are disturbed only by the whistling of marmots or the chuntering of a stream spilling its way from one level to the next. Small lakes and ponds lie in shallow scoops, some half-hidden by a chaos of rock and boulder; others seem more welcoming, set among flower meadows or on a high plateau of pastureland. Habitation is sparse; a small village here, a workaday hamlet there. There are no real resorts to match Chamonix, Zermatt or Grindelwald, and even the main centres of Bourg d'Oisans, La Grave, Vallouise and La Bérarde have none of the glamour of their counterparts in other well-known districts of the Alps. These are simple, unpretentious communities: solid, sturdy and weatherbeaten. Most would

still be recognised by Whymper, who came here to climb in the 1860s; but in their timeless simplicity lies much of their charm.

Located between Mont Blanc and the Mediterranean, a sizeable portion of this rugged, uncompromising landscape lies within the Parc National des Écrins, the largest and highest of France's national parks, with an area of some 91,800ha. It has scores of peaks over 3000m high and the Alps' most southerly 4000m summit, the 4102m Barre des Écrins, from which the district takes its name. La Meije, one of its consorts, towers over La Grave and was the last major Alpine peak to be climbed. Bronzed by the alpenglow, it stands as a mighty cornerstone, lording it over the Vallée de la Romanche.

This is the background to the GR54, otherwise known as the Tour of the Oisans. Why Oisans? Well, the Massif des Écrins answers to several names: Haut Dauphiné, Massif du Pelvoux, or l'Oisans. And Tour of the Oisans has become the established signature of the Grande Randonnée 54.

La Meije turns bronze with the alpenglow, seen here from Le Chazelet

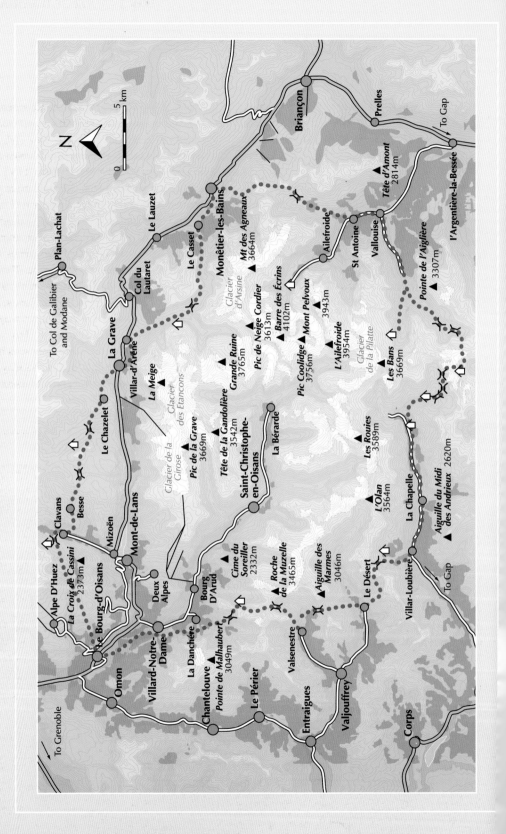

Tour of the Oisans

N

5 km

0

To Col de Galibier
and Modane

Plan-Lachat

Briançon

Prelles

To Gap

Tête d'Amont
2814m

l'Argentière-la-Bessée

Le Lauzet

Le Casset

Monêtier-les-Bains

Mt des Agneaux
3664m

Ailefroide

St Antoine

Vallouise

Pointe de l'Aiglière
3307m

Col du
Lautaret

Glacier
d'Arsine

Pic de Neige Cordier
3613m

Barre des Écrins
4102m

Mont Pelvoux
3943m

L'Ailefroide
3954m

Glacier
de la Pilatte

Les Bans
3669m

Villar-d'Arène

La Grave

La Meige

Glacier
des Étancons

Grande Ruine
3765m

Pic Coolidge
3756m

Le Chazelet

Glacier de la
Girose

Pic de la Grave
3669m

Tête de la Gandolière
3542m

Saint-Christophe-
en-Oisans

La Bérarde

Les Rouies
3589m

La Chapelle

Aiguille du Midi
des Andrieux 2620m

Besse

Mizoën

Mont-de-Lans

Clavans

Alpe D'Huez

La Croix de Cassini
2373m

Le Bourg-d'Oisans

Deux
Alpes

Bourg
D'Arud

Cime du
Soreiller
2332m

Roche
de la Muzelle
3465m

Aiguille des
Marmes
3046m

L'Olan
3564m

Le Désert

Villar-Loubière

To Gap

Omon

Villard-Notre-
Dame

La Danchère

Chantelouve

Pointe de Malhaubert
3049m

Le Périer

Valsenestre

Entraigues

Valjouffrey

Corps

To Grenoble

A circular route of around 176km, it takes between 10 and 12 days to complete, and with more than 12,800m to climb across a series of cols, it's an undeniably tough route. Some claim it's one of the toughest of all Alpine treks, and when you consider the lofty ridges that act as spokes pushed out from a hub of mountains – spokes or ridges that confuse, interrupt and challenge the way – there should be no surprise at this claim.

The first half of the trek works around the north and eastern fringes of the massif, from Bourg d'Oisans to Vallouise, and though less demanding than the second half, which goes around the western side, it still has its 'moments'. One of these comes right at the start, as we shall discover.

Bourg d'Oisans to La Grave

Within minutes of leaving the heart of **Bourg**, a waymarked path edges alongside the lovely Cascade de la Sarenne, then suddenly arrives at the foot of rock slabs that support the east wall of the Sarenne gorge. GR54 ascends these slabs by a series of minor ledges, narrow, grit-strewn and sufficiently tricky to demand caution. Here the steepness and severity of the slabs will make you curse any unnecessary weight in your rucksack, but fortunately lengths of fixed cable safeguard the route where it is especially narrow or smooth, and as you gain height, so the town comes into focus below and across the Romanche. Though of only modest size, Bourg is the administrative capital of the Oisans district, and flanked by steep-walled mountains it acts as a gateway to the Écrins National Park. Reached by bus from Grenoble, it's the obvious place from which to begin the Tour of the Oisans. But the way up those slabs above the Sarenne cascade makes for a tough initiation.

En enchanting region of little meadows, streams and pools lies below the Cirque d'Arsine

When the slabs peter out, meadows and patches of woodland lead to tiny hamlets that gather the sunlight. Linked by tree-shaded paths and stretches of tarmac, practically every step from one to the other is upward. Until, that is, you come to the huddled buildings of La Rosay, 830 muscle-stretching metres above Bourg. Here you leave tarmac, inch past renovated stone houses and a small chapel, cross a meadow with grasshoppers exploding around your boots, then descend into the gorge to find the stone-built **Pont Romain** spanning the Sarenne – a narrow stream which pounds and pummels water-smoothed rocks among deciduous trees that turn yellow and gold at the tail-end of summer.

On a summer's day the walk through the wooded gorge makes a welcome interlude, but then you emerge to another road easing through a shadeless scoop of a valley up to the 1999m **Col de Sarenne**, with a smart, privately owned refuge snug in the pastures nearby.

Over the col you leave the road to plunge steeply down into the Vallée du Ferrand, from which the Roche de la Muzelle can be seen far off. The penultimate col of the trek passes just below this peak, but that will be several days and a lot of puff away. For now the route passes through Clavans-le-Haut and its much smaller neighbour, Clavans-le-Bas (no accommodation at the first, but two options at the second), before making an abrupt climb to the one-time customs post of **Besse-en-Oisans**. With its well-preserved traditional stone and timber houses, Besse is a charming village and an opportunity to restock with supplies. It also has a hotel, a gîte, and a basic campsite 1km further on up the road.

Out of Besse the way passes the campsite and takes a footpath angling up a steep hillside to gain the grassy crest of Col Nazié at 1902m. It's not much of a col, just a dip in a ridge from which the way continues upward for another 300 vertical metres to reach **Col Bichet** overlooking a vast open pastureland. Way ahead, above and beyond the hidden Vallée de la Romanche, La Meije and Le Râteau rise above their glaciers – it's an exciting view.

The Tour of the Oisans crosses the pastureland known as the Plateau d'Emparis with La Meije appearing seductive all the way, while a short diversion from the trail leads to the Lacs Noir and Lérié, which make a perfect foreground to the big peaks and glaciers.

From the far side of the plateau the trail dips steeply into a groove scoured by the Torrent du Gâ, climbs through the village of **Le Chazelet** (two gîtes and a hotel), then swoops down yet another

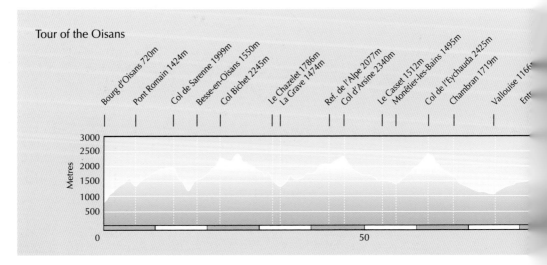

knee-aching hillside to **La Grave** on the true right bank of the Romanche at 1474m. La Meije soars a giddy 2500m above the village.

La Grave to Vallouise

Out of La Grave a very pleasant and fairly easy trek leads to a refuge set upon a shelf of grassland above the infant Romanche, amid an arc of big mountains. Should you have time, **Refuge de l'Alpe de Villar d'Arène** (2077m) is a near-perfect location to relax for a day or two, for there's some spectacular country to explore nearby. But even without time off from the trek, a night at the refuge is recommended. When you finally leave, it will only take an hour to reach the 2340m **Col d'Arsine**, a trough-like saddle below a massive rib of black moraine, overshadowed by stark rock peaks and loud with the call of marmots, and this leads to a wonderland of streams and pools gathered in the most enchanting of meadows and natural rock gardens below the Cirque d'Arsine. It's almost impossible to resist the temptation to throw off the rucksack and either lie in the grass or perch upon a rock to dream for an hour. Or two.

It's a long descent from Col d'Arsine to **Le Casset** in the valley of the Guisane. Or at least it seems long, for there are so many idyllic places on the way that threaten to delay progress. Streams disappear and reappear 200m lower down the valley. Waterfalls spray in long ribbons; there's a tiny lake, milky blue with the run-off of a fast-shrinking glacier. Mountains loom on either side; there are delicate flowers, wild raspberries and bilberries to pick in season; then fragrant larch-woods whose paths are carpeted with needles. At last Le Casset appears; a village of thick-walled houses, a gîte and a bar/restaurant where you can slake your thirst at a marble-topped table, and downvalley, less than an hour's walk away, lies **Monêtier-les-Bains**, the largest habitation since leaving Bourg d'Oisans. As well as hotels and a gîte, Monêtier also has restaurants, a supermarket and a bank with a cash machine.

Sadly, the pass that takes the Tour of the Oisans out of the valley of the Guisane and on to Vallouise has been partially desecrated by cableways and bulldozed pistes, for here on the outer edge of the national park the Serre-Chevalier ski circus leaves its indelible mark long after the snow has melted. However, the trail begins innocently enough, rising through woodland behind Monêtier, and up into a green hanging valley before arriving at the first pylon. But an hour's grimly determined march through this sorry mess takes you over the 2425m **Col de l'Eychauda** and into the comparative serenity of the Vallon de Chambran.

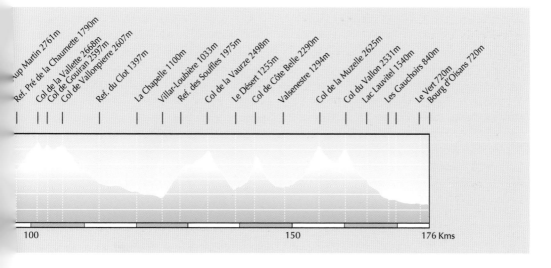

Twisting back and forth, the trail makes a long and winding descent of a very steep slope to arrive in the upper reaches of the valley, where a *buvette* serving welcome refreshments is reached soon after. Beyond the summer-only hamlet of **Chambran** the way dodges down narrow trails, on and off a feeder road, then along tree- and shrub-crowded paths with a view of Mont Pelvoux, to a clutch of small villages that direct you into **Vallouise**. This small market town at the confluence of the Gyr and l'Onde boasts two gîtes, hotels, a campsite, a few bars and restaurants, a shop or two and another opportunity to tease cash from a hole in the wall, should you be running low on funds.

Vallouise to Valgaudemar

Vallouise marks a turning point on the Tour of the Oisans, for now the more-or-less circular trek explores the south and western sides of the massif. From now on the way has a greater sense of remoteness; the passes are higher, steeper, more challenging and more rewarding.

A morning's walk leads to the roadhead in the Vallée d'Entraigues (also know as Vallée de l'Onde). Some trekkers choose to take a taxi along this road to shorten the unrelenting hike over two high passes on the way to the Refuge du Pré de la Chaumette, but I prefer to take the riverside path and continue to the head of the valley, where the old, traditional Refuge des Bans is perched in a wild cirque of mountains crowned by the 3669m mountain after which it is named.

Having spent a night among the high peaks, it's essential to rise early and descend back to **Entre-les-Aygues**. Cross the river on a long footbridge, then head off up the narrow Vallon de la Selle on a trail that eventually slants up and across long fans of black scree (dodgy in bad weather or when masked by snow) to gain **Col de l'Aup Martin**. At 2761m, this is the highest pass on GR54, but instead of descending on the far side, you then traverse more slopes of rock and scree to the 2735m Pas de la Cavale. Only then can

you begin the remorseless zigzag descent into the Vallée de Champoléon, where the **Pré de la Chaumette refuge** offers welcome food and shelter after a long and tiring day's hike.

That two-pass crossing makes for a brutal stage, but one of the toughest stages of the trek follows, with no fewer than three high passes on the itinerary: **Col de la Vallette**, **Col de Gouiran** and **Col de Vallonpierre**. Linked by eroded ribs and fins of unstable shale and grit, the first and last of these cols contain some extremely steep and exposed sections, and are not for the faint-hearted. A slip could have serious consequences, so pray for settled conditions and remain alert at all times.

A vertiginous descent from Col de Vallonpierre takes you to a refuge set beside a small tarn, then loses another 1100m of altitude before reaching **La-Chapelle-en-Valgaudemar**, where there's gîte and hotel accommodation, a bar/restaurant, a small grocery store – and some level ground for a change.

Valgaudemar to Bourg d'Oisans

The valleys of Valgaudemar and Valjouffrey flow in roughly parallel lines, divided by a lofty ridge system emanating from the 3564m L'Olan, and to get from one to the other the Tour of the Oisans chooses to cross that ridge via **Col de la Vaurze**, whose height is variously quoted as 2490m, 2498m, or 2500m.

After a gentle valley stroll of about an hour from La-Chapelle the small village of **Villar-Loubière** appears, its buildings apparently cascading down the hillside. It is here that the long five-hour climb to Col de la Vaurze begins, at first through a ravine-like valley, with trees and shrubs growing in its upper reaches. Roughly midway between the village and the col, the small but well-appointed **Refuge des Souffles** stands on a bluff just above a trail junction, and even if you decide against spending a night there, the opportunity to stop by for refreshments is hard to resist.

Beyond the hut the trail works its way into a profound combe topped by Pic des Souffles. Part of this combe is confused by rocky spurs

Shimmering reflections of the alpenglow in Lac de Vallonpierre. A refuge sits on the bank of this tarn

The view looking back over the previous day's route from just below Col de la Muzelle

interspersed by stream-cut gullies, but once this is behind you long switchbacks angle across an open hillside to gain the narrow col; this is a memorable vantage point from which to study not only the way ahead, but also the deep trench of Valgaudemar, the valley system you're about to leave. On the northwest side of the col a giddy view looks directly down on the rooftops of **Le Désert**, a tiny huddle of buildings 1250m below. It will take about two hours of very steep descent to reach this small farming community, whose facilities for trekkers include three simple gîtes d'étape and a bar/restaurant.

The next pass on the tour lies almost directly above Le Désert. At 2290m, **Col de Côte-Belle** is one of the lowest on GR54, and by comparison with many of its predecessors, the crossing is straightforward, albeit steep in places and with some impressive shattered rock formations along the way. Straightforward it may be in good conditions, but should the weather turn nasty, or snow

and ice remain on the trail (as they may, early in the season), then this crossing could be a very different undertaking.

On the northern side of the pass **Valsenestre**, an attractive hamlet of old stone houses, boasts a welcoming gîte, Le Béranger, in which to spend the night before tackling the 2625m **Col de la Muzelle** next day.

Flanked by the Roche de la Muzelle, the ascent to the col is undemanding until the final 200m, where the route struggles up a very steep cone of compacted shale and slate, some of which is sharp-edged and threatening. But views back the way you came can be exhilarating.

From the col you gaze down onto a green lake set among rucked pastures. In the mid-distance can be seen the ski resort of Les Deux Alpes, while far off the tiny snowfields of Les Grandes Rousses shine in the sunlight. And once again a steep slope of shale has to be negotiated before an easy trail meanders across the pastures to reach the timber-built Refuge de la Muzelle set upon a grass slope not far from a shepherd's *cabane*, just above the lake. Towards dusk hundreds of sheep are brought back from their grazing to be coralled for the night nearby.

The original route of the Tour of the Oisans plunged directly down to Bourg d'Arud in the Vallée du Vénéon, then followed this valley all the way to Bourg d'Oisans. That was a pleasant enough way to finish the tour, but by rerouting this final stage across the 2531m **Col du Vallon** to the west of Refuge de la Muzelle, a much more rewarding stage has been created, and one that retains the essence of GR54 much longer.

There's nothing difficult about the normal way up to Col du Vallon from the refuge, and as you gain height, so the views grow in extent and interest, with the shapely Aiguille du Plat de la Selle demanding your admiration from the east. The pass is a surprisingly gentle saddle of grass and rock, but before long the descent demands caution as it picks a way along and over an abrupt spur of rock, with one section teetering along a narrow exposed ramp with **Lac Lauvitel** far below.

The lake is one of the gems of the Parc National des Écrins. Trapped in a cirque of rocky peaks, its northern end is dammed by a great tip of rocks and boulders, among which there are tangles of wild raspberries, while marmots sun themselves or frolic at the water's edge.

Down then, steeply down, to **Les Gauchoirs**, and a track which runs between meadow and woodland, passes below the Cascade de la Pisse and then spills onto a narrow tarmac road. On the outskirts of Bourg d'Oisans gîte accommodation can be found in the hamlet of **Le Vert**; then it's a last easy stroll into the little town where the trek began, and you're left with a host of memories to replay on the journey home – and in the months and years to come.

Lac Lauvitel is one of the gems of the Écrins National Park

FRANCE
Tignes
Val d'Isère
Pralognan-
La-Vanoise
Bonneval
-sur-Arc
Bessans
Bramans
Modane   Moncenisio
ITALY

Trek 4
Tour of the Vanoise
by Kev Reynolds

La Grande Casse, Grande Motte, Dent Parrachée, Pointe de l'Echelle – all these and countless other peaks form a backdrop to this figure-of-eight tour in the heart of the Vanoise National Park. Glaciers and snowfields too, play their part in the landscape, as do the lakes and pools that turn mountains on their heads, and the chamois, ibex and marmots that inhabit the inner valleys and add daily excitement to the trek. The first five days remain above any habitation except for mountain refuges and isolated farms, but then a descent is made to handsome Bonneval-sur-Arc before crossing Col de l'Iseran on the way to Val d'Isère. Returning to the sanctity of the national park takes the route across Col de la Leisse and Col de la Vanoise, and after visiting Pralognan a valley walk leads to the lofty Col de Chavière, from which a long descent revisits Modane, where the trek began.

Plan du Lac is a tranquil site from which to study La Grande Casse (left) and La Grande Motte

Route summary

Location	The Vanoise National Park, northeast of Grenoble, France
Start/Finish	Modane, in the Maurienne
Distance	154km
Duration	10–12 days
Maximum altitude	2796m
Accommodation	Mountain refuges, gîtes d'étape and hotels
Grade	Moderate
Guidebook	*Tour of the Vanoise* by Kev Reynolds (Cicerone Press, 2nd edition, 2009)

It was mid-afternoon on a July day when, descending below the final col on the Tour of the Vanoise, I became conscious of movement among the grass hummocks ahead. My two friends and I paused, held our breath and stayed silent as a female ibex (*bouquetin* to the French) wandered nonchalently across the trail. Almost immediately

she was followed by another, then another. Then a pair of youngsters pranced and frolicked into view; a mother snuffled and snorted, then took to grazing as yet more adults and kids appeared, blissfully unconcerned by our presence. So we slumped among the rocks and for the next 10 minutes or more, were entertained by these graceful, perfectly-at-ease wild mountain goats that inspected the hillocks and hollows around us. We could smell the musky scent of their short-haired beige coats, hear their teeth tearing at the grass, the sound of their hooves tinkling on rock. One would sneeze; another twist her head and scratch her neck with a hind foot. None took any notice of us, and time stood still as we soaked in the beauty of each moment until they finally drifted away. Magic. Pure magic.

The Parc National de la Vanoise was established in 1963 largely to protect the dwindling ibex population. That protection has proved successful, for there are now around 2000 individuals roaming the district, and each time I've trekked the Tour of

Lac des Vaches is crossed on a causeway of stone slabs

the Vanoise I've seen ibex on several stages of the route. Not only ibex, but chamois and marmots, a rich variety of birds and butterflies, stoats and lizards, and the most extravagant flower meadows of any region in the Alps. With its sparkling lakes

Trekkers pause to appreciate the scene in the Aussois combe

and backdrop of glacier-hung mountains, it's also a region of great scenic beauty.

Located between the upper valleys of the Isère (Tarentaise) and Arc (Maurienne) in the *département* of Savoie, the Vanoise shares a common boundary with Italy's Gran Paradiso National Park, and when the two were twinned in 1972, they created the largest nature reserve in Western Europe.

Not surprisingly, the Vanoise contains some very fine walking opportunities. The epic GR5 makes its way through the region, and several short circular tours are publicised locally. The most popular of these among French walkers, is the five-day Tour des Glaciers de la Vanoise, and the trek described here shares some of its trails. But our route is twice as long as that, and it makes almost a figure-of-eight tour of the very best the district has to offer. It's not a difficult route, nor particularly strenuous, but it is without question a richly rewarding one.

Modane to Plan du Lac

With bus and rail access from the airports of Lyon and Grenoble, and the fast and convenient Paris to Turin TGV service stopping there, the unpretentious little town of **Modane**, snug in the Maurienne on the southeastern edge of the national park, makes an obvious starting point for our trek. Should you arrive there too late in the day to begin trekking straightaway, there's a choice of modest hotels in which to spend a night before setting out on the steep uphill climb that leads to the first hut of the tour.

It is a steep uphill climb, too, but among trees for much of the way, so at least shade is guaranteed on a hot day. Modane is soon left behind, and across the rushing waters of the Arc, waymarks direct you through the 'suburb' of Loutraz to a signed footpath angling up the forested slope with no concessions made to muscles not yet ready for the demands of a trek in the Alps. The moral is clear: get fit before you go.

Several refuges in the area have been converted from one-time dairy farms. But not the comfortable **Refuge de l'Orgère**, which stands almost 900m and half a day's hike above Modane on a sloping meadow, backed by the sharply

Tour of the Vanoise

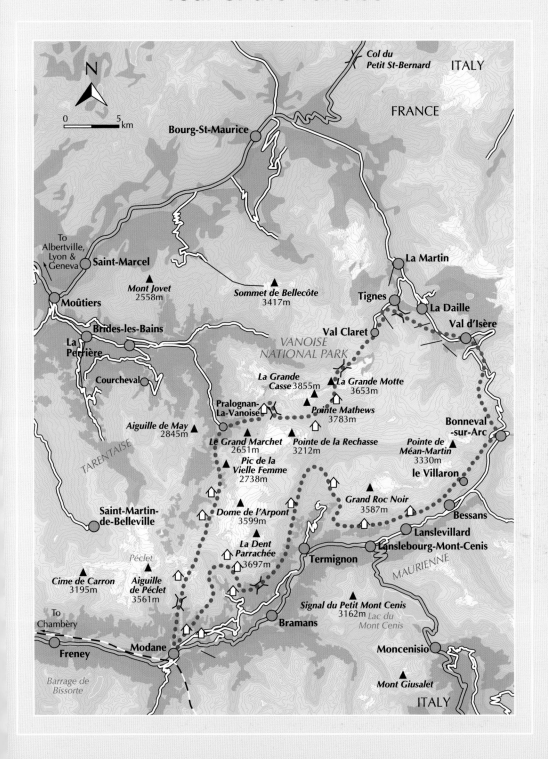

N

0   5 km

Col du
Petit St-Bernard

ITALY

FRANCE

Bourg-St-Maurice

To
Albertville,
Lyon &
Geneva

Saint-Marcel

La Martin

Mont Jovet
2558m

Sommet de Bellecôte
3417m

Tignes

La Daille

Moûtiers

Val Claret

Val d'Isère

Brides-les-Bains

VANOISE
NATIONAL PARK

La
Perrière

Courcheval

La Grande
Casse 3855m

La Grande Motte
3653m

Bonneval
-sur-Arc

Pralognan-
La-Vanoise

Pointe Mathews
3783m

Aiguille de May
2845m

Le Grand Marchet
2651m

Pointe de la Rechasse
3212m

Pointe de
Méan-Martin
3330m

le Villaron

Pic de la
Vielle Femme
2738m

TARENTAISE

Grand Roc Noir
3587m

Bessans

Saint-Martin-
de-Belleville

Dome de l'Arpont
3599m

Lanslevillard

Lanslebourg-Mont-Cenis

La Dent
Parrachée
3697m

Termignon

MAURIENNE

Péclet

Cime de Carron
3195m

Aiguille
de Péclet
3561m

Signal du Petit Mont Cenis
3162m Lac du
Mont Cenis

To
Chambèry

Bramans

Moncenisio

Freney

Modane

Barrage de
Bissorte

Mont Giusalet

ITALY

Snow still lingers well into July as trekkers make their way from Arpont to Plan du Lac

pointed 3041m rock peak of the Aiguille Doran. Owned by the national park authority (PNV), the

refuge has excellent facilities and each time I've stayed there delicious meals have been served in

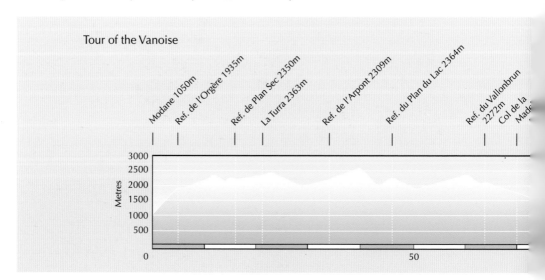

Tour of the Vanoise

generous portions, and films about the park and its wildlife were screened in the common room during the evening.

The next four days are spent high above the river, well away from towns and villages, as the route weaves along the Maurienne flank of the mountains, then pushes deep into the heart of the region before returning to the Maurienne slope once more. Trails are mostly good, waymarks adequate, and overnight accommodation is simple but welcoming, providing all that one needs after a day's exercise amid fine scenery.

Leaving l'Orgère the GR5 trail is adopted as it takes an undulating course along the hillside 1000m above the river, gradually rising past a pair of old stone huts to gain the broad grass saddle of Col du Barbier at 2287m. After this, the way curves into a deep combe with two lakes below and the big block of the Dent Parrachée (3697m) standing proud on the far side. The path pushes towards the head of this combe, crossing grass slopes littered with rocks and boulders and running with streams, before losing height among alpenroses on the way to the Pont de la Sétéria which spans the torrent of the Rau de Saint-Benoit. Now on the eastern side of the combe, the trail takes you just below Refuge de la Fournache

and continues high above the lakes to bring you to **Refuge de Plan Sec**. This attractive, privately owned refuge was once a summer farm. Of the three buildings, one contains the dormitories, another the dining room (one-time stables), while the third houses the showers and toilets. There's also a small camping area nearby.

Day three is a little more demanding, for within a few minutes of leaving Plan Sec the trail zigzags up a steep gully, edges against overhanging cliffs, then comes to a spectacular section where it has been cut into a precipitous slope. After this you twist up a spur to gain the 2363m saddle of **La Turra**, then climb another 100m before contouring across a steep-walled combe giving access to the valley sliced by the Doron gorge which almost divides the Vanoise region in two.

The ruins of one or two old farms are being reclaimed by the land from which they were built. There are small meadows and the remains of a rockfall to cross. Slips of old winter snow hug north-facing gullies, and as you progress towards the heart of the region, long slender cascades come pouring down the left-hand slopes, draining the unseen Glaciers de la Vanoise. And there's a glimpse of the snow-draped 3855m La Grande Casse, the highest of the Vanoise summits, at the

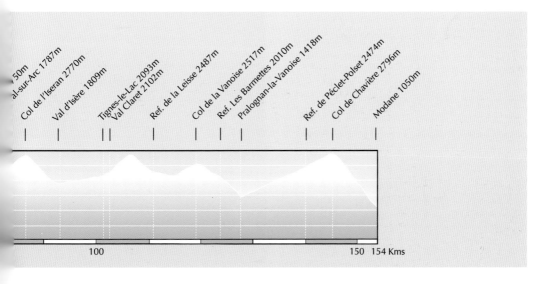

head of the valley as you approach the PNV-owned **Refuge de l'Arpont**.

La Grande Casse and its neighbour, La Grande Motte (3653m) are joined by a long, high ridge that effectively walls the northern end of the valley, and on the stage leading from Arpont to Refuge du Plan du Lac, that wall is on show for most of the way. It's a seductive view, and one that is constantly being rearranged as the trail eases along the hillside, curves towards Mont Pelve and the Roche Ferran, passes between the two Lacs de Lozières and rising over glacier-polished slabs visits another small tarn to reach a high point from which you gaze down into the Doron gorge. Shortly after, the trail comes to the Mont de la Para junction where you swoop down the hillside to a confluence of streams below Refuge d'Entre-Deux-Eaux (another lovely old converted farm), then begin a climb of about 400m which leads to **Refuge du Plan du Lac**.

The neat mottled stone building of Plan du Lac is another refuge owned by the national park authority, and it enjoys an uninterrupted view of La Grande Casse to the north, and across the hinted depths of the gorge to the Glaciers de la Vanoise in the west. But an even better view is gained when you leave next morning, for a short stroll brings you to the glorious lake after which the area is named, from whose southern end both La Grande Casse and La Grande Motte are mirrored in its waters. It's one of the many highlights of the trek.

Plan du Lac to Bonneval

Later, after you've turned away from the valley of the Doron de Termignon and resumed above the Maurienne, the trail passes an isolated farm, rises to the end of the Crête de la Turra, then descends through the most spectacular natural rock gardens I've seen in all my Alpine wanderings. On my last visit dense, damp mist clung to the hillside, but nothing could detract from the beauty of the flowers that crowded every nook, cranny and open space, that blazed their colours

through the mist and filled the air with fragrance. Sheer heaven.

It's a longish stage of about 18km and six hours or so of actual trekking before the **Refuge du Vallonbrun** comes in view. A longish stage with plenty of ups and downs, all of which make arrival at the refuge extra welcome. It's another fine building owned by the PNV. Recently refurbished, it retains the traditional style of a Maurienne mountain farm, and sits comfortably on a grass slope in a peaceful back-country. There are no dramatic peaks on show, but both the refuge and its setting are utterly charming.

On departing a short uphill stroll leads to a tiny chapel at about 2300m, behind which a path sweeps down in steepening zigzags over a hillside lavish with flowers and loud with insects, eventually spilling out at the hamlet of Le Collet on the

1752m **Col de la Madeleine**. Having regained the Maurienne valley for the first time since leaving Modane, a gentle walk beside walled meadows promises a morning without effort, and a little over two hours after leaving Vallonbrun you have an opportunity to cross the river to raid the bakeries and cafés of **Bessans**.

The continuing trek resumes on the west bank of the river, squeezing through the crowded little hamlet of **Le Villaron**, in which there's a popular gîte d'étape, and passing alongside the huge Rocher de Château which from a distance appears to block the valley, and on which Neolithic settlers painted at least eight deer. Sadly, only one of these can now be recognised, the others having faded into oblivion.

Bonneval-sur-Arc is one of the most attractive of French villages. It's a delight of medieval stone houses huddled one against another at the foot of a steeply sloping hillside, and with its gîte d'étape, two or three hotels and unmanned French Alpine Club (CAF) chalet-refuge, is an obvious place to spend the night before tackling the Col de l'Iseran.

Bonneval to Refuge de la Leisse

Bonneval is roughly the halfway point on the Tour of the Vanoise, and the stage leading away from it is one of the most demanding, for there's a long 980m uphill climb to gain **Col de l'Iseran**, which marks the transition from Maurienne to Tarentaise. The Iseran is a road col, of course, and often features on the Tour de France cycle marathon, but fortunately we have little to do with the road, for our trail seeks out some 'hidden' country with its own appeal.

A steep pull above Bonneval brings you into the Vallon de la Lenta, noted for its waterfalls and stunning view of l'Albaron and La Grande Ciamarella astride the Italian border. From the head of the vallon the way climbs through a gorge (watch for ibex and chamois) and emerges at the Pont de la Neige, from where you then tackle the left-hand slope of an open basin to reach Col de l'Iseran (2770m) about three and a half hours after leaving Bonneval. Refreshments are available at the pass, but traffic and crowds spilling from coaches and cars can seem brutal intrusions into the tranquil nature of the trek, so escape is found on the descent to **Val d'Isère** which takes you away from the road and down grass slopes and woodland, and eventually into the sprawling town with its many hotels, restaurants, shops and banks. Primarily known as a ski resort, Val d'Isère is much quieter in summer than in winter, and a night spent there can be more relaxing than may be imagined.

But it's good to escape once more to the peace of the hills. Fortunately, it's not long before the

From Vallonbrun a trail descends flowery slopes to the Col de la Madeleine

town is left behind as you wander through larch-woods into the pastoral Vallon de la Tovière, where marmots abound and the meadows are full of flowers in early summer. At its head the 2252m Pas de la Tovière provides a distant view of Mont Blanc, while below the high-rise resort of **Tignes-le-Lac** seems as out of place as Benidorm in the mountains.

Our route skirts the lake and enters another collection of high-rise buildings at **Val Claret**; a rash of architectural vandalism on the edge of the national park. All you can do is grit your teeth and, head down and eyes averted, march through as fast as possible.

The sanity of the national park is restored on the crossing of Col de la Leisse, a wild little pass at 2758m, with La Grande Motte soaring above, and a trough-like valley below in which two lakes lie among rocks, boulders and long fans of scree. The trail descends into this trough, and from the far end, descends again to reach the three timber buildings of **Refuge de la Leisse**, set upon a pro-jecting spur of land overlooking the lower Vallon de la Leisse.

Refuge de la Leisse to Modane

Early morning in the Vallon de la Leisse can be rewarding. As night's shadows are chased out of the valley by the intruding sun, the dew-damp grass sparkles, rivulets sneak across the trail, tiny alpine flowers open their blooms, and chamois gaze on tres-passing hikers. The val-ley is flanked on either side by abrupt moun-tain walls, too high and too steep for their sum-mits to be visible, but when it curves towards the south views open to scenes familiar from the early part of the trek. And when you

reach the old stone bridge, Pont de Croé-Vie, you're only a stone's throw from Refuge d'Entre-Deux-Eaux and the trail that led to Plan du Lac. Given time, it would be worth straying to Entre-Deux-Eaux and maybe devoting a few hours to exploring the nearby Vallon de la Rocheure.

But for the continuing trek, you cross the bridge and begin a steady ascent to the Col de la Vanoise. At first the path is edged with alpenroses, but as you progress, so the landscape becomes more stony and austere until you enter a high, almost level scoop of a valley lying between Pointe de la Réchasse on the left and Pointe Mathews on the right. The valley is marshy in places; elsewhere you walk alongside shallow tarns, then rise to another level from where a close view can be had of the glaciers and huge moraines of La Grande Casse. But it's not just La Grande Casse that holds your attention, for impressive rock peaks with vast slab faces and sharp summits intrude on the scene; there are pools and lakes and immense screes, and marmots bounding from burrow to burrow.

The two large buildings of a refuge stand on the **Col de la Vanoise** at 2517m. Owned by the French Alpine Club (CAF), Refuge du Col de la Vanoise is also known as Refuge Felix Fauré after a French president who came here in 1897. Although rather large and impersonal (it has 148 places), the ref-uge rewards with magnificent views, and even if you have no intention of spending a night there, refreshments are worth stopping for.

Beyond the refuge the path plunges below the slabs of the Aiguille de la Vanoise to Lac des Vaches, which is crossed on a causeway of stone slabs where it is worth pausing to enjoy the retrospective views. Below the lake the path continues down to the privately owned Refuge

Pralognan is entered down a flight of stone steps

On the final descent to Modane the trail passes below the Aiguille Doran

Les Barmettes, then down and yet more steeply down to **Pralognan-la-Vanoise**, a small resort town with all modern facilities at 1418m.

Hemmed in by crowding mountains, Pralognan is a popular walking centre, just two days' walk from Modane where the Tour of the Vanoise ends. From the town an easy 14km valley walk leads to **Refuge de Péclet-Polset**. At 2474m, the refuge lies within striking distance of Col de Chavière, the final pass of the trek, but there are other possibilities for accommodation between the hotels of Pralognan and Péclet-Polset; namely, a gîte in the hamlet of Les Prioux, and a chalet-refuge beside the little chapel of La Motte, so itineraries can be adapted to suit.

Two previous Péclet-Polset refuges have been destroyed by fire, and the architecture of the present building is in stark contrast to the more traditional stone-built huts of the PNV. Clad in timber and with large solar panels, it looks out at a rugged landscape rimmed with big mountains rising from a jumble of rocks that conceal several small pools and lakes.

At 2796m, **Col de Chavière** is the highest point reached on the Tour of the Vanoise. From the refuge a trail picks its way across rocky terrain, skirts a grass-fringed tarn, edges limestone slabs and finally strikes up a ramp of unstable grit to gain the pass. Views back and ahead are filled with mountains as far as the eye can see. Mont Blanc and the Aiguille Noire feature in the backward view, while ahead it is the Écrins Massif that dominates. Given settled conditions, this is a wonderful scene to absorb and to treasure before you begin the long descent that concludes the trek where it began 10 days or more ago in Modane.

SWITZERLAND
Mont Blanc
Courmayeur
ITALY
La Thuile
Planaval
Cogne
Chardonney
FRANCE
ITALY

Trek 5
Gran Paradiso Alta Via 2

by Gillian Price

*T*his is a trek to test both lungs and legs with some hefty ascents and descents on a journey from the shadow of the Gran Paradiso to the foot of Mont Blanc. A string of lofty cols, the highest topping out at 3299m, offer views to take your breath away – if you have any breath left, that is. Many of the trails adopted for this route have a royal pedigree. Paved and generously graded, they owe their existence to the days before the Italian king's hunting grounds metamorphosed into the Gran Paradiso National Park. Now that the hunting is long gone, the region teems with wildlife. Out of the park, and working towards Mont Blanc, streams and tarns sparkle in Alpine perfection to temper fatigue on some of the toughest days, and when you reach the top of the final col you really will feel you are in Paradise!

Beautiful Lago di Lauson is a must-see

Route summary

Location	Valle d'Aosta, Graian Alps, Italy
Start	Chardonney in Valle di Champorcher, near Hône-Bard
Finish	Courmayeur in Valle d'Aosta
Distance	143km
Duration	12 days
Maximum altitude	3299m
Accommodation	Village guesthouses and mountain huts
Grade	Strenuous to demanding
Guidebook	*Gran Paradiso. Alta Via 2 Trek and Day Walks* by Gillian Price (Cicerone Press, 2008)

It was pretty early on in my Alpine walking life when I made my first visit to the Gran Paradiso National Park, and it took the best part of a day on a train to reach the Valle d'Aosta in Italy's northwest. The season was well advanced and September was on its way out. My first impression was of sombre, uninviting mountains, stark valleys and shrivelled vegetation. Not very promising, I mused, as I laboured up the path from the Cogne valley to Rifugio Vittorio Sella. The air temperature dropped rather rapidly as late afternoon shadows cast their purple veil over rocky slopes, and walkers going in the opposite direction rushed downhill, keen to reach the comfort of their hotels before nightfall. Frequent pauses became necessary for me to catch my breath, which was still set at sea-level, and my attention was captured by a movement nearby. A fully grown ibex, head down, calmly

grazing only metres from me. I was enthralled. Talk about beginner's luck. Pointing excitedly I frantically sign-languaged passing walkers to hush and walk on tiptoes, but was puzzled not to be eliciting anything more than a polite half smile. 'Ignorant lot,' I thought as I clicked away with my trusty Minolta camera, 'They don't know what they're missing.' On arrival at the hut I learnt the reason for their indifference ... the vast surrounding arc filled by a pasture basin was choc-a-bloc with hundreds of ibex and chamois peacefully enjoying their evening munch. You could hardly see the grass for the animals!

Needless to say my diary for that day contains more animal entries than path

Top A baby marmot leaves the safety of its burrow to go exploring
Bottom Male ibex have magnificent grooved horns

Gran Paradiso Alta Via 2

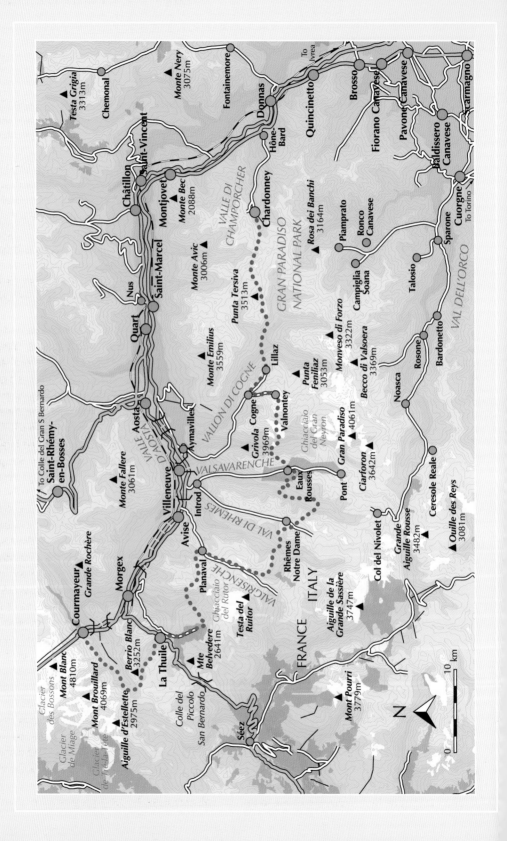

description: later on came bold foxes scavenging for dinner leftovers outside the kitchen, marmots frolicking, and even a flock of courageous choughs chasing a golden eagle out of their aerial territory. I began to understand the significance of the name Gran Paradiso – it is truly wildlife heaven! This was the start of a long-lasting love affair with this region – and the Alta Via 2 would prove to be the perfect way to explore it at leisure. Strictly speaking the trek only spends half of its 12 days within the borders of the park, but luckily animals can't read signs.

Once you realise this all used to be a royal game reserve, the remarkable abundance of wildlife becomes understandable. Back in the 1800s the ibex and chamois populations were boosted when the king banned hunting (though naturally he and the privileged members of his retinue were exempt from the ruling). Local hunters were taken on as track builders and expert gamekeepers. Their descendents are still on patrol, but nowadays as *guardiaparco*, as in 1922 this was declared Italy's very first national park by King Vittorio Emanuele III. On my subsequent visits I had the privilege of spending time with these dedicated guardians, unassuming characters who dwell in a tiny high altitude *casotto* hut for weeks at a time – in solitude, except for the wildlife whose every movement they monitor, never interfering.

Valle di Champorcher to Cogne

Branching off south from the major traffic artery of Valle d'Aosta, **Chardonney** in the little-visited Valle di Champorcher marks the start of this adventure. The Alta Via embarks on one of the king's game tracks that has survived intact to this day, a broad paved lane that ascends in generous curves through flowered slopes. Hours on and well above the treeline, an especially evocative spot is reached; surrounded by rugged ridges and the gentle contours of Rosa dei Banchi, a broad grassy basin opens up, housing pretty Lago Miserin and the ancient refuge of the same name. In times long gone by, labourers crossing to the neighbouring Cogne valley to work in the mine would be fed and watered at the squarish stone buildings of this former hospice, along with pilgrims visiting the sanctuary.

The pass which follows, the 2828m Fenêtre or **Finestra di Champorcher**, acts as a superb lookout taking in the Gran Paradiso peak itself, along with the superb pyramid of the Grivola and Torre San Pietro. The two names (meaning 'window') are a pointer to the area's linguistic heritage as the entire Valle d'Aosta is bilingual French and Italian, though a deep-seated patois can also be overheard in many a local café, and is evident in the toponomy.

Not far below is a converted mountain dairy, now a spacious hut and restaurant, **Rifugio Péradzà**, completely rebuilt with sturdy local stone and timber and inaugurated in 2003. This is a good spot to taste local food before heading down the ample trough that is Vallon de Urtier, run through with cascading streams carrying run-off from higher ice fields, watering the dense and brightly coloured blanket of wild flowers that the path traverses. Simply beautiful! Opposite, and clinging to the heavily eroded mountainside facing south, are the old Colonna mine buildings. Extraction operations ceased in 1979, bringing to a close an activity that had been going on since the 1500s. Hundreds of metres below stands the pretty village of **Cogne**, which now relies wholly on eco tourism for its livelihood. It favours cross-country skiing and has a lot going for it, thanks to a spider's web of walking trails linking beauty spots. A good bus service and plenty of accommodation and eateries complete the picture. But don't settle in here as the wonders of the trail await.

Across Col Lauson to Eaux Rousses

Not far from Cogne, on a glacial torrent downstream from a vast amphitheatre hemmed in by the ice-bound Roccia Viva and Tribolazione groups, stands a cluster of chalets. Known by the name Valnontey, this spot has a secret that will momentarily delay progress. The Giardino

The old hunting lodge close to Rifugio Vittorio Sella

Botanico Alpino Paradisia is a beautifully laid out garden that puts on a summer show of thousands of flowers, both common and rare, each one carefully labelled. Named after a graceful white lily that flourishes on high meadows, this is the perfect chance to put the (correct) name to those pretty blooms you've been immortalising on film for days, and prepare for those yet to come.

But that climb can be postponed no longer. Alta Via 2 follows an easy mule track in wide curves, gradually leaving the forest of conifer trees well behind. The spectacle at the southern head of Valnontey improves with every step taken, sprawls of glaciers broken up by rocky points.

Early arrival at **Rifugio Vittorio Sella** (2584m) is essential as an extra hour or so must be allowed

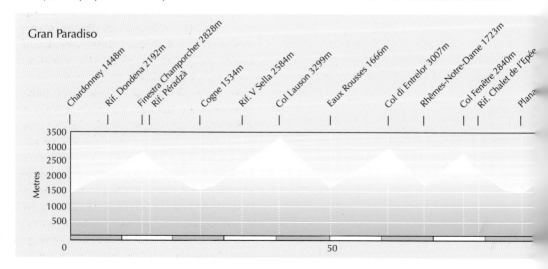

for the ritual stroll to Lago di Lauson at sunset. An atmospheric paved stretch of a former game track winds up to a magnificent lookout, en route passing through pasture where herds of ibex and chamois take their meal of an evening, quite oblivious of humans. Lucky visitors will even witness the mock battles fought by young male ibex trying out their horns in a ritual clash.

The next day, the approach to **Col Lauson** follows a long open corridor that becomes increasingly bare and austere as height is gained. Walkers are dwarfed by soaring reddish tinted flanks where the odd splash of spring snow sticks to the stone surface. A final climb negotiates a rather tricky passage, where a steady foot is essential. The airy col stands at a record-breaking 3299m, which easily makes it the loftiest point on the whole of this Alta Via. It was well known to pioneer mountaineers like George Yeld and the Reverend WAB Coolidge back in the late 1800s, who said it was 'probably the highest path traversed by horses and not leading over a glacier in the Alps'. However, as views are a little limited here, it's well worth making the extra effort to reach Punta del Tuf on the adjacent crest. Marginally exposed, it entails a further 100m in ascent and half an hour more. But all fatigue becomes ancient history as your head starts turning this way and that, south and north,

west and east, to drink in the sight of giants Monte Rosa and the Matterhorn. Sensational!

Valsavarenche is gained an exhausting 1600m in height loss later, over loose scree, pasture valleys thick with marmot burrows, and woodland. A good welcome is laid on at the **Eaux Rousses** guesthouses.

To Val di Rhêmes

The following stage needs to be taken slowly so you can savour the wonderful surroundings. On the margin of woodland alive with squirrels is a clearing housing Orvieille (2164m), a long photogenic building right out of a history book. Of old, this was a favourite base for both hunting and partying, and sepia photographs show it surrounded by ranks of tents for staff, and wonder of wonders, even a telegraph line. It does not require a great stretch of the imagination to visualise the flurry of activity this spot must have seen, with a veritable army of beaters, horsemen, cooks, servants and the rest. These days, at the most, a park ranger might drop by.

Two inspirational lakes are encountered beneath the Cime di Gollien. The first, Lac Djouan, is vast and shallow, perfect for alpine charr, a type of salmon, easily spotted in the crystal clear water. Further on is steep-sided Lac Noir, which belies its name as it actually has deep green hues. The trail becomes rougher and harder as broken scree is traversed on the approach to another dizzy pass, **Col di Entrelor** at 3007m, where a glimpse of Mont Blanc is enjoyed.

An initial plunge that puts even the sturdiest knees to the test leads to wonderful Vallone di Entrelor, a lush verdant corridor looking over to the dramatic looming bulk of Grande Rousse. Close at hand is a useful landmark for walkers, a huddle of ancient shepherds' buildings with characteristic vault ceilings, standing on the immense pasture flats of Pian de la Feya. In the early months of summer, once the snowmelt has drained away, these double as animal nurseries. Marmots emerge from hibernation with their young in search of

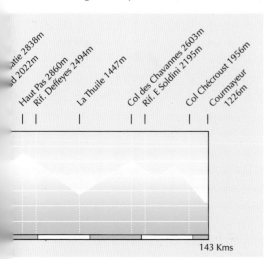

...atie 2838m
...d 2022m
Haut Pas 2860m
Rif. Deffeyes 2494m
La Thuile 1447m
Col des Chavannes 2603m
Rif. E Soldini 2195m
Col Chécroust 1956m
Courmayeur 1226m

143 Kms

tender greens, which they share with grazing families of chamois. The maxim 'there's safety in numbers' was the perfect description for the events that unfolded one July before our amazed eyes as we sat quietly whiling away hours observing the youngsters at play. The far-sighted marmots had posted an experienced sentry on duty on a prominent rock with a good view. Out of the blue, he launched into a tirade of piercing whistling and screeching, though for the life of us we couldn't see a sign of any danger – not a shadow of an eagle. He went on and on, never letting up, the atmosphere becoming ever more tense as adults herded their offspring together, never losing a munch, but always alert. When the intruder finally showed his face it was almost a disappointment – a young and clearly inexperienced fox for whom the sight of countless dinners on legs had been too much to bear. He crept cautiously onto the meadow, and of course the animals scattered helter-skelter, utterly bewildering the poor fox who slunk away, hungry.

Rhêmes-Notre-Dame. Any visit to this charming village must include the Visitor Centre to admire the lammergeier. OK, it's a stuffed exemplar, left over from the time when they were hunted, deemed a threat to livestock. But it's a rare chance to see this exceptional creature close up. As explained in the permanent exhibition, this bearded vulture boasts a mind-boggling wingspan up to 3m, constructs precarious cliff nests and feeds on bones of animal carcasses, cracking them open with great cunning by dropping them from a height. The good news is that this magnificent bird has returned to the skies of the Alps through a careful schedule of reintroduction, and sightings are increasing along the Valle d'Aosta.

Valgrisenche to La Thuile

In neighbouring Valgrisenche, Alta Via 2 touches on a string of hamlets with huddles of traditional farming houses in stone, and artistic communal fountains. All very low key and relaxing. Towards the lower northernmost reaches of the valley is **Planaval**, a peaceful farming settlement that time seems to have ignored. It is overshadowed by soaring cliffs, where trees hang on with difficulty amidst crashing waterfalls. The trek branches off on a path used by generations of shepherds to accompany their flocks to precious

high-altitude pasture. In fact the lush upper slopes are well watered thanks to myriad streams trickling through terraces of marsh, run-off from the huge spread of the Ruitor glacier that dominates the following two stages. The original trek routing actually crossed it – an arduous enterprise – but now swings north using ice-free passes.

Col de la Crosatie opens up at 2838m and comes as a breathtaking surprise, as the vast Mont Blanc line-up of glacier-spattered ridges and soaring peaks is suddenly clearly seen and almost touchable. And the icing on the cake? The odds are good that you will have all this magnificence to yourself.

Afterwards it's time to brace for a knee-bashing plunge to the isolated dairy hamlet of **Promoud**. The local council has constructed new bivouac premises here, a boon for trekkers who prefer self-catering and choose this as their stopover. On our first visit it was still a 'work in progress', so we took a pretty woodland detour to La Haut for a cosy B&B. The affable owners took us for a superb meal at their rustic restaurant, and we did try to feel guilty as next door a group of hardy French walkers had slept in the barn and picnicked on the lawn.

Next morning comes with a hefty 1200m slog picking its way over a boulder field set at a challenging angle. The imaginatively named **Haut Pas** opens up at 2860m to reveal a dreamy undulating landscape of sparkling turquoise tarns, the Lacs des Usselettes. Once again the Alps do not fail to repay energy expended with gifts of 'on top of the world' sensations. A delightful path drops into the magical atmosphere of the Comba des Usselettes, where trickling streams thread through marshy terrain studded with the dainty swaying stems of white cotton grass, contrasting with bright purple orchids. Everyone has a hard time of it here deciding which of the perfect picnic spots to choose for a relaxed lunch. One feasible alternative is to press on to **Rifugio Deffeyes**, where a cool drink and a tasty, filling plate of pasta can be had, along with a stunning outlook over the Ruitor glacier that extends beneath majestic 3846m Testa del Ruitor and the breadknife-shaped Grande Assaly. It's eerie to imagine that according to an ancient legend, all this was once fertile pasture. A curious tale is told of divine punishment meted out to a bad-mannered shepherd who overturned a milk pail rather than quench the thirst of Christ himself – disguised as a tramp. Alas! A vast freezing wave overtook everything, the milk turning into ice and snow. Nowadays the glacier melt feeds three magnificent crashing waterfalls that fling spray over passers-by and accompany the winding path to **La Thuile**.

Ten stages into the trek, fatigue combined with great satisfaction usually sets in, as does excitement in anticipation of the grand finale – 'the cherry on the pie', as the Italians say. Not that things have been boring so far. In any case make sure you get a good night's sleep and recharge all those batteries.

To Val Vény and Courmayeur

Emerald green Vallone di Chavannes conducts you gently uphill, though almost four hours will have passed before **Col des Chavannes** (2603m) is finally attained. The broad grassy ridge has a panorama that will take your breath away, as Mont Blanc opens out in wave upon wave of rock and endless cascades of ice. This spectacular pass is a hard spot to leave, and with one of the best outlooks on the trek, it is well worth savouring at length.

At your feet stretches the awesome Vallon di Lex Blanche (or Vallon de la Lée Blanche), which once hosted an ancient Roman road that channelled trade and civilisation back and

The Miage glacier sweeps into the valley below Lac Combal

Amazing views onto the Mont Blanc massif are the reward at Col des Chavannes

forth across the Alps. In this day and age it sees the constant passage of trekkers, both on the Alta Via 2 and the renowned Tour of Mont Blanc. Human figures are dwarfed by the graceful, soaring limestone of the Pyramides Calcaires, unique formations. Now all roads lead to **Rifugio Elisabetta Soldini**; a bustling, welcoming hut run by a local family, it is set on a minor

outcrop that feels shiveringly close to the ice fingers of the Lex Blanche glacier.

With every step taken the ice show gets better and better. The gigantic frozen river of the Miage does its best to invade Val Vény, englobing rubble and vegetation bulldozed by the walls of moraine that build up with the gradient in descent. Soon after pretty Lac Combal, there's a fascinating detour up a ridge and into the realms of the glacier to Lac Miage, a body of meltwater. Constantly reshaped by shifting ice, this milky lake can vary from murky green to grey-green, and is even crossed by the occasional wave as slender ice pillars topple.

The main itinerary climbs easily across open meadows, every step complete with a breathtaking panorama of the vastness of the Miage and Brenva glaciers and huge southern walls of the Mont Blanc massif. A final spot for contemplating all this splendour is **Col Checrouit** over an al fresco lunch.

From here you may prefer to take the handy cable-car that transports walkers and their weighty rucksacks down to the Alpine capital of **Courmayeur**; though naturally a decent path goes the same way for knees still capable of a steep but mere 700m descent and the trek's conclusion. Phew!

FRANCE
Martigny○
Trient○
Champex○
Argentière
St-Gervais-les-Bains○ Chamonix○ Ferret○
▲
Mont Blanc
Les Contaminès○
Courmayeur○
ITALY
Les Chapieux○

Trek 6

Tour of Mont Blanc

by Kev Reynolds

Ten passes, seven valleys and three countries makes a crude summary of one of the world's most famous mountain treks. But the popularity of this wonderful multi-day tour survives not because of numbers, but through the ever-evolving grandeur of the scenes to be won along the trail. With Chamonix below its north flank and Courmayeur to the south, the highest mountain in Western Europe makes a giant hub around which the Tour of Mont Blanc (TMB) pays homage not only to Mont Blanc, but to the entourage of granite aiguilles, graceful snow domes, chaotic glaciers, screes, moraines and fragrant meadows that lie at its feet. Whether tackled in a clockwise or anticlockwise direction (as on the standard tour), this is a trek to savour. It has its challenges, its demanding cols, its long days and never-ending descents, but every step is one to cherish.

The steep slab section of trail below Le Brévent – Mont Blanc across the valley

A laden pony carrying baggage for a French trekking party rests on Col du Bonhomme

Route summary

Location	The Mont Blanc range; France, Italy and Switzerland
Start/Finish	Les Houches
Distance	168km
Duration	10–12 days
Maximum altitude	2665m
Accommodation	Hotels, gîtes and mountain refuges
Grade	Strenuous
Guidebook	*Tour of Mont Blanc* by Kev Reynolds (Cicerone Press, 2nd edition, 2009)

Towering over Chamonix, Mont Blanc appears as a regal snow dome, a benign monarch, seductive and alluring. But from the southeast it takes on a very different aspect, for here the Brenva face and razor-sharp Peuterey spire lend the mountain a defiant, almost intimidating stance. It does not stand alone, but is linked by ridges and glaciers to numerous other peaks, virtually all of which are noteworthy in themselves: the elegant shaft of the Drus, the massive Grandes Jorasses, the upthrust finger of the Dent du Géant, the granite ramparts of the Chamonix Aiguilles, the cornerstone of Mont Dolent whose summit gathers the borders of France, Italy and Switzerland. Numerous other satellite peaks, less well-known than these perhaps but majestic nonetheless, stand alongside ice fields such as the long tapering tongue of the Mer de Glace and the frozen cascade of the Bossons glacier, whose deeply cut surfaces glimmer blue in the summer sunlight. Over all these Mont Blanc stands supreme, dominating the surrounding valleys and dictating their climate.

Making a circuit of this Monarch of the Alps, the Tour of Mont Blanc is Europe's most popular mountain trek. Over a period of 10–12 days it provides opportunities to study the massif in all its glory from every side, visiting seven valleys in three separate countries and, depending which variations are taken, crossing at least 10 passes, gaining and losing approximately 10,000m of height in a journey of about 170km. Ideal both for newcomers to the Alps and old hands, the TMB serves as a perfect introduction to Alpine trekking, and is rewarding whether you follow it just once or a dozen times. Its trails are mostly well defined and waymarked, some tracing balconies from which the finest views are gained, and as accommodation is both plentiful and varied there's no need to be burdened with a heavy rucksack.

In 1767, Horace Bénédict de Saussure made the first-known pedestrian tour of Mont Blanc. With an entourage of guides, porters and mules, he left the Chamonix valley and journeyed by way of the Col du Bonhomme, Col de la Seigne, Courmayeur and the Grand St Bernard Pass. In those days there were no refuges, and inns were scarce, so when he was unable to find a bed for the night, he would sleep in the hay of a simple alp chalet. In all, de Saussure made three full tours of the Mont Blanc range, and others were not slow to follow in his footsteps. His contemporary Marc-Théodor Bourrit ('mountaineering's first great publicist' according to Walt Unsworth) made a similar tour in 1785, and in

1839 JD Forbes, the young Professor of Natural Philosophy at Edinburgh, completed his own circuit, concluding that 'the most successful of Alpine travellers will … admit that the happiest, if not the proudest, moments of their experiences, had been spent on some of the more majestic passes of the Alps'.

Those sentiments have been echoed by tens of thousands of TMB trekkers ever since.

Les Houches to Les Contamines

Being a circular route, the tour could begin in any one of a number of different places, although tradition favours **Les Houches**, the village which stands on the left bank of the Arve about 7km downvalley of Chamonix. When taken in an anticlockwise direction, the first pass to cross is the modest 1653m **Col de Voza**, little more than 600m above the start. Modest in altitude it may be, but from the col the Chamonix valley is laid out for inspection in a backward view, flanked by the Aiguilles Rouges on the left and the Chamonix Aiguilles on the right. It's a fine

Col de Voza is crossed on the first day after leaving Les Houches

Tour of Mont Blanc

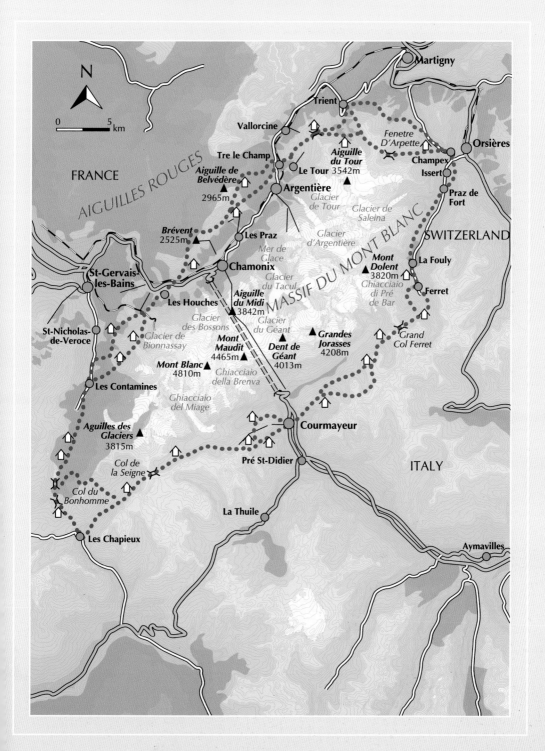

view, but many others will surpass it in the days ahead.

From Col de Voza the standard route descends via the hamlet of Bionnassay to **Les Contamines** in the Val Montjoie. But longer, and certainly more demanding than the main route, a variant rises alongside the track of the historic Tramway du Mont Blanc to the aptly named Bellevue, then descends a wooded slope into the upper reaches of the Bionnassay valley. Here, glacial meltwater thunders through a stony channel, which is crossed on a Himalaya-style suspension bridge, followed by a steep climb leading to the grassy Col de Tricot (2120m). A little over half an hour later it's tempting to call a halt at a private refuge in a meadow far below the col, in full view of the Dômes de Miage, while those who prefer to continue to Les Contamines face almost two more hours of walking.

Les Contamines to Courmayeur

Beyond Les Contamines the walk through Val Montjoie is gentle and undemanding as far as the pilgrimage chapel of Notre-Dame de la Gorge, where the TMB adopts an old mule path dating from Roman times. Rising through a wooded ravine, it enters the Réserve Naturelle des Contamines-Montjoie, and heads south towards

the Aiguille de la Pennaz. A path then climbs to Col de la Croix du Bonhomme at 2329m before angling across patches of old snow to reach **Col de la Croix du Bonhomme**, an easy 45 minutes and a little over 150 vertical metres further on.

The traditional TMB descends past a CAF refuge, and keeps heading downhill to the group of buildings at **Les Chapieux**, where there's an auberge. But a very fine alternative cuts left from the pass to reach the bare 2665m saddle of Col des Fours, before sweeping down towards the head of the Vallée des Glaciers and the converted dairy farm of **Refuge des Mottets**, where the standard route from Les Chapieux meets the Col des Fours variant. Refuge des Mottets is an atmospheric building, ideally placed for the crossing of **Col de la Seigne** (2516m), which serves as the gateway to Italy, for the ascent to the pass is neither long nor arduous. An easy ascent it may be, but the view on arrival at the col will stop you in your tracks.

Ahead the Vallon de la Lée Blanche drains past the twin Pyramides Calcaires to the Val Veni, which in turn leads to Val Ferret, at whose head the Grand Col Ferret can be seen far off. Across that distant col the TMB enters Switzerland, but for now Switzerland can wait, for it is the Italian face of Mont Blanc that attracts most immediate

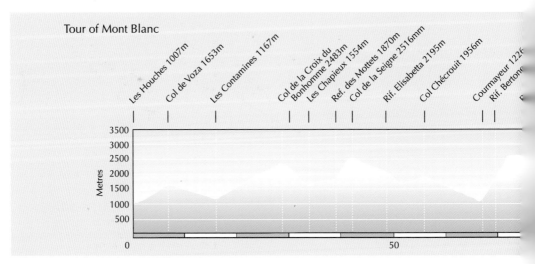

On the Italian side of Mont Blanc trekkers climb to a wonderful balcony trail that eventually leads to Courmayeur

attention – that and the spear-like Aiguille Noire de Peuterey beyond the Pyramides Calcaires.

A straightforward descent leads to the Alpe Inférieure de la Léx Blanche below the busy **Rifugio Elisabetta**, perched on a spur backed by a chaos of glaciers. Then down again to Lac Combal in a flat plain almost blocked at its far end by the Miage glacier's moraine wall. Val Veni spills below that moraine, offering a gentle valley stroll to Courmayeur. But conditions would have to be very poor indeed to take that route, for by far the better option angles up and across the right-hand

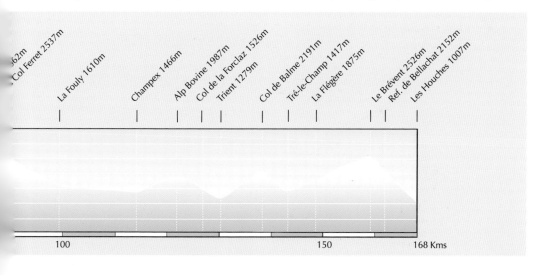

hillside to a ruined building, then more steeply to gain one of the finest of all balcony paths near a tiny pool rimmed with flowers. This trail takes an undulating course high above Val Veni, where every step rewards with an unfolding panorama of crag, spire, rockface, snow dome and tumbling glacier. None could fail to be moved by such a scene, and on arrival at **Col Chécrouit**, it's good to relax outside the Maison Vieille refuge, and with drink in hand gaze in awe at the wonderland revealed. It takes a strong will to drag yourself away to descend to Courmayeur.

Courmayeur to La Fouly

Wedged between steep mountain walls, and with a direct view of the Dent du Géant, the small yet bustling town of **Courmayeur** has a surprisingly relaxed atmosphere, and with a variety of hotels and restaurants is the perfect place to indulge in a little luxury before moving on.

The next stage takes the TMB along or above Val Ferret. Although it would be feasible to walk through the bed of this boulder-strewn valley, another magnificent section of the TMB takes a high route over the classic vantage point of Mont de la Saxe, and by way of Col Sapin, Pas Entre-Deux-Sauts and the Vallon de Malatra, brings the trekker to **Rifugio Bonatti**. Throughout, the way admires an array of glacial ribbons and big mountains: Mont Blanc, Aiguille Noire, the Géant, Grandes Jorasses and Aiguilles of Leschaux and Triolet among them. It's a truly spectacular walk, but if conditions should make this high route a dubious choice, yet another option is worth considering; a mid-height trail joined at a knoll above the privately owned **Rifugio Bertone**, two hours from Courmayeur. Contouring along the northwest flank of Mont de la Saxe among juniper, bilberry and stands of larch, the trail crosses open meadows with nothing to obscure more wonderful views across the unseen depths of the valley. Marmots whistle, streams chunter through shallow runnels, and cloud-shadows ripple across the hillsides. It may be an easier walk than its higher counterpart, but the rewards are no less memorable.

Named after the great Italian mountaineer, Rifugio Bonatti is one of the nicest of all lodgings on the TMB, with one of the finest outlooks from its dining room where the alpenglow on Mont Blanc adds an unforgettable bonus to the walk.

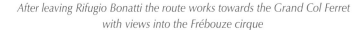

After leaving Rifugio Bonatti the route works towards the Grand Col Ferret with views into the Frébouze cirque

Nearby, derelict alp buildings mark the continuing route towards the Pré de Bar glacier. It then angles down to the valley floor beside Chalet Val Ferret, and an hour or so later brings you to **Rifugio Elena**, set on the hillside below the Grand Col Ferret, but looking across the valley to the Pré de Bar combe headed by Mont Dolent.

The 2537m **Grand Col Ferret** on the Swiss–Italian border is gained without undue effort. A backward view draws the eye to Col de la Seigne, while soaring above Val Ferret the Grandes Jorasses may be seen end-on, dwarfing the pastoral Mont de la Saxe opposite. However, the snowy Grand Combin entices the TMB into Switzerland, and after descending a short way from the col, a brief diversion from the main trail rewards with an overview of the Swiss Val Ferret, into which the route now descends.

Lower and more gentle than its Italian counterpart, the Swiss Val Ferret is dotted with small villages. The first, Ferret, is little more than a hamlet with a hotel and a tiny white-walled chapel, but a short stroll downvalley via a good path on the west bank of the river, **La Fouly** boasts a handful of shops, a sprawling campsite, several hotels and a tourist office – not to mention a direct view into the A Neuve cirque, crowned by Mont Dolent and the Tour Noir. In an earlier age, La Fouly was a renowned climbing centre and a favourite haunt of mountain writers such as Emile Javelle and Charles Gos. Today it's perhaps better known as an overnight halt on the TMB.

La Fouly to Trient

The four-to-five hour walk from La Fouly to Champex is an easy one – perhaps the least demanding of any on the TMB – but it's not without its charms, despite being dismissed by some commentators who advise taking a bus. The way leads through meadows and alongside rock walls. It teeters along an old tree-crowded moraine, and glances into the Saleina side valley. It squeezes through villages seemingly untouched by time, their timber-and-stone chalets resplendent with

flowers at almost every window, the fragrance of drying hay in every alley. Big mountains have no prominence here, but you know they're not far away. In their absence it's possible to concentrate on other things: grasshoppers that leap away from your boots, tiny clusters of alpines in crannies in the rocks, the blotched stain of lichens on wayside boulders, the sound of rushing water – all of which add substance to the bigger picture, and to the observant trekker are the very essence of mountain wandering.

Approached through open meadows, Issert stands astride the valley road, and 100m beyond the hamlet's last buildings a sign directs the TMB along a lane, over a stream and up a track, before a footpath leads into forest and the only real uphill stretch of the day. This emerges at the lakeside resort of **Champex**, where in la belle époque before the First World War the well-heeled would congregate in grand hotels, but where today trekkers make for more modest lodgings or the village campsite, and day-trippers enjoy the scene from a row of bars and cafés. Champex may have lost some of its former sheen, but the distant snow-crowned Grand Combin, turned upside down in the lake, underscores the resort's genuine appeal. There may be no major peaks to crowd the scene, but Champex is nonetheless firmly embedded in the mountains.

There are two options to progress the route from here. The main TMB makes a loop round the northern slope of a rocky spur pushed out from Point d'Orny; this is a largely wooded stage with a few short demanding sections, that goes by way of the **Bovine alp** and ends at **Col de la Forclaz**. It is a fine walk, of that there is no doubt, but the alternative via the lofty Fenêtre d'Arpette is simply stunning. Should the weather be doubtful, or fitness waning, the lower Bovine route should be taken. But given good conditions and lungs full of puff, the Arpette variant is a must for all keen trekkers.

Out of Champex the trail follows an irrigation channel, or *bisse*, through woodland, before emerging in Val d'Arpette, an unspoilt little valley with a hotel at its entrance, stands of larch and fir in its middle section, and a turmoil of rocks and scree leading to a cleft in a ragged skyline ridge. This cleft is the 2665m Fenêtre d'Arpette which, along with the Col des Fours, is the highest point reached on the TMB.

Breaking through the gap, the Trient glacier is revealed ahead, its frozen cascades tipping from the Plateau du Trient, while the deep valley below frames a multitude of peaks stretching as far as the eye can see. At first working through a jumble of rocks, the descent into the valley soon becomes a steep switchback overlooking a maze of crevasses, although as the glacier is shrinking at an alarming rate, it will only be a matter of time before it disappears below the icefall.

The path forks a few paces below the Chalet du Glacier buvette. Remaining on the right bank of the valley, one trail follows a well-made bisse to Col de la Forclaz and the Bovine route of the TMB. The alternative path crosses the torrent and forks once more. One branch climbs to the often unmanned Refuge Les Grands, and continues to Col de Balme, but the other slopes downvalley and is the one to be taken by trekkers opting to stay overnight in the tiny village of **Trient**.

Trient to Les Houches

This final two-, or three-day section sees a return to France via the 2191m **Col de Balme**, and despite the rise of 900m from Trient, the ascent along the TMB's standard route is generously graded. A rather soulless refuge stands astride the Franco-Swiss border on the grassy col, but the view of Mont Blanc, Aiguilles Verte and Drus, and the long trench of the Chamonix valley is truly inspiring. As RLG Irving once wrote: 'If that view does not thrill you you are better away from the Alps.'

Once more there are route options to consider, and again the weather (or conditions under foot) will be the deciding factor. An easy variant swoops straight down to Le Tour, the highest village in the

Refuge de Bellachat is the last opportunity to spend a night high in the mountains before completing the TMB

Chamonix valley, but the official route is far more rewarding. Edging the right-hand hillside, it then picks a way along the crest of the Aiguillette des Posettes, with one of the finest panoramic views

The onward route climbs away from the road through open patches of woodland, then by way of a series of steep metal ladders bolted to abrupt rock walls from which a birds-eye view reveals Argentière's rooftops more than 800m below. For those with a tendency to vertigo, an easier alternative takes a path from Col des Montets, and joins the ladder route at the massive cairn of Tête aux Vents below the Aiguilles Rouges. Yet another tremendous panoramic view stretches from Col de Balme to Col de Voza, and remains with you as far as Le Brévent.

The celebrated Grand Balcon Sud which takes the TMB from the Tête aux Vents to Le Brévent is one of the classic walks of the Alps, although it must be said that the ski industry has rather spoilt the way in some places, but those views of the Mont Blanc range, and of the Aiguilles Rouges above you, serve as a perfect distraction. Halfway along the trail the cableway station of **La Flégère** has accommodation, while it's also possible to stay overnight at the refuge beside Lac Blanc, which lies in a combe under the Aiguilles Rouges on a TMB variant.

Above Plan Praz the trail twists up to the bleak Col du Brévent, then continues through a wilderness of rocks and boulders to a piste easing the way up to **Le Brévent** at 2526m. It's not essential to visit the summit of this outstanding vantage point, but a brief diversion is recommended, especially as refreshments can be had on the terrace of a café built just above the cableway carrying visitors up from Chamonix, whose buildings huddle like toys far below.

There follows a long and knee-crunching descent to the valley, passing on the way the timber-built **Refuge de Bellachat**, the last opportunity to spend a night in a spectacular location where you can gather memories and watch the sunset stain the summit snows of Mont Blanc across the valley. After that it's downhill all the way to the railway station below Les Houches.

of the whole tour, before descending through forest to a road below Col des Montets. Overnight accommodation can be found at a nearby gîte in the hamlet of **Tré-le-Champ**.

Trek 7

GR5: Through the French Alps

by Paddy Dillon

Not only is the GR5 trail from Lac Léman at Geneva to the Mediterranean a true classic of near-epic proportions, it samples several other great treks along the way, the Tours of Mont Blanc, the Vanoise and the Queyras among them. And in between it explores wild and lonely terrain where few other walkers are to be seen. Given the freedom to spend a month or so trekking in the Alps, this would be a route to satisfy any experienced hillwalker. But, with numerous variants also waymarked, walking from A to B could take on a fresh dimension and lead to a series of energetic summer holidays, until each stretch has been walked, leaving very few corners of the French Alps untrod. GR5 from lake to sea is an enticing prospect, for the most imposing mountains in France lie between the two.

Cotton grass beside a lake on the way up to Col du Palet

Route summary

Location	French Alps, bordering the Swiss and Italian Alps
Start	St Gingolph or Thonon-les-Bains
Finish	Nice or Menton
Distance	645–725km
Maximum altitude	2770m
Accommodation	Refuges, gîtes d'étape and hotels
Grade	Demanding
Guidebook	*The GR5 Trail – Through the French Alps – Lake Geneva to Nice*, by Paddy Dillon (Cicerone Press, 2008)

Eddie, a seasoned Swiss walker from the Jura mountains, was a worried man. He'd been watching me for several days while I was walking the GR5, writing, photographing, detouring off-route and back again to check nearby services and facilities. He broke his silence as we entered the Vanoise. 'Do your publishers know how hard you work?' he asked. 'No,' I replied, 'They just think I'm on holiday.' I should have told him that I was enjoying myself so much I didn't want it to end, and it never once occurred to me to take a day off in 10 weeks of trekking.

Some years earlier, while crossing the Col du Bonhomme on the Tour du Mont Blanc, someone mentioned the GR5. I knew the trail was a classic, but I never realised

Pause for reflection at Plan du Lac on the way to Entre-Deux-Eaux

that it traversed the whole of the French Alps between Geneva and Nice. I made a mental note to chase up further details, but was distracted by the rumblings of a thunderstorm, followed by torrential rain and purple forks of lightning all the way down to Les Contamines, where the campsite flooded, save for the slight hump where my tent was pitched. Returning home, my feet were distracted by other trails over the next few years.

It was late one night after a mountain film festival that my publisher said, 'The GR5 may be coming your way, if you're interested.' From that moment, 'interested' was the wrong word – the correct word was 'obsessed'. Maps were ordered, and as they weighed a kilo, were attacked with scissors. In fact, everything I packed was brutally pared to the bare minimum. The more I researched the route, the more it

seemed to bristle with alternatives and variants. The main route alone would take a month to walk, while the variants needed another two weeks, and that was just one-way, since I planned to walk the route both ways. The 'season' for walking the GR5 is generally understood to run from mid-June to mid-September, and it was clear that I'd be one of the first to set foot on the trail, and one of the last to finish. Could I wait until summer? Not at all – I set out in the middle of winter to check the ins-and-outs of travel around Geneva and Nice, and potter around the foothills of the Alps, so that in the summer I could launch straight onto the trail and limit the time spent in the cities.

A complete north to south traverse of the French Alps takes around a month to walk and involves climbing and descending between 1000 and 2000m a day. Put in such blunt terms it sounds daunting, but walkers who pace themselves, neither dawdling nor rushing, will fall into a routine that allows the journey to be completed without undue stress, while being immensely satisfying and enjoyable throughout.

St Gingolph or Thonon-les-Bains to Les Houches

The GR5 has two starting points on the southern shore of Lac Léman – St Gingolph or Thonon-les-Bains – and the approach par excellence is on a slow and expensive ferry. Buses or trains get there quicker and cheaper. The climb from **St Gingolph** is steep, maybe too steep so early in this long trek, but it allows walkers to reach Chapelle d'Abondance in a day, compared to the

The Pre-Alps of Chablais rise above the Chalets de Bise

GR5: Through the French Alps

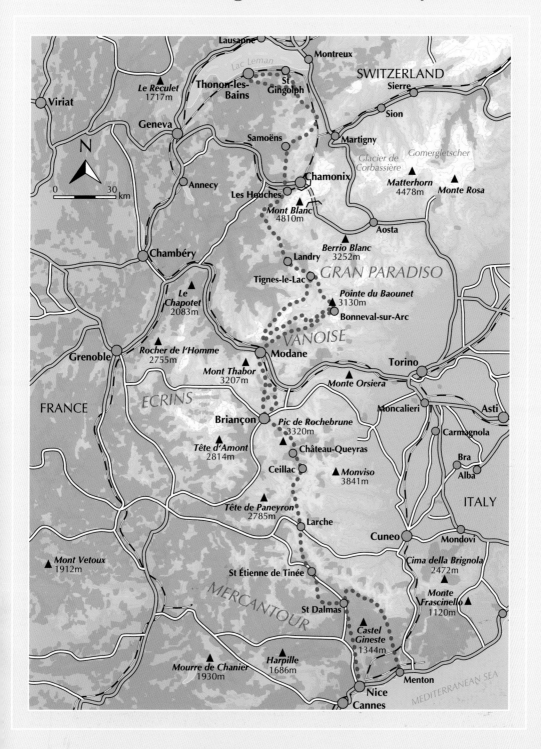

The Dents Blanches are seen on a brief incursion into Switzerland

gentler two-day trek from Thonon-les-Bains. The first mountains on the trail are merely the pre-Alps of Chablais; nevertheless they are a formidable barrier on the way to the mighty mountains of Haute Savoie. Herds of goat-like bouquetin (ibex) should be seen at an early stage in the trek.

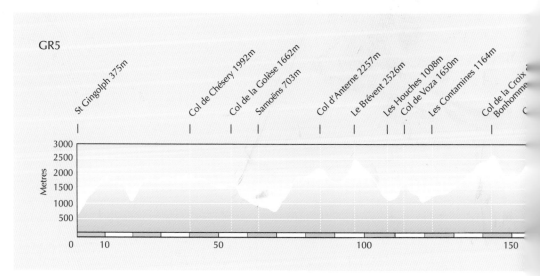

After a morning spent climbing round the sprawling shoulders of Mont de Grange, gentler gradients feature on the **Col de Chésery** between France and Switzerland. The likelihood is that a night will be spent at the Refuge de Chésery, so that in the morning walkers cross the Portes de l'Hiver, where there are sudden and magnificent views of the Dents Blanches. A series of easy tracks lead from farm to farm and over the Col de Coux back into France. Drop downhill and admire the boilerplate slabs of Les Terres Maudites, then cross the **Col de la Golèse**. The rustic little village of Les Allamands, named after German settlers, is passed on the way down to **Samoëns**. As for Samoëns, this busy town has spread far beyond its central 500-year-old lime tree and is a thriving centre for all kinds of outdoor activities.

After easy riverside walking beside the Giffre Torrent, iron ladders are used to climb through the intriguing, well-wooded Gorges des Tines. A series of splendid waterfalls are passed while climbing back into the mountains, so don't moan if it rains – rejoice at their power and fury! The Refuge Alfred Wills, named after an original member of the Alpine Club, sits on level turf at the Chalets d'Anterne. Waking up one morning to find blanket snow coverage, most people turned back to Samoëns, but I convinced three Englishmen to at least attempt a crossing of the **Col d'Anterne**. We ploughed a deep furrow through the snow in whiteout conditions, and found a lone walker sitting on the 2257m col. He had climbed from the Refuge de Moede Anterne, but was concerned he might not be able to find the Refuge Alfred Wills. We offered him our footprints in that direction, and we followed his footprints in the other direction – a fair exchange!

Le Brévent is a huge, steep and rocky mountain subject to fickle weather, and a dangerous place to be in a thunderstorm. Sudden snowfall quickly leads to avalanche conditions, and once the steep and narrow path is buried, route-finding is incredibly difficult. On a clear day there are wonderful views of Mont Blanc, and the only jarring note are the crowds who arrive on the 2526m summit using the cable-car from Chamonix. A steep and rugged, knee-jarring descent drops in tandem with the Tour of Mont Blanc. Walkers pass the delightful Refuge de Bellachat and continue down through forest, deep into the valley, to finish in the bustling village of **Les Houches**. Trekkers aiming to cover week-long 'bite-sized' chunks of the GR5 will find this a handy place to break their journey.

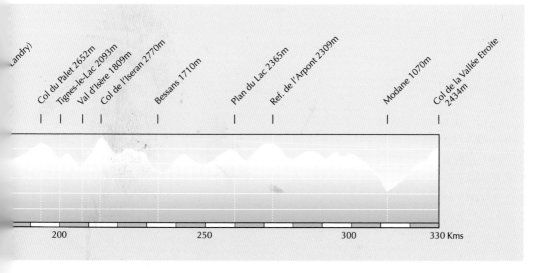

The rock tower of La Pierra Menta near Col du Bresson

Les Houches to Landry

From Le Brévent to Croix du Bonhomme, the GR5 runs concurrent with the Tour of Mont Blanc, and in high season accommodation comes under considerable pressure. The TMB gets very busy and some large groups now have their baggage carried along the trail by mules. I once came across a couple walking almost the whole of the GR5 with a mule, but the clouds of horse-flies it attracted were driving them to distraction. A simple climb from Les Houches uses winding tracks to reach **Col de Voza**, where the Tramway du Mont Blanc is crossed. By all means use the tram to climb to its terminus at Nid d'Aigle, at 2372m, otherwise wave it on its way and keep walking. Originally, it was planned to run to the summit of Mont Blanc, at 4810m – an impossible dream.

There is a choice of routes to **Les Contamines**. The simplest runs down to the village of Bionnassay, which was used as 'base camp' for early attempts to climb Mont Blanc in 1784 and 1785, then drops low into the valley to reach Les Contamines. A more challenging and scenic variant climbs towards the snout of the Glacier de Bionnassay, crosses the 2120m Col de Tricot and naturally takes longer and descends more steeply into the valley. It is well worth the effort on a clear day for views of the glaciated flanks of Mont Blanc. Make the most of the shops, bars and restaurants at Les Contamines, then start the long and gradual climb up through the valley of Le Bon Nant. As the trees thin out, snow might be noticed ahead on the 2329m Col du Bonhomme. A rocky traverse leads to the Refuge du Col de la Croix du Bonhomme.

The Tour of Mont Blanc drops down to Les Chapieux, and sometimes GR5 trekkers must go the same way. It all depends on the weather, since strong winds or snow and ice make the airy traverse of the Crête des Gittes difficult and dangerous. Normally, it won't be a problem in the summer and the GR5 later drops down grassy, flowery slopes grazed by stocky brown cows.

They produce the rich milk used in the famous Beaufort cheese, possibly the best cheese you'll taste anywhere in the Alps, and it may well be served after meals at many refuges, including the simple refuges down at Plan de la Lai. Cheese is a serious business in the Alps: as one Frenchman told me, 'Fromage, en France, est une religion.' The bongling bells of contented cows are heard as height is gained, and grassy slopes give way to steep, rocky mountainsides at 2469m **Col du Bresson**. Remarkable rocky peaks, pinnacles, cliffs and monstrous boulders flank the col, and the trail quickly leads down below La Pierra Menta to the Refuge de Balme.

Easy walking on paths and tracks leads down to the villages of Valezan and **Bellentre**, then there is a choice of routes. Anyone continuing along the GR5 can climb to the villages of Montorlin and Montchavin, while those wanting to leave the route can head for Landry, which has a handy railway station.

Landry to Modane – The Vanoise

The Vanoise national park is fascinating, but the GR5 really only skirts around its fringes. Some trekkers switch to the GR55 in order to climb higher and explore the remote interior of the park. In case of foul weather a third option is available, following the GR5E gently down through the Arc valley, from village to village instead of refuge to refuge. (See Trek 4: Tour of the Vanoise for an exploration of the national park.)

The GR5 climbs from Landry, passing a handful of villages to reach the Chalet-Refuge de Rosuel, which has a curious avalanche-shedding roof. The terrain becomes remote, though the route remains a simple valley walk. The Refuge d'Entre le Lac cowers at the foot of a monstrous cliff, beside a lake; Refuge du Col du Palet, as its name suggests, lies close to the 2652m **Col du Palet**. Tantalising views of the higher parts of the Vanoise are spoilt by the sudden appearance of high-rise buildings and the tangled cableways of the brash and busy resort of **Tignes-le-Lac**. Skiing is available throughout the summer, courtesy of the Glacier de la Grande Motte.

The GR55 offers a remote and exciting variant route to Modane; otherwise stay on the GR5, which crosses easily over a grassy shoulder to reach the neighbouring resort of **Val d'Isère**. A relentless climb short-cuts a winding road over and over again, where cyclists test their muscles and lungs, and everyone takes a break on the **Col de l'Iseran**, the highest point on the trail at 2770m. Looking ahead, snow-capped peaks straddle the border between France and Italy, while snow patches persist well into summer on the way down to the Vallon de la Lenta. The GR5 stays high, and later descends into the Arc valley at the village of **Bessans**. However, there is a chance to drop straight into that valley, picking up the low-level GR5E at Bonneval-sur-Arc. The low-level route generally appeals in foul weather, but a succession of Haute Maurienne villages are delightful on sunny days, when their heavy schist-slab roofs glisten with an almost metallic sheen.

The GR5 climbs and contours high above the Arc valley, passing only a few farms and refuges. Advance planning is essential as options to buy food are limited. Few walkers realise there is a summer bus service linking the remote Entre-Deux-Eaux with the village of Termignon and the railway station in Modane, or that there is a simple path linking the GR5 and GR55, if anyone wishes to switch from one to the other in a matter of minutes. A particularly rugged part of the trail runs to the **Refuge de l'Arpont**, climbing to 2589m at one point, and herds of bouquetin should be seen along the way. In fine weather the onward traverse is splendid and scenic, but in foul weather note that there are options to descend to villages such as Termignon or Aussois.

The final descent from the mountains to **Modane** is mostly forested, and it can be difficult to gauge progress, especially as the signposts bearing walking times seem to have been planted in the wrong order. Don't be in too much of a hurry, or you'll risk rolling on the pine cones that cover the slope. Bear in mind that the trail splits low in the valley – one leg runs through the centre of Modane, which has shops, but little else, while the other leg heads for nearby Fourneaux, which has accommodation and a railway station.

Modane to Ceillac

The two variant routes climb from Modane, up through a steep, forested valley, joining near

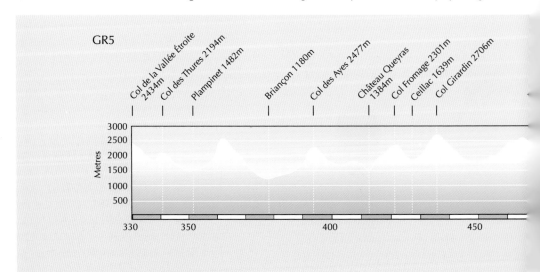

the ski resort of Valfréjus. As the trees thin out, a few farms give way to a gentler, empty valley dominated by Mont Thabor. The mountain can be climbed as an 'extra' by staying at the Refuge de Thabor, but this is a popular excursion in its own right and beds are limited. Crossing the **Col de la Vallée Étroite** used to lead into Italy, but France annexed the Vallée Étroite after the Second World War, and the 2434m col is now the boundary between Savoie and Hautes-Alpes. Nevertheless, the valley is ethnically Italian, with most of the properties owned by Italians, and Italian is the dominant language among residents and visitors. The refuges in the valley are called *rifugios* and serve Italian food. Pointe Balthazar, Pointe Melchior and Pointe Gaspard dominate the valley and are named after the biblical Magi, the Three Wise Men.

The GR5 crosses the 2194m **Col des Thures**, formerly on the France–Italy border, and descends crumbling, forested slopes to Névache, later passing through **Plampinet** on the way to Briançon. The GR5B offers a rugged, mountainous variant staying high above Plampinet, but lacks lodgings or services. A further variant, the GR5C, follows an exciting, narrow ridge route directly from Névache to Briançon. Once again,

trekkers must juggle between these variants depending on the weather and fitness levels. In calm and clear conditions, the GR5C is highly recommended, climbing to 2645m on La Grande Peyrolle, but the descent to Briançon is punishingly steep, rocky and stony. The GR5 main route crosses the Col de Montgenèvre, used in the past by the armies of Caesar, Charlemagne and Napoleon. From 1907 it was regarded as a major winter sports venue, though it has been eclipsed in recent years by other developments. If you can't choose between these variants, bear in mind that there are bus services between Névache and Briançon that allow you to cover all three, one after the other!

Briançon boasts of being the highest city in the Alps. It also boasts massive fortifications, constructed over several centuries, with the most obvious ones designed by Sébastien le Prestre de Vauban in the late 17th century. Anyone with an interest in military history should spend a couple of days exploring the city. A rather fiddly route leaves Briançon in order to avoid busy roads, and the scenery increases in charm as a valley is followed up to the 2477m **Col des Ayes**. In clear weather, views stretch to distant Monte Viso in Italy, as the trail enters the Queyras natural park.

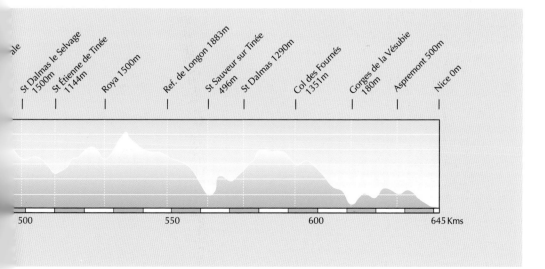

A valley route from village to village leads to **Château Queyras**, an iconic Alpine structure strengthened by Vauban, which also features an interesting Alpine geology exhibition. A long climb through a forested valley reaches the 2301m **Col Fromage**, where a short, steep and crumbling descent leads to **Ceillac** in the middle of the Queyras. This charming village is a notable woodworking centre (there being no shortage of raw material in the surrounding forests), with lots of wooden buildings and a number of wooden wayside crosses in and around the settlement (see Trek 2: Tour of the Queyras for more on this village).

Ceillac to Auron

While Ceillac occupies a pleasant pastoral niche in the Alps, the trail quickly leaves it to climb steep, forested slopes and even steeper mountainsides. The **Col Girardin** is crossed at 2706m and a steep descent splits, either for Maljasset or La Barge. Either way, an uncharacteristically long road walk leads down through the Ubaye valley. Jagged mountains rise impressively on both sides, but the road walk is tiresome. The trail crosses a narrow stone bridge, the Pont Châtelet, spanning an alarmingly deep and rocky gorge. An attempt to destroy this bridge with explosives during the Second World War failed, so the structure is a credit to its builders. After climbing through the village of Fouillouse, passing huge stone water troughs, the GR5 heads for the high mountains, reaching a remarkable derelict border fortress at Viraysse. After crossing the Col de Mallemort at 2558m, the trail descends to **Larche**, a village with a long history of transhumance, passed by shepherds and drovers travelling between Provence in France, and Piémont in Italy, over the course of thousands of years.

The Mercantour national park is entered at a point where visitors feed dozens of chubby marmots, next to signs telling them not to. A long, gradual, incredibly scenic climb leads to the **Pas**

The GR5C offers a splendid ridge walk from Névache to Briançon

de la Cavale at 2671m. Care is needed on the descent, as unstable piles of rock are prone to collapse onto the path without warning. Derelict barracks, once home to border-patrolling soldiers known as Les Diables Bleus, or Blue Devils, are passed as the route crosses the Col des Fourches, and descends to Bousieyas, the highest hamlet in the Maritime Alps at 1883m. Although the GR5 is now confined to the Tinée valley for its final week, the trail is anything but a valley walk, and there are still considerable ascents and descents to chart on both sides of the valley. The Col de la Colombière is crossed, followed by a rugged drop to the village of **St Dalmas le Selvage**. The easier, forested Col d'Anele is followed by a descent to **St Étienne de Tinée**. For a little extra effort walkers can climb up a steep, forested slope to reach the resort of Auron, and if ending or starting a stage hereabouts, both towns have good bus links with Nice.

Auron to Nice or Menton

The final stage to the Mediterranean involves a choice between two remarkably different routes – something to mull over for a couple of days. First, there is a fairly simple ascent from Auron, followed by a descent to **Roya**, then take stock of the weather, for the GR5 climbs very close to the summit of Mont Mounier, which often attracts late-afternoon thunderstorms. The climb onto its shoulder, crossed at 2587m, may offer a view ahead to the distant Mediterranean. There is a long descent to the only place offering lodgings, the simple **Refuge de Longon**. On a hot day, it is hard to believe that this refuge was built to replace a nearby structure that was demolished by an avalanche. The following day the descent continues, down and down, deep into the valley to **St Sauveur sur Tinée** . On a hot summer's day this may feel like a furnace, and there is a long and gradual climb up the other side, from village

Lac Miroir is passed on the climb from Ceillac to the Col Girardin

Steep, rocky slopes are a feature of the GR52 variant to Menton

to village to reach **St Dalmas**. Now it is time to decide whether to stay on the GR5 or switch to the GR52 to reach the Mediterranean.

If pressed to recommend a 'favourite' option I would urge trekkers to use the GR52, but bear in mind that it finishes on the France–Italy border at Menton, a long way from Nice. Compared to the GR5, the GR52 is longer, climbs higher, and is a much more rugged trail, which would appeal to anyone who prefers to stay in the mountains for as long as possible. The scenery is often astounding, for example, the amazing view gained soon after leaving St Dalmas while crossing the 2452m Col du Barn, and again crossing the 2448m Pas des Ladres. At that point a short variant offers a detour to the Col de Fenestre, where there is a peep into the Maritime Alps national park in Italy.

Monstrous boulders cover the mountainsides on both sides of the 2548m Pas du Mont Colomb and 2693m Baisse du Basto, where bouquetin and chamois are often seen. The trail runs through the Vallée des Merveilles, noted for its archaeology, featuring over 36,000 prehistoric rock carvings. Using walking poles, or leaving the trail without a guide is forbidden, and national park staff watch your every move!

Beyond the Refuge de Merveilles, the GR52 follows a long and arid mountain crest, with no lodgings or facilities until the distant town of Sospel is reached. On the whole, the walking is fairly easy, but start early, don't dawdle, and bear in mind that it may be a late finish. The final day's walk includes an option to climb Le Grand Mont at 1378m, otherwise it is a case of crossing col after col, then dropping steeply downhill to finish on the shore of the Mediterranean at Menton. Rugby fans should note that the founder of their sport, William Webb-Ellis, is buried in the ornate old hilltop cemetery.

Backtracking to St Dalmas, the main GR5 route features one of its longest days when it leaves the village. The climbing is gradual, scraping as high as 2000m for one last time. Only water and dairy produce is available in the middle of the day, at Granges de la Brasque. The trail continues along or beside a lengthy mountain crest that becomes increasingly rough and rocky, especially around Brec d'Utelle. Turning a corner here, I surprised a fox about to pounce on an eagle that was making a meal of a dead sheep. To this day I can't decide who the winners and losers were, but it happened too quickly for me to get a picture! The rugged ridge leads to the little village of Utelle, huddled on a hilltop where past inhabitants were able to defend themselves.

The altitude is considerably less towards the end of the GR5, and the only option available to climb above 1000m requires taking a slight variant route out of Utelle. The slopes, however, remain steep and rocky, traversed by airy mule tracks. A drop into the **Gorges de la Vésubie** is followed by a steep climb, but when the village of Levens is reached, there is a remarkably flat, grassy plain known simply as Les Grands Prés. Easy walking leads to the **Aspremont**, then only a whaleback crest stands between this fortified village and the city of Nice. Walkers who like to stick religiously to their routes will need to keep their eyes open to navigate through **Nice**, and it takes time, since

this is the fifth largest city in France, with crowded streets, traffic, hustle and bustle.

Technically, the GR5 finishes at a nondescript city square, Place Alexandre Médecin, but every trekker with a heart will press onwards through the city to reach the shore of the Mediterranean. I managed this in record time when the Avenue Borriglione was completely closed to traffic while a tramway was being laid through the city centre. The Plage Beau Rivage is the easiest beach to find, where you can declare this long trek through the French Alps well and truly completed. Alternatively, you can do what I did, and turn on your heel to walk all the way back. When a trail is as good as this, why not?

The hilltop village of Utelle, perched above the Gorges de la Vésubie

Trek 8
Tour of Mont Ruan

by Hilary Sharp

*A*lthough almost within touching distance of the Mont Blanc massif, the Tour of Mont Ruan is unknown to the vast majority of those who flock to Chamonix, and while the bristling summits of the Dents du Midi are clearly seen by travellers journeying south alongside Lac Léman, what lies behind them remains unguessed by all but the most inquisitive of trekkers. If ever there were an excuse to go exploring, this is it! Making a clockwise circuit of this hidden land of lakes and mountains, the Tour of Mont Ruan touches prehistory with the imprints of dinosaur tracks embedded in the rock; it crosses cols and invites walkers to divert onto non-technical summits that serve as grandstands from which to study Mont Blanc, and it plunges into valleys carpeted with flowers in the early summer. Unknown to all but a few, the Tour of Mont Ruan is a secret worth sharing.

Checking the map above the Giffre valley

Emosson lake – man-made but wildly beautiful

Route summary

Location	French Haute Savoie, Swiss canton of Valais
Start/Finish	Emosson (or Le Buet)
Distance	about 67km
Duration	5–6 days
Maximum altitude	2830m (Mont Buet 3096m)
Accommodation	Mountain huts and inns
Grade	Strenuous/Demanding
Guidebook	None; but a good website in French www.tourduruan.com

It is sometimes said that there's no wilderness left in the Alps. This may be how it seems when you're in the heart of the Chamonix peaks, or trailing along in an endless line, jostling with mountain bikes on some of the more frequented trails. However, once you've embarked on the Tour of Mont Ruan there may be times in certain weather conditions when you'd welcome a few more folk on the trail, for this route takes you into some of the lesser-known areas of the Haute Savoie and

Valais Alps, and even though the region is very close to those over-frequented Chamonix mountains, it tends to feel quite remote when the fog comes down or the storms hit.

This little-known trek circumnavigates the equally little-known summit of Mont Ruan (3054m), which forms the north end of the cirque that surrounds the Emosson lake above the Vallorcine valley to the northwest of the Mont Blanc massif. Mont Ruan is not a prominent peak, and in fact I've read that Willy Fellay, president of the Swiss walking organisation ValRando and inventor of this trek, mistook the peak that inspired him for Mont Ruan when it was, in fact, the nearby Tour Sallière! But by then the name of the trek was chosen.

Unlike many Alpine treks, the Tour of Mont Ruan does not have any famous name in its title or go through any major tourist resorts, but it does provide one of the most adventurous multi-day walks in the northern Alps. It takes an intricate route through the huge limestone foothills on the edge of the main Mont Blanc massif, which straddles the Franco-Swiss frontier. Along its length numerous summits beckon to be climbed, without the hassles of glacier travel or scrambling. *Via ferratas* aid the passage of a couple of ascents, and for the rest of the tour the walking is on small trails, unfortunately quite eroded in places, with friendly refuges each night. The trek is consistently on the edge of the high glaciated Alpine massif, so views are predictably stunning. You will not only become familiar with the striated limestone hills of the Giffre valley, the bulky mass of Mont Buet, and the prominent point of the Haut Cime, but your views will almost always encompass the glistening snow slopes of Mont Blanc and occasionally the far off point of the Matterhorn, its east ridge mimicking the profile of the Haut Cime.

All nights are spent high in the mountains giving extra-long daylight hours to savour the calm and tranquillity of the Alps. You'll revel in misty dawns when the cloud rises out of the valleys, and dusky twilights when the sun's last rays stain the summits rosy pink.

Important note: There's a long-term pump storage construction going on at Emosson, which will continue until at least 2015. Hopefully the work will not greatly affect the area, and in the long term, as far as hikers are concerned, there should be few changes. Up-to-date information on the project and details of any access limitations at Emosson can be found at www.emosson.ch/PublicEN/Visites.htm. As this work could impact on the Vieux Emosson area in the next few years, I have given two options for the first part of the trek.

Emosson to Grenairon:
option one, the normal route

Being a circular tour it can be started anywhere, so why not at the **Emosson** lake? At nearly 2000m, this gives a good high start to the trip and is accessible by road or by the rather fine funicular from Châtelard, reputed to be the steepest in the world with its alleged 87° section. From the far side of the lake a trail goes up into the Veudale valley

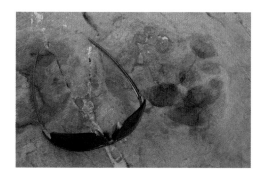

Dinosaur footprint, above the Vieux Emosson lake

and is then waymarked across rocky ground to the Cabane de Vieux Emosson, situated next to the higher dammed lake at 2181m. A night spent here allows an early start the next day, in which case you can slot in an ascent of Mont Buet en route.

On the far side of the Vieux Emosson lake, dinosaur tracks dating from the Triassic era are definitely worth a look. First discovered in 1976, they are now protected by chains but, because climate warming means they are exposed to the elements for longer each year, it is predicted that they will erode away in the next half century. How amazing when they have existed in one form or another for millions of years!

Beyond and to the southwest the beautiful cone-shaped summit of the **Cheval Blanc** will be the first of the trek. From this 2830m summit views of the Mont Blanc massif are really splendid and it would be easy to linger here. There's often a herd of male ibex chilling out just below the summit, seemingly unaware of the splendid backdrop behind them. If the plan is to include Mont Buet on this first day then you need to press on, but be sure to take time to gaze not only at the Mont Blanc massif, but also in the other direction towards the verdant slopes of the Giffre valley far, far below.

Returning to **Mont Buet**, the north ridge is equipped with cables and can only be envisaged in good weather. This ridge has to be descended, too,

Tour of Mont Ruan

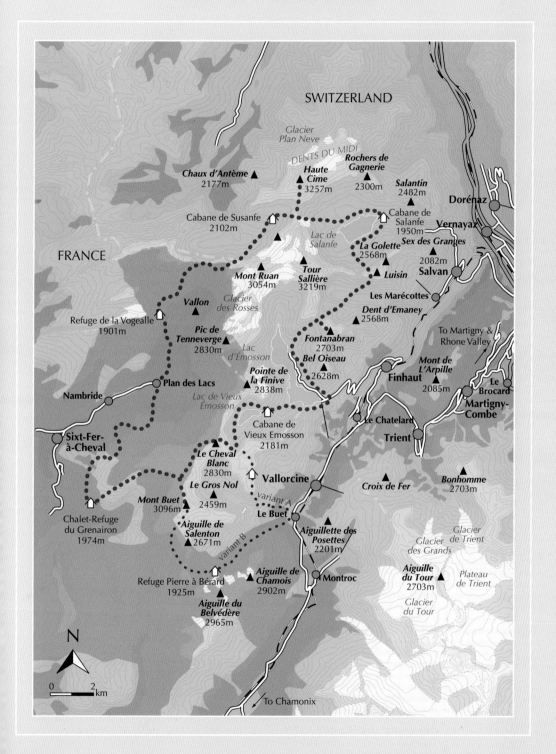

SWITZERLAND

Glacier Plan Neve

DENTS DU MIDI

Chaux d'Antème ▲
2177m

Haute Cime
3257m

Rochers de Gagnerie
2300m

Salantin
2482m

Dorénaz

Vernayaz

Cabane de Susanfe
2102m

Cabane de Salanfe
1950m

Sex des Granges

Lac de Salanfe

La Golette
2568m

2082m

Salvan

FRANCE

Mont Ruan
3054m

Tour Sallière
3219m

Luisin

Les Marécottes

Vallon ▲

Glacier des Rosses

Dent d'Emaney
2568m

Refuge de la Vogealle
1901m

Pic de Tenneverge ▲
2830m

Lac d'Émosson

Fontanabran
2703m

Bel Oiseau
2628m

Mont de L'Arpille
2085m

To Martigny & Rhone Valley

Le Brocard

Plan des Lacs

Pointe de la Finive ▲
2838m

Finhaut

Martigny-Combe

Nambride

Lac de Vieux Émosson

Le Chatelard

Sixt-Fer-à-Cheval

Cabane de Vieux Emosson
2181m

Trient

Le Cheval Blanc
2830m

Vallorcine

Croix de Fer

Bonhomme
2703m

Le Gros Nol

Glacier de Trient

Glacier des Grands

Mont Buet
3096m

2459m

Variant A

Le Buet

Chalet-Refuge du Grenairon
1974m

Aiguille de Salenton
2671m

Aiguillette des Posettes
2201m

Aiguille du Tour
2703m

Plateau de Trient

Variant B

Refuge Pierre à Bérard
1925m

Aiguille de Chamois
2902m

Montroc

Glacier du Tour

N

Aiguille du Belvédère
2965m

0   2 km

To Chamonix

The higher slopes of the Cheval Blanc are equipped with sparse chains to secure progress

so anyone who dislikes such steep slopes should abstain – this is an optional extra. The summit of Mont Buet at 3096m is the highest in the Aiguilles Rouges massif and is considered a good training climb for the higher glaciated peaks. Its local name of the Mont Blanc des Dames gives an insight into the effort required for Mont Buet, as well as into the macho nature of the Chamonix residents. If you're

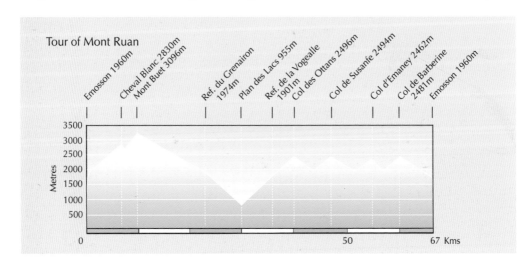

Tour of Mont Ruan

Emosson 1960m
Cheval Blanc 2830m
Mont Buet 3096m
Ref. du Grenairon 1974m
Plan des Lacs 955m
Ref. de la Vogealle 1901m
Col des Ottans 2496m
Col de Susanfe 2494m
Col d'Emaney 2462m
Col de Barberine 2481m
Emosson 1960m

Metres

3500
3000
2500
2000
1500
1000
500

0   50   67 Kms

sure of the weather, leave sacs on the col below the ridge to allow unencumbered walking to the top. On any sunny day in the summer season the summit itself will be busy – many people ascend by the long trail up the Bérard valley, but the north ridge is usually fairly quiet.

Returning from Mont Buet, the Tour of Mont Ruan takes the trail down from the col at the bottom of the cables. This leads to the Plan du Buet, from where a signpost optimistically gives one and a half hours to the **Chalet Refuge du Grenairon**. Don't be fooled – it is at least two hours, if not more, but the walking is stunning. The trail wends in and out of limestone towers before a polished rocky descent to the hut, perched high above the Giffre valley.

This is a very typical French refuge with a friendly welcome and good mountain food. An evening spent here gives the chance to relax and reflect on a long and exciting first day.

Vallorcine Valley to Grenairon: option two, variants A and B

Starting in the Vallorcine valley is hardly less logical than starting at Emosson, except that it is not officially on the tour. From the hamlet of Le Buet, a couple of kilometres away from the true centre of Vallorcine, the Bérard valley runs southwest towards Mont Buet. A stroll up here leads past the impressive Cascade de Bérard. Exit the valley at the next bridge, go past Sur le Rocher and out of the forest at Les Granges and you'll find yourself on the main trail to Loriaz, where there is a traditional refuge and working farm (variant A on the map). Alternatively, you could just follow the Bérard valley as far as the Refuge Pierre à Bérard

Savouring the exposure on Mont Buet's north ridge

(variant B on the map). It is advisable to stay at one or other of these huts, as the day to Grenairon is so good and interesting that it deserves not to be rushed.

From the Loriaz refuge, the rather steep Col de la Terrasse gives access to the Vieux Emosson combe, and the dinosaur tracks will require a diversion down towards the lake before picking up the trail over the Cheval Blanc as described in option one. From the Refuge Pierre à Bérard, Mont Buet is directly en route to Grenairon, but the Cheval Blanc will be missed out on this variation.

Grenairon to Susanfe

I first did this trek in the torrid heat of summer 2003 and the next day's descent to the valley was a slow and sweaty affair. Luckily the views made up for it as we ambled down to the Sixt valley, flanked by the impressive rocky summits of Tenneverge and the Pointe de Bellegarde. Lethargy caused by the heat prevented us from taking time out to explore the wild valley, aptly named Le Bout du Monde. But this was nothing compared to the subsequent sultry ascent from the 40°C temperatures in the valley to **Refuge de la Vogealle** (1901m), which left us all gasping from thirst at the Buvette du Boret about halfway up. Arriving at the hut an hour later we found that the water supply had dried up – luckily they had just had a helicopter delivery of 100 bottles of water – all of which had been sold by the next morning. On that occasion I remember being relieved that we'd not had any rain during the night, despite the water shortage, since the dormitory was tiny, cramped and the roof liberally decorated with holes. On a subsequent visit I had the opposite experience, with a full day of rain for this section. And that's when I found out that a heat-wave was far preferable.

The descent from Grenairon becomes very treacherous in rain because the limestone is so slippery. There are sections of trail that traverse gullies worn smooth by water run-off, and even

the slightest incline on these channels in rainy weather feels extremely precarious. Eventually this scary terrain gives way to meadows, extremely muddy ones in the wet, but less terrifying than what's gone before. However, beware the climb out of the Sixt valley in such conditions. In dry weather a short cut can be taken up the Pas de Boret, which not only cuts the distance of this section considerably, but is also quite fun if you like steep, narrow trails up limestone cliffs. There are chains to aid progress and the height is gained easily as you're concentrating on where to put each foot. However, in rain this path absolutely should not be taken. Instead, a long detour has to be made up towards the head of the valley, to eventually pick up a trail that heads up then cuts back above the cliff band ascended by the short cut. This way is long and tortuous – the path is bordered by lush vegetation which once wet quickly ensures that anyone walking through is also quickly soaked.

The good news is that the Refuge de la Vogealle has been recently restored and is now big, modern and comfortable. The rooms are pleasant and the food good. And, in case of rain, there is plenty of space to dry out gear in the entrance room – a rarity in Alpine huts.

Leaving the hut, the trail wends through meadows, which in the first part of the summer are carpeted with flowers. The 2295m Tête de Perua is a great viewpoint before taking the traverse across to the Col des Sageroux at 2395m, from where the little mound of the Tête des Ottans is crossed to **Col des Ottans** (2496m). This section of the route from the Tête de Perua cuts across numerous water run-off gullies and has become quite eroded. Beware on these crossings, as the path is slippery and worn away in several places.

A short detour can be taken to the 2847m summit of the Petit Mont Ruan, which is basically a shoulder on the west ridge of the main Ruan summit. Cairns lead the way but are not easy to spot and the ascent is only advisable if you have time to spare, and good weather.

The descent from Col des Ottans is exciting enough in its own right. A short slope leads to a rather intimidating void at the top of a via ferrata that facilitates the descent of a chimney and access to the cirque where the Cabane de Susanfe is situated. The first step into the chimney is the worst, after that you're encased in the rocky walls and less aware of the steepness, but take care and check that you can fit in with your sac. Best to give each other some space and let any ascending hikers exit first – there are no passing places!

After the excitement of the climb down, the path onwards is basically good, but in at least one place there are red and white flashes in opposite directions so you need to concentrate, as there are steep cliffs below and it would be somewhat tedious to get stuck above these and have to climb back up.

The Susanfe hut is typically Swiss – friendly but firm guardians make it clear exactly how they wish you to behave, and everything runs like clockwork. Sunset from here is rather impressive.

Susanfe to Emosson

A short climb from the hut leads through grass and boulders to a final barren moraine slope and the **Col de Susanfe** (2494m). From the col it's a short walk to the Salanfe lake (very confusing, these names that are almost identical) and a completely different accommodation experience. The so-called Cabane de Salanfe bears little resemblance to the *cabanes* used so far on this trip. The place lacks the character of a real mountain hut, but after several nights of traditional mountain accommodation most people will be more than happy to have big spacious dormitories with lots of coat hooks (rooms are also available), and a café that seems to stay open all day. Apparently the building was originally constructed for a firm that made and tested arms. Around the lake there are disused arsenic and gold mines. The views are good, notably of the Tour Sallière and Le Luisin, and the very popular Haut Cime des Dents du Midi, whose 3257m summit is a feasible proposition on this short day – so long as the weather is

The Susanfe Hut with Col Susanfe in the background, and the Haut Cime des Dents du Midi on the left

good. Starting from the Col de Susanfe, the climb takes shaly scree and moraine slopes, with the trail indistinct at times. Cairns mark the way but the loose rocky slopes are forever sliding and on some parts of the path it is really just a question of two steps up and one back. Care must be taken not to knock rocks onto people below – especially when descending.

It's also important to have good visibility for this ascent. It may seem difficult to lose the way on such a summit, but in fog the trail is impossible to see and a mistake could lead to disaster – big cliffs line the base of the slopes. Finally, from personal experience I can tell you this is a place to avoid in storms – and they can come very quickly; having been caught at the Col des Parresseux, just 200m before the top, in a barrage of lightning, thunder and hail that came from nowhere, I can only say, be careful!

However, having given all the warnings, on a good day this summit is really special – and

generally very busy too. The views are immense (from Mont Blanc to the Matterhorn with everything in between) and the sense of having achieved a real Alpine summit is very rewarding. Afterwards you can sit out on the terrace at Salanfe and bask in your summit pride.

It's perhaps important to note here that there is a very small bivouac hut on the Col de Susanfe – just room enough for two people to lie down but it could be a lifesaver in bad weather. It's also a possible shelter if some of the group wish to ascend the peak and others don't.

From Salanfe to Emosson there are two options. Either way involves a first climb over the 2462m **Col d'Emaney**. The summit of Le Luisin (2785m) is worth doing from here if time permits, and provides great views over the Emaney valley, but usually time constraints make it unfeasible because there is no alternative accommodation on this section. Going on, the path descends to the western end of the Emaney combe. Below

is the Emaney alpage where in the summer they make their own cheese, and a visit is highly recommended to see the cheese cellars and sample the local fare. If you do this the continuation of the hike would be over the 2451m Col Fenestral and down to Fenestral alpage, from where a nice balcony path returns to Emosson.

Otherwise the higher trail stays above Emaney itself and skirts to the west, not losing too much height, to then climb west-facing slopes past imposing red and grey cliffs to the **Col de Barberine** (2881m). These slopes often hold névé well into the summer and can be somewhat hazardous.

On the other side of the col the Emosson lake beckons, but it would be a shame to miss out the final summit of the trek. Fontanabran (2703m) is reached by a short climb of about 45 minutes and gives a fantastic panorama – all the way from the Mont Blanc massif to the Valais peaks.

Back at the col the descent path begins with a delicate traverse across scree, then becomes an easy trail down the grassy Barberine meadows to the track above the lake. This goes past the only remaining farm at **Emosson** – a poignant reminder that before the dam there were high pastures and a whole summer farming community up here. This road contours above the lake, through a couple of dark tunnels where, in truly Swiss squirrel fashion, boats and other machinery are stored away in nooks and crannies. Finally you emerge into daylight at the Gueulaz car park, with the Emosson café just a few weary steps away.

There's no accommodation here. If you began your trek in Le Buet then there is a choice: a bus service descends to Châtelard where you can pick up the train to Le Buet; if you have plenty of cash then the funicular journey is a far more exciting way to get to Châtelard. Finally, if you have time and leg-power then head for the Col de Passet on the far side of the Emosson dam and follow the trail down towards Barberine, cutting off to Vallorcine where signed – a long finish!

Sunrise at the Vieux Emosson lake

SWITZERLAND

Gasenried
Gruben
Zinal
Verbier
Trient
Arolla
Champex
Zermatt
Chamonix

ITALY

Trek 9
The Walker's Haute Route

by Kev Reynolds

To trek across the grain of the Pennine Alps is to unfold a succession of panoramic scenes unrivalled for their dramatic beauty. This 'haute route' is a fairly tough and adventurous one, but despite the rigours involved in a journey that crosses so many high passes and areas of chaotic wilderness, there are no technical difficulties to deter the experienced hillwalker, and as it also visits a number of small villages and low-key resorts in valleys that lie between the passes, the trek alternates a sense of remoteness with the orderliness of habitation that has long been part of Swiss culture. Reckoned to be one of the most beautiful treks in Europe, the Walker's Haute Route rewards those who accomplish it with a rich palette of experience.

The regal Combin massif is clearly seen from the Sentier des Chamois

Route summary

Location	Mont Blanc massif (France) and the Pennine Alps of canton Valais, Switzerland
Start	Chamonix
Finish	Zermatt
Distance	180+km
Duration	12–14 days
Maximum altitude	2965m
Accommodation	Mountain huts, gîtes d'étape and hotels
Grade	Demanding
Guidebook	*Chamonix to Zermatt, the Walker's Haute Route* by Kev Reynolds (Cicerone Press, 4th edition, 2007)

From Mont Blanc to the Matterhorn; what a dream of a route!

Who would not want to trek from one to the other; from the highest mountain in western Europe, to one of the most elegant, and certainly the most easily recognised of all mountains? Not from summit to summit, for that would take the trek into another league, but beginning at the base of the first and ending at the foot of the second.

And in between? In between there are no less than 11 passes to cross, with an accumulated height gain of more than 12,000m – that's almost one and a half times the height of Mount Everest. Each pass is a window that opens to a scene of dramatic grandeur, for in the two weeks it takes to walk from one to the

The flower-covered chalets of Clambin are met halfway to the Mont Fort hut

other you will gaze upon the greatest collection of 4000m peaks in all the Alps, visit some of its most spectacular valleys, and start and finish in two of the world's most important mountaineering centres – Chamonix and Zermatt. Surely that is a guarantee of the trek's pedigree?

The original high route (*haute route*) from Chamonix to Zermatt was conceived in the 19th century by the pioneers of mountaineering. And in those days it was very much a mountaineering expedition, for it traced a line across the Pennine Alps by linking a number of glacier passes, with the opportunity to bag a few summits on the way. Then, in the early years of the 20th century that haute route concept was hijacked as a springtime skiing expedition; an expedition that has grown in popularity over the years as the number of competent ski-mountaineers has expanded.

But the Walker's Haute Route described here has become well established as a true classic that owes nothing to its predecessors, other than its

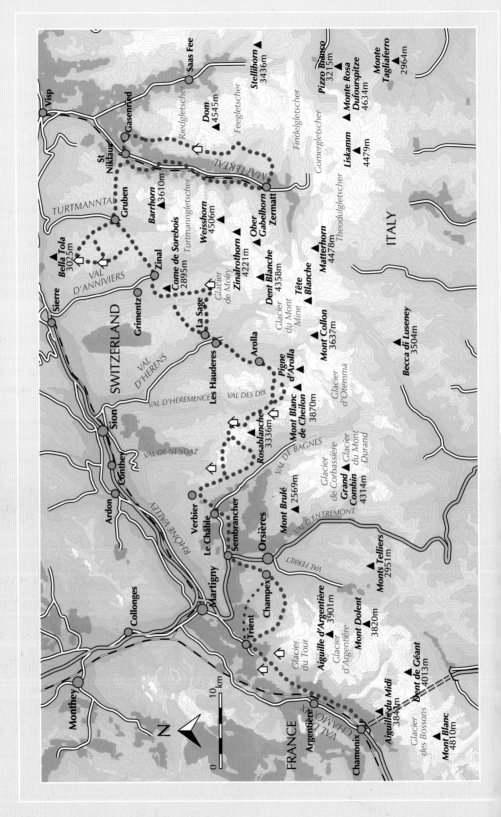

The Walker's Haute Route

name and the fact that it links those two iconic mountains. It may not cross any glacier passes, stray to summits, or top 3000m; it may not require any technical mountaineering skills, nor specialised equipment to ensure safe passage on its journey across the ridges that push north from the Alpine backbone. But it rewards with views of some of the most dramatic high peaks imaginable, among them Mont Blanc and the Chamonix Aiguilles, the snow-domed and glacier-clad Grand Combin, Mont Blanc de Cheilon and Pigne d'Arolla, Mont Collon (a great iced gateau of a mountain), the Tête Blanche and vast rocky tooth of the Dent Blanche. There's the Grand Cornier, Ober Gabelhorn, Zinalrothorn and Weisshorn, the Dom, Täschhorn, Breithorn and Matterhorn, and a long list of supporting peaks, glaciers and snowfields that form a background to the trek and invade your dreams.

Chamonix to Cabane du Mont Fort

Chamonix is a bustling place in summer, with a buzz of excitement, of anticipation, of longing, as mountain lovers of all persuasions shuffle through the streets, congregate at the many bars and restaurants, and inevitably – often without conscious thought – find themselves gazing up at the great snow dome that looms above the town. Chamonix belongs to Mont Blanc. Without that dominating presence, it would be just another town. But because of Mont Blanc, Chamonix is famous throughout the world, and it's impossible to spend time there without being caught up in Mont Blanc fever.

But if you are to achieve the trek to Zermatt, with the promise of gazing at the Matterhorn instead of Mont Blanc, it's necessary to resist catching that fever, so you weave a way through the crowded streets and make your escape as

Within minutes of leaving Chamonix, the Aiguille Dru appears on the right-hand side of the valley

Coated with a dump of summer snow, Aiguilles Verte and Dru look magnificent from Col de B

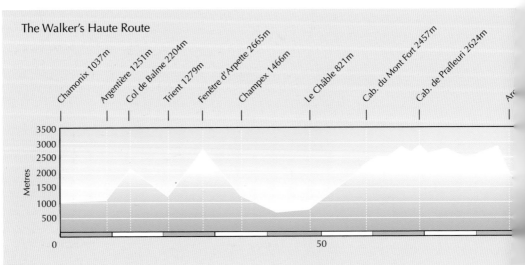

The Walker's Haute Route

Chamonix 1037m · Argentière 1251m · Col de Balme 2204m · Trient 1279m · Fenêtre d'Arpette 2665m · Champex 1466m · Le Châble 821m · Cab. du Mont Fort 2457m · Cab. de Prafleuri 2624m · Ar

soon as possible. Within the first half-hour you're free of the town and find your gaze is directed not at the Monarch of the Alps, but at the Aiguille Dru, a graceful granite shaft that stands erect on your right above the dark green of forest, defending a trench scoured by the icy bulldozer of the Mer de Glace.

Depending on your time of arrival in Chamonix, it's quite possible you will choose to spend the first night in nearby **Argentière**, just far enough from the start to underline the fact that the trek has begun. Argentière is about two hours' walk from Chamonix, and one and a half from Le Tour, the tiny village at the head of the valley where Michel Croz, one of the greatest guides of mountaineering's Golden Age, was born. Le Tour lies below the Col de Balme, which takes the route into Switzerland, and it's comforting to know that from the village a fairly undemanding path works directly up the hillside towards that col.

The 2191m **Col de Balme** is crossed by trekkers on the Tour of Mont Blanc, but usually in the opposite direction from that of the Walker's Haute Route. From it, retrospective views of Mont Blanc and the aiguilles on one side of the Chamonix valley, and the Aiguilles Rouges on the other, are truly memorable, while Switzerland

beckons beyond the refuge that stands astride the international border. In the valley below, among sloping meadows flanked by steep hillsides, **Trient** has become a haven for trekkers from around the world.

Trails used by the TMB are also adopted by the Haute Route for the stage which leads from Trient to Champex. The easier option is the so-called Bovine route which begins on the Col de le Forclaz above Trient; the other crosses the challenging 2665m **Fenêtre d'Arpette** at the end of a weary climb alongside the fast-shrinking Trient glacier. The Fenêtre route is the preferred option, given suitable conditions, that is, for it represents the very essence of Alpine trekking, and provides stimulating views throughout. But beware of storms, and take great care on the initial descent from the pass into the turmoil of screes, rocks and boulders of the upper Val d'Arpette. Lower down, the valley is seductive with larchwoods and rough pastures, and the trail eventually spills into the little lakeside resort of **Champex** – a complete contrast to the uncompromising upper reaches of Arpette.

Champex offers a choice of hotels, gîtes and a campsite, and is a restful place in which to relax after a tough day on the trail. A cold beer clutched

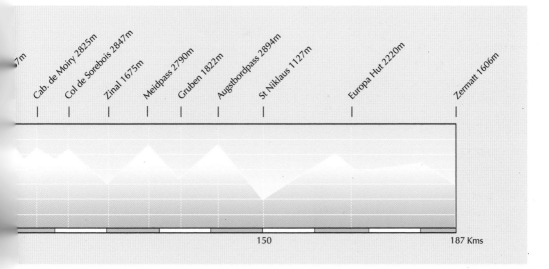

Cab. de Moiry 2825m · Col de Sorebois 2847m · Zinal 1675m · Meidpass 2790m · Gruben 1822m · Augstbordpass 2894m · St Niklaus 1127m · Europa Hut 2220m · Zermatt 1606m

150   187 Kms

in your hand as you gaze across the lake to the distant Grand Combin is another of the joys of Alpine trekking.

A tough day on the trail is followed by one of the easiest, for there's very little height gain on the stage leading to **Le Châble** in Val de Bagnes. Most of the way is downhill through a workaday Swiss landscape dotted with farming communities. Then, from Sembrancher which lies at a confluence of valleys, the way swings into Val de Bagnes, cuts through woodland and meadow and enters Le Châble by the back door, so to speak.

The next stage is another tough one, for there's a hefty 1636m of ascent to face in order to reach Cabane du Mont Fort. Of course, you could always take a cable-car that would deliver you onto a trail with a short walk to the hut, but that would rather defeat the object of choosing this trek. Better to accept the challenge and revel in it – although there may well be moments on the long, steep haul up the mountainside when you will question the wisdom of that decision!

After twisting uphill through forest, about halfway up the mountainside you emerge at the flower-smothered buildings of Clambin, whose restaurant exploits a charming view of the distant Mont Blanc range. I defy anyone to wander past that restaurant without stopping for a drink, at the very least. But don't forget there's another 700m or more to climb before you reach the hut.

Cabane du Mont Fort stands on a 2457m bluff at a junction of trails due south of Mont Gelé, facing across the deep Val de Bagnes to the Mont Blanc massif in one direction, the Dents du Midi in another, and the Combin massif off to the southwest. Comfortable, and with an ambience that suits its location, it makes a perfect overnight lodging, and sunset views can be spectacular.

Mont Fort to Arolla

The route that heads away from Mont Fort soon joins the dramatic Sentier des Chamois. Never was a trail more aptly named, for it really is a 'chamois path' that contours along the mountainside hundreds of metres above the valley, and chamois and ibex are often seen from this path, for the area is protected as a nature reserve and the wildlife obviously knows it. Exposed in places, but safeguarded with fixed chains or cables, there's a breathtaking view across the valley to the beautiful Combin massif, whose long tongue of the Corbassière glacier is such a prominent feature.

Turning away from that view, the trail edges above the Louvie basin to reach Col de Louvie, the second of the day's three passes – the first was Col Termin, less a col than a spur. From Col de Louvie you descend into a wilderness of rocks, screes and old moraines, skirt round the tail end of the Grand Désert glacier and mount a seemingly never-ending wasteland to gain the 2965m Col de Prafleuri. Since *prafleuri* means 'the plain of flowers' you may well expect to peer down from the pass into a meadowland. But reality is very different, for below the col a depressing scene reveals a much-abused mountain basin, scarred by quarry works dating back to the 1950s and the construction of the Grande Dixence hydro scheme. But on the edge of that sorry basin stands the comfortable **Cabane de Prafleuri**, from which you can sometimes watch ibex grazing nearby.

Prafleuri may have been sacrificed for the creation of electricity, but just 20 minutes above the hut, Col de Roux (2804m) reveals another side of that industry, for a lovely scene opens out as you look onto the 5km long Lac des Dix spreading through the valley below. Its huge concrete barrage is not seen, so unless the water level is low the lake appears to be natural, while at its far end old moraines and minor rock peaks lead the eye to Mont Blanc de Cheilon and its neighbours.

A pleasant walk through pastures and on a lakeside track ends at a junction of paths. One crosses the glacial torrent feeding into the lake; the other remains on the west side of the Glacier de Cheilon to visit Cabane des Dix, perched atop a curious plug of rock near the foot of Mont Blanc de Cheilon. Across the glacier east of the hut walkers have a choice of two routes by which to

The climb to the Fenêtre d'Arpette looks over the Trient glacier

As evening settles at the Mont Fort hut, the Mont Blanc massif appears to float on a raft of mist

scale a low ridge for the continuing trek to **Arolla**. The first of these ridge crossings is the 2919m Col de Riedmatten above a steep and gritty gully; the other is the Pas de Chèvres (2855m), reached by three near-vertical steel ladders bolted to the rockface. The ladder route is the easier and shorter of the two, but is definitely not for anyone suffering vertigo.

Both crossing points reveal the distant tip of the Matterhorn as one small but eye-catching feature in an exciting panorama, while the two descending trails meet in a rough basin of pasture to continue as one all the way down to Arolla. This small climbing centre appears to have grown very little since being 'discovered' by Alpine Club pioneers during the Victorian era, and is over-looked by Mont Collon, whose regal presence far exceeds its modest 3637m height.

Arolla to the Mattertal

An hour's walk from Arolla leads to the tiny Lac Bleu, after which you descend to Les Haudères, another mountaineering centre at the head of Val d'Hérens. Reached far too early to make an overnight stay worth considering, most trekkers continue up the east flank of the valley for another hour or so to **La Sage**, where a small hotel, and dormitories above the Café-Restaurant l'Ecureuil, provide accommodation at the end of an easy day's trekking.

Between La Sage and Zinal lies Val de Moiry, a glacier-carved tributary of Val d'Anniviers, whose exquisite icefall is admired in all its chaotic glory from **Cabane de Moiry** – my preferred overnight option for the stage after leaving La Sage. To get there entails crossing a long ridge system emanating from the Grand Cornier. Of the several cols in that ridge, the trekker's choice usually falls between the 2868m Col du Tsaté, or 2919m Col de Torrent. Despite its slightly lower altitude, the

Below the Augstbordpass the Dom suddenly reveals itself across the depths of the Mattertal

first is a tougher proposition than the second, but both send their descending trails down to Lac de Moiry, where a path teeters along a moraine rib, then up broken rock slabs to gain Cabane de Moiry at 2825m. Few overnight lodgings on the Haute Route have a more imposing location than this.

Having gained more than 400m of height from the shores of Lac de Moiry, it's necessary to lose most of that height next morning, before contouring over abrupt grass slopes above the lake to a junction with a path which then climbs to the 2847m **Col de Sorebois**. This is the way into Val de Zinal, the upper stem of Val d'Anniviers, and on the way down into that valley, a great arc of icy mountains, topped by the mighty Weisshorn, demands your attention. The slope grows steeper as you approach **Zinal**, and at the end of a brutal 1172m descent, you'll be anxious to rest aching leg muscles. Though only a small mountaineering centre, Zinal has no shortage of facilities, and a restful night spent there will prepare you for the next stage of the route.

That stage has a variety of options, including a choice of overnight accommodation on the Val d'Anniviers side of the next dividing ridge, or the opportunity to cross that ridge into the Turtmanntal and thereby reduce the trek's overall length by one day. But first a trail leads away from the high mountains that crowd the head of the valley, and at midheight it ripples along the hillside heading north to the large Victorian-era Hotel Weisshorn below the 2790m **Meidpass**. An hour's walk beyond the hotel, the privately owned Cabane Bella Tola offers alternative accommodation, and is also well situated for the next day's crossing of the Meidpass. But before you even reach Hotel Weisshorn on the walk from Zinal, there's an opportunity to break away from this well-trod route in order to cross the 2874m pass of the Forcletta, which leads into the Turtmanntal by a route even more beautiful than that allowed via the Meidpass.

Whichever crossing is chosen, the little summer-only village of **Gruben** is the eventual destination. Snug among meadows in the peaceful Turtmanntal, at whose head glaciers spill from Weisshorn and Bishorn, Gruben is the first German-speaking community on the Walker's Haute Route. From Chamonix to the Forcletta/Meidpass crossing, all was French-speaking, but from Gruben to Zermatt, German (or Swyzerdütsch) to be precise, is the local language.

The windy 2894m **Augstbordpass** is the final col, giving a stiff 1072m climb straight after breakfast. There's no gentle lead-in to this climb, for it begins the moment you set out from the village, and barely relents until the pass is reached. Overlooking a rock-strewn wilderness, there's also a distant view of the Fletschhorn and northern outliers of the great Mischabel wall, before you descend into the rocky bowl below. Picking a way with care among those rocks, the way curves to the right and, on turning a spur, presents one of the most exhilarating views of the Haute Route. It's a view guaranteed to stop you in your tracks.

Hundreds of metres below, the deep trench of the Mattertal is little more than a hint, while across that valley, the Dom – highest mountain that lies entirely in Switzerland – rises above its snow-shining neighbours and casts down the long tongue of the Ried glacier between dark shoulders of rock. At the head of the Mattertal Liskamm, Castor, Pollux and the long white crest of the Breithorn all challenge for supremacy. The Matterhorn, however, cannot be seen from this angle as it remains hidden behind the black outline of the Mettelhorn.

When you can at last tear yourself away from that view, the descent continues on an old partly paved mule trail, and 600m below that wonderful viewpoint, enters another place of romantic beauty: the tiny alp hamlet of Jungen (1955m). Also known as Jungu, the cluster of chalets, haybarns and a minuscule chapel appears to hang from the precipitous hillside. As only limited accommodation is available, most trekkers continue all the way down to **St Niklaus**, a small town deep in the Mattertal 800m below the hamlet.

The Mattertal to Zermatt

For many years the only walking route from St Niklaus to Zermatt led from village to village along the bed of the Mattertal. That route is still valid, making a day's journey of about 18km. But in 1997 an alternative high route,

the so-called Europaweg, was created along the east flank of the valley. A route of extraordinary beauty and complexity, it must be admitted that in several places it is also potentially dangerous, and the rockfall to which it is vulnerable has often closed it for weeks at a time. The route changes from one year to the next.

To reach the start of the Europaweg entails a short uphill walk from St Niklaus to Gasenried, a lovely little hamlet at the foot of the Ried glacier, with just one hotel for overnight accommodation. From there a six-hour hike (plus rests) takes the determined trekker to the **Europa Hut** on an ever-interesting and often heart-racing route. The hut is perched halfway along the trail, on a dizzy slope with a direct view across the valley to the Weisshorn. Upvalley the Matterhorn is also on show.

The final day continues along that amazing trail to Täschalp. From Täschalp an easier walk leads to Tufteren, from where a highly recommended but devious route stretches the glory of this trek to its ultimate conclusion, with the elegant Matterhorn in view all the way. And by way of Findeln you descend at last to **Zermatt**, overshadowed of course by that great icon of the Alps.

What a trek to celebrate!

The Europaweg crosses several unstable sections where caution is paramount

Trek 10

Alpine Pass Route

by Kev Reynolds

A long route that not only makes close acquaintance with the renowned giants of the Bernese Oberland, but becomes familiar with peaks and passes known only to the true Alpine addict, the Alpine Pass Route (APR) crosses the Swiss mountains from east to west in a journey of classic proportions. The terrain walked is as varied as the scenery, while a number of rustic villages along the way introduce the walker to a workaday Switzerland rarely portrayed in the glossy brochures, but which is every bit as interesting as that which surrounds world-famous resorts such as Grindelwald, Wengen or Mürren visited midway along the trek. Impressive mountains may be what entice you to go trekking in the Alps, but the APR also illustrates the charm of village and valley that brings a human dimension to the Alpine scene.

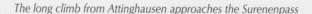

The long climb from Attinghausen approaches the Surenenpass

Descending to the Lauterbrunnen valley the trail passes through Mettlenalp, overlooked by the Mönch

Route summary

Location	East to west across the Swiss Alps
Start	Sargans, near Liechtenstein
Finish	Montreux on Lac Léman
Distance	326km
Duration	15+ days
Maximum altitude	2778m
Accommodation	Hotels, gasthofs, dormitories (*massenlagers*) and mountain huts
Grade	Demanding
Guidebook	*Alpine Pass Route* by Kev Reynolds (Cicerone Press, 2nd edition, 2004)

The idea of walking from one side of a country to the other is an imaginative concept that has spawned several great treks, among them the popular Coast to Coast route in Britain, three epic treks along the length of the Pyrenees from the Atlantic to the Mediterranean and, in Switzerland, the Alpine Pass Route.

The APR is a truly challenging route. Beginning in the ancient town of Sargans near the Liechtenstein border, it works a way southwestward across the mountains via no less than 16 passes, to end in Montreux on the shores of Lac Léman. The central part of the route crosses the north flank of the well-known Bernese Oberland, but elsewhere – and particularly this is true at the start and finish – the hills, valleys and mountains are largely ignored by all but a very few enthusiasts. It seems hard to believe that in the 21st century there are regions of Switzerland where, even in summer, you can walk for hours at a time and see no-one. But this is the reality which gives the lie to the oft-repeated myth that the Alps are overcrowded.

Alpine Pass Route

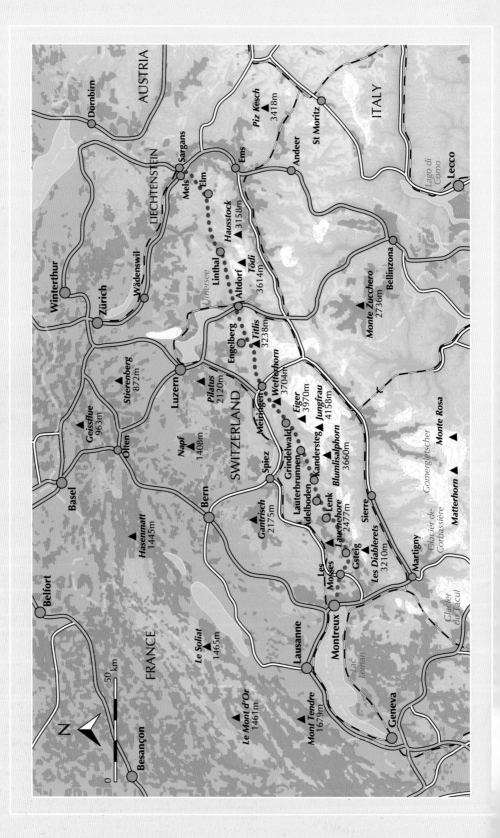

Consider the statistics. Apart from the 16 passes that give the route its name, between Sargans and Montreux there's a walking distance of around 326km, and an accumulated height gain of more than 15,000m. The APR may not claim to be the longest or toughest in the Alps, but the combination of challenge, history, cultural variety, opportunities to study wildlife, and the sheer quality of mountain landscapes among which the trek weaves its course, ensures an unforgettable experience for all who complete it.

To walk from end to end will take most seasoned trekkers at least 15 days, but the route splits neatly into two or three multi-day sections, so if time is limited, it would be feasible to tackle the APR over several holidays. A few trekking companies organise holidays that concentrate mostly on the central section, but it's not at all difficult to do this independently. It should also be noted that some individual stages are very long, yet for all but the most dedicated of purists transport options exist that enable you to shorten some of those stages without detracting too much from the experience.

As there are few mountain huts actually on the route, accommodation will be found in small hotels, gasthofs and dormitories, known here as either *massenlagers* or *matratzenlagers* – literally, 'mattress rooms' – which are located in a number of villages; check the guidebook for details.

Sargans to Altdorf

Conveniently reached by train from Zürich, **Sargans** directs the APR into the pastoral Weisstannental in readiness for the first pass crossing, and together with the next three stages, it makes a fine, albeit low-key, introduction to the trek. On the way to Altdorf there'll be four passes and a clutch of neat villages as you wander through a back-of-beyond country with attractive

Snowpeaks at the head of the Sernftal are seen from above Wichlenmatt

mountains on show that need a map for identification. In most European countries some of those peaks would be notable, but here they remain little known bit-part players, a chorus line standing back to allow the star cast to parade their beauty as the trek progresses.

The Weisstannental is a peaceful valley flanked by wooded hillsides, and guarded at its entrance by a defile that forces the APR along its western side. About four hours from Sargans the first night's accommodation is found in the village that lends its name to the valley. With two small hotels to choose from, **Weisstannen** is a modest farming community with the pungent smell of cows and silage to lend it a truly bucolic atmosphere.

Next day the 2223m **Foopass** is the first on the route to be crossed. Located on the headwall of an amphitheatre enclosing the valley between the Foostock and Piz Sardona, it's reached by way of a couple of farms and a solitary alp with its own marmot colony. Waterfalls feature in the landscape on both sides of the pass, and descending the western side through more alps,

After crossing the Klausenpass a trail passes below the impressive waterfall at Äsch

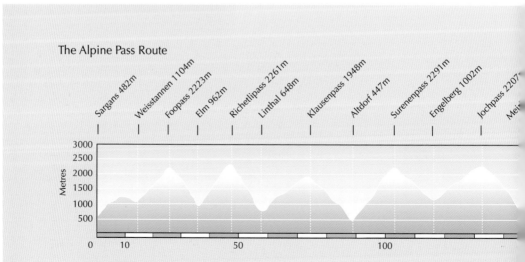

The Alpine Pass Route

the Tschingelhoren comes into view on the way down to meadows that lead into the Sernftal and the flower-decked village of **Elm**, backed by Piz Sardonas and Piz Segnas.

The second full day of the trek is more demanding than the first, with 22km to cover and the forcing of two passes (of sorts) on the way to Linthal. The first of these is an unnamed saddle of 2156m; the second is the 2261m **Richetlipass**. Between the two lies the Wichlenmatt basin ringing with the sound of cowbells in summer. This is a pastoral land. Not for us yet the big glacial mountains with their moraines, boulder fields and screes; here the trail cuts across grass slopes running with streams. But a dump of unseasonal snow can transform the way in moments, demanding caution and navigational skills for the descent into the deep valley of the Durnachtal.

Linthal is the highest village in the Linth valley which is headed by the Tödi, the so-called 'King of the Little Mountains' and one of the first of the Alpine massifs to be explored. The village has several modest hotels and a *gasthaus*, and an opportunity to ride a postbus for part of the next day's 32km stage. By all means do so to avoid the initial section of the route which criss-crosses a road, or the last weary downhill trek to Altdorf, but on no account should you miss the walk through the glorious flat-bottomed valley of Urner Boden and across the 1948m **Klausenpass** to Unterschächen, for this is a delightful hike, packed full of interest.

Overlooked by the Gemsfairenstock and handsome Clariden (3268m), the valley of Urner Boden is a vast pastureland dotted with dairy farms and herdsmen's huts, flanked on the north by abrupt limestone peaks rising from terraces of flowers. Below Clariden a waterfall cascades down the headwall to drain its snowfields and last glacial remnants. There's a small village (Urnerboden) from which a trail makes for the Klausenpass. This is crossed by a road, but a walker's route keeps away from tarmac until the actual pass itself is reached, then you skirt away from it to descend against a rockface on a steeply zigzagging path safeguarded with wooden handrails. At the foot of this the continuing path takes you past the dark timber chalets of Äsch, behind which one of the finest of Swiss waterfalls erupts from a band of cliffs. Rainbows appear in its spray, while the thunder of its force echoes across the valley. And when you reach Unterschächen, having walked for about seven hours from Linthal, you've still a very long way to go to Altdorf. If ever there were an excuse to hop on a bus, this is it.

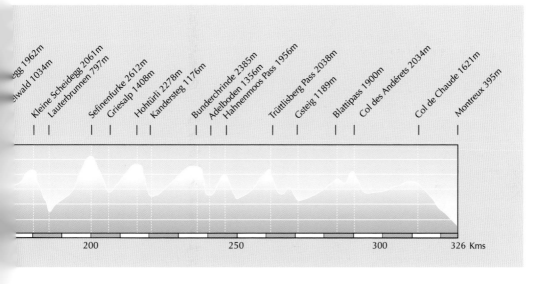

Altdorf to Grindelwald

Altdorf makes much of William Tell, the Swiss hero who was born in nearby Bürglen, but 30 minutes beyond his bronze statue in the town's Rathausplatz, Attinghausen puts you in touch with the long steep climb to the 2291m **Surenenpass**. This is the finest crossing so far, with stunning views from both sides, the best of which is revealed as you emerge through the cleft of the pass with the tranquil Seewen tarns lying below in a rumpled grassland, while the distinctive Titlis forms a backdrop of majesterial proportions. For much of the descent to **Engelberg** it will be the Titlis that commands most of your attention.

Next day the APR crosses the Titlis massif on the way to Meiringen, but for the first time on this trek, a string of cableways partially detracts from the impact of the scenery. A gondola lift swings up to the Trübsee on a mid-height plateau; other cableways continue to the Titlis summit, while another rattles its way to the **Jochpass** at 2207m. The APR trekker crosses in an easy hour's walk from the Trübsee, and although the Jochpass may be voted the least satisfying of any on the trek, once over it the way improves greatly. The large oval Engstlensee lies 300m below in the lovely Gental, and on each of the route options that proceed to Meiringen, the first real hint of Oberland giants brings a frisson of excitement.

It is at Engstlenalp that the onward route to **Meiringen** forks. One takes a trail along the right flank of the Gental; another descends through the valley itself, while yet another option strays onto the Melchsee plateau, then wanders along the crest of a ridge overlooking the Gental. It's difficult to know which is best, but whichever is

Welcome refreshments on the long valley walk to Engelberg

Trübsee, on the way to the Jochpass

chosen, at the end of a long day's walk Meiringen welcomes with a choice of accommodation and the knowledge that over the next two days you will become familiar with those icons of the Bernese Oberland: Eiger, Mönch and Jungfrau.

The first part of the walk to Grindelwald takes the APR through the Reichenbachtal. Narrow and wooded in its lower reaches, the valley opens to the sun as you advance towards the Grosse Scheidegg. On the left the multi-pinnacled wall of the Engelhörner is popular with rock climbers, while the valley itself has a high moorland-like quality that changes to pasture and clusters of alp farms as you wander through, but on reaching the **Grosse Scheidegg** at 1962m, the outlook changes as the lush green Grindelwald basin is revealed below. Towering over the pass the Wetterhorn is so near it's impossible to gain a true evaluation; ahead the Eiger is seen end-on with the snowy Mönch peering over the razor-sharp Mittellegi

ridge, while the saddle of tomorrow's pass, the famous Kleine Scheidegg, forms part of the west wall of the Grindelwald basin.

The walk down into that basin dodges from meadow to woodland and from woodland to pasture, and as you descend it's worth looking back to see the Wetterhorn growing in familiarity, its coronet of peaks now easily recognised. And as you enter the resort itself, gaze off to the left where, through the cleft of a glacier gorge, the big wall of the Fiescherwand gleams with snow and ice.

Without question **Grindelwald** is the busiest and most popular of resorts on the Alpine Pass Route, and as it comes roughly halfway through the journey to Montreux, this is as good a place as any to have a day off. Perhaps take a gondola lift and a short walk to the Bachsee for views to die for (see Trek 11: Tour of the Jungfrau Region), or just sit at a café table with a drink and a pastry and gaze in awe at the mountains that surround you.

Grindelwald to Adelboden

A steep descent to Grund below Grindelwald leads to an even steeper ascent to Alpiglen, the cluster of farm buildings, *berghaus* and narrow-gauge railway station that nestles at the foot of the Eiger's notorious north face. But beyond Alpiglen the way eases towards the 2061m **Kleine Scheidegg**, from where the sublime Jungfrau appears in all her glory. Eiger and Mönch are also seen to good effect from here, while the walk down to Wengernalp and Wengen gradually brings the deep trough of the Lauterbrunnen valley into focus. Overnight is usually spent in the depths of that valley in **Lauterbrunnen** itself, in view of the wispy cascades for which the village is known.

The next day is tough, with more than 1800m to climb to reach the craggy Sefinenfurke. The first part of that climb is up the near-precipitous valley wall to Mürren, but a cable-car gives the option of 'cheating' and reducing the effort by about one and a half hours. From Mürren to the pass is largely over pastureland with stunning views south to the head of the Lauterbrunnen valley, and ahead to the equally impressive Gspaltenhorn, but when you finally reach the **Sefinenfurke** at 2612m, it is the glacier-hung Blümlisalp massif that grabs your attention.

The west side of the pass is steep and tricky, with long sections of fixed cable to safeguard the descent. Caution is imperative, although once you've reached the foot of the initial slope of shale and grit, a trail takes you over grassy hummocks, past farm buildings and onto a farm road that leads gently down to **Griesalp**, a tiny hamlet ranged around a square at the head of the little-known Kiental.

After a night in Griesalp the next crossing is the highest on the APR, beyond which there's a

On the trek from Grindelwald to the Kleine Scheidegg the Eiger's north face rises out of morning cloud

The Hohtürli is the highest pass on the APR

very long descent to Kandersteg to look forward to. The 2778m **Hohtürli** is gained after four or five hours of steady uphill work, the last hour being the toughest, with steep moraine deposits, runnels of shifting black grit and a final series of fixed cables, ladders and a lengthy stairway of timber-braced steps beneath overhanging crags. Arrival at the pass comes with no small amount of relief, and an eye-dazzling view of shrinking glaciers hanging from the Blümlisalp crest. About 15 minutes' walk above the pass the Blümlisalp Hut gives the promise of welcome refreshment – although the few metres of uphill effort needed to reach it can seem daunting.

With 1600m to descend in order to reach Kandersteg, you know you're in for a muscle-straining afternoon. The trail is good for the most part, on well-graded zigzags, but it's still a long descent that takes you beside glacial slabs, along the crest of an old moraine, into a rough basin littered with rocks and boulders, and down into well-like depths that contain the lovely Oeschinensee. Beyond that lake, and another 400m lower, **Kandersteg** offers the promise of a bed for the night and an opportunity to rest weary legs.

Between Kandersteg and Adelboden it is the 2385m **Bunderchrinde** that enables the trek to cross the dividing mountain wall. This pass is a mere nick in a craggy ridge at the head of a slope of scree, and is gained about four hours after leaving Kandersteg. It's the last of the major passes on the APR, for thereafter they are mostly grassy cols at modest altitudes, with only two exceeding the 2000m mark.

The Bunderchrinde, however, is a rugged pass with screes on both flanks, but with a much less strenuous descent on the western flank than was the case with the Hohtürli. On the way down to **Adelboden** the broad, level-topped Wildstrubel captures your imagination to the south, where the main line of the Bernese Alps is now becoming more remote from the course of

Col de Chaude is the final crossing on the APR, with Lac Léman 1200m below

the APR. There are cross-country routes that stay closer to the high mountains, but the APR trail keeps its distance for a while, choosing instead a more gentle, soft series of landscapes to continue the route from Adelboden to Lenk, Lauenen and Gsteig.

Adelboden to Montreux

Out of Adelboden the way follows a river upstream towards its source, crossing and recrossing the Geilsbach before taking to woodland and higher pastures, and then adopting a minor road to reach the **Hahnenmoospass** at 1956m. After the efforts of the previous few days, this pass is reached (comparatively speaking) almost without breaking sweat. It's well-known to skiers, and the *berghotel* on the pass offers not only refreshment, but beds and dormitory places for those who fancy a night with the Wildstrubel as a neighbour. For APR purposes, it is reached far too early in the day to consider settling down, so continue walking on a track that leads to a series of footpaths descending over romantic flower-rich hillsides shaded in part by linden trees, down to Lenk, a small resort and a choice centre for walking holidays in the upper Simmental.

Next day there are two passes to contend with. The first, the 2038m **Trüttlisberg** which leads to Lauenen, is gained via fairly steep woodland trails and meandering paths over grass slopes, while the much lower Krinnen Pass (1659m) is concealed among trees on a ridge running north of the Arpelistock. Neither crossing is difficult, and at this stage of the trek a two-pass day will not be too demanding. From the Krinnen Pass you drop down to **Gsteig**, nestling at the foot of Les Diablerets, the big limestone massif that effectively marks the western limit of the Bernese Alps, and below which the Alpine Pass Route turns more directly towards Lac Léman with the

knowledge that there's only two more full days of trekking left.

Those two days take you away from the big mountains, heading west from alp to alp through the pastoral country of Canton Vaud, a region that attracts little publicity and therefore remains virtually unknown to walkers from outside Switzerland. But that is not to suggest for one moment that it is uninteresting. In common with the first few stages of the trek, the final two provide balance and create an overall picture of the Swiss Alps that will never be realised by those whose holidays are focused forever on centres such as Grindelwald or Zermatt. These little-trod regions with their sudden exciting vistas help make the Alpine Pass Route an experience to treasure.

The first of those sudden vistas comes a little over two hours after leaving Gsteig when you arrive on the **Blattipass**. This 1900m saddle on a grass- and shrub-covered ridge is not even marked on most Swiss maps, yet the panorama it shows is one of the best of the whole APR. If you're blessed with good weather the full length of the Bernese Alps is on show, from the Wetterhorn to Les Diablerets. It's a view to absorb and savour.

After that another hour or so brings you to Col de Voré at 1910m; then you reach the 2304m **Col des Andérets** on a ridge marking the Rhône/Rhine watershed. It's a day of passes, none of which challenges, but each of which has its own features. The final one on this stage is Col des Mosses, a modest resort spread across a plateau at the head of two valley systems at just 1445m.

The walk from Gsteig to Col des Mosses required a full day's commitment, and so will the final stage leading to Montreux. It begins by making for the eastern end of Lac de l'Hongrin in the Pays d'Enhaut (note the French names now), and passing lovely grey shingle-roofed farms makes the ascent through a strip of deciduous woodland, and on (and on) to finally gain the **Col de Chaude** (1621m) and a first view onto Lac Léman. It's at once an uplifting and a disheartening view. Uplifting because after more than two weeks of trekking the end at **Montreux** is in sight. Disheartening, because there are more than 1200m of descent, and almost four hours of knee-strain to reach it.

Trek 11
Tour of the Jungfrau Region

by Kev Reynolds

The outlook from Schynige Platte is one of the finest in the Alps. More than that, it's one of the world's great mountain views, as exciting as many a Himalayan panorama, with the added frisson of including a large portion of the tour described in this chapter. Some 1400m above the valley, it's an eyrie from which to launch out on this momentous trek. Despite having some of the best-known mountains, valleys and resorts in the Alps, the Jungfrau region also has its secretive corners where few tourists intrude, leaving wonderlands for the trekker to discover. Peaceful valleys, spectacular peaks and pinnacles, huge waterfalls and the most romantic of mountain inns and secluded huts: such are the temptations on this circular tour that has a fair selection of alternative routes and variations to consider. And every one's a winner.

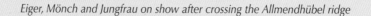

Eiger, Mönch and Jungfrau on show after crossing the Allmendhübel ridge

Route summary

Location	Bernese Oberland, Switzerland
Start	Schynige Platte, above Wilderswil
Finish	Wilderswil
Distance	111–135km
Duration	9–11 days
Maximum altitude	2970m
Accommodation	Mountain huts and inns
Grade	Moderate +
Guidebook	*Tour of the Jungfrau Region* by Kev Reynolds (Cicerone Press, 2nd edition, 2009)

Forty-odd years ago the Bernese Oberland gave me my introduction to the Alps, and it's retained a special place in my affections ever since. Countless times I've walked the trails, visited the huts, crossed its passes and climbed a few of its minor summits. There are winter nights when I can wake with a start and find myself transported to a particular alp, an old moraine meadow perhaps, or a viewpoint guaranteed to catch my breath with surprise, no matter how many times I've been there, nor how many photographs I've taken in an attempt to capture its essence.

Who could fail to be mesmerised by that iconic trio of Eiger, Mönch and Jungfrau? Or their neighbours, Wetterhorn, Schreckhorn, Finsteraarhorn and the vast open wall of the Fiescherwand? Who would not be impressed by the depth of the Lauterbrunnen valley, its stupendous

The trail from Schynige Platte to the Faulhorn gives magnificent views every step of the way

limestone walls down which countless waterfalls spray in steaming ribbons? Or the headwall of that valley, topped by a succession of lofty summits and crowned by the Lauterbrunnen Breithorn? Then there's the Gspaltenhorn with its extensive east ridge and a mind-boggling northeast face to rival that of the Eiger; it's the highest most consistently steep face in the Alps, blocking the narrow moat of the Sefinental.

All these, and more, retain an undeniable magic whose spell is impossible to break. For there are insufficient days in the year to breed contempt by familiarity, nor enough trails nor summers in a wanderer's lifetime to exhaust all the possibilities contained within its boundaries. Yet experience told me it should be feasible to condense some of the very best of the Oberland into a single journey.

So by linking the most scenic of its paths, and staying in the most idyllic of locations – avoiding busy resorts

Tour of the Jungfrau Region

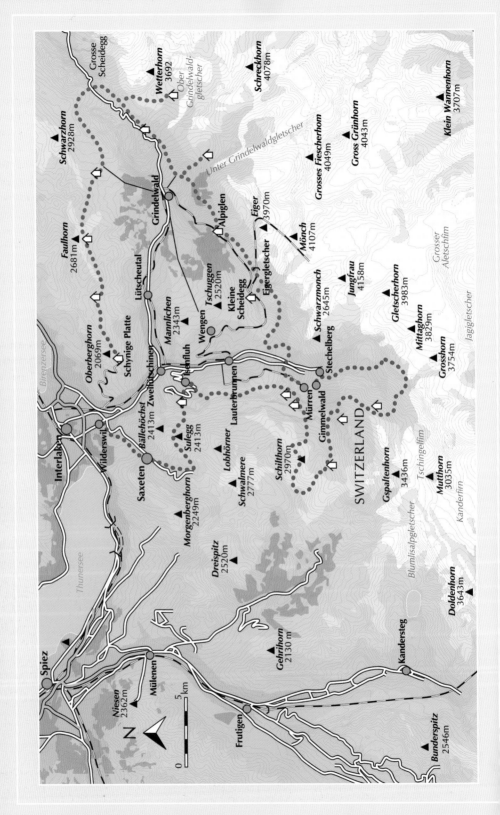

Spiez

Niesen 2362m

Mülenen

Interlaken

Wilderswil

Saxeten

Morgenberghorn 2249m

Frutigen

Gehrihorn 2130 m

Bunderspitz 2546m

Kandersteg

Doldenhorn 3643m

Blümlisalpgletscher

Kanderfirn

Mutthorn 3035m

Tschingelfirn

Gspaltenhorn 3436m

SWITZERLAND

Dreispitz 2520m

Schwalmere 2777m

Lobhörner

Schilthorn 2970m

Lauterbrunnen

Gimmelwald

Mürren

Stechelberg

Schwarzmonch 2645m

Schelberg

Jungfrau 4158m

Gletscherhorn 3983m

Mittaghorn 3829m

Grosshorn 3754m

Grosser Aletschfirn

Jagigletscher

Thunersee

Brienzersee

Bällehöchst 2413m

Sulegg 2413m

Zweilütschinen

Isenfluh

Schynige Platte

Oberberghorn 2069m

Mannlichen 2343m

Wengen

Tschuggen 2520m

Kleine Scheidegg

Lütscheutal

Faulhorn 2681m

Schwarzhorn 2928m

Grindelwald

Alpiglen

Eigergletscher

Eiger 3970m

Mönch 4107m

Grosses Fiescherhorn 4049m

Gross Grünhorn 4043m

Klein Wannenhorn 3707m

Schreckhorn 4078m

Wetterhorn 3692

Ober Grindelwald-gletscher

Unter Grindelwaldgletscher

Grosse Scheidegg

N

0   5   km

where possible – I began to devise a multi-day tour among these mountains that would stand comparison with any trek in the Alps. It would be a celebration of all that is uplifting and exciting in a rugged landscape, a potpourri of trekking delights.

The maps came out. Well-thumbed, and stained with bilberry juice and sweaty fingers, curled at the edges, torn and worn in places, they covered the sitting room floor. Favourite trails were highlighted; huts, remote mountain inns and matratzenlagers circled; timings jotted down, altitudes noted. And as the blue line wound its way across the paper like a grown-up version of a dot-to-dot sketch, the journey took on a fresh dimension.

The first summer's outline worked like a dream. It became reality, as all one's daydreams should, for one day's trek led to another. And then another. Each stage blended seamlessly into the next until the circle was closed and our dot-to-dot was transformed into one of the finest mountain tours we'd ever made.

But still I was not completely satisfied. There were other wonderlands just off-route but within reach that would be worth diverting to, worth visiting, exploring, enjoying. So out came the maps and the highlight pen once more, and the route was refined and expanded. And when we returned to the Alps we soon agreed that this new Tour of the Jungfrau Region achieved all we wanted of it.

Wilderswil to the Wetterhorn

South of Interlaken, just a few short minutes away by public transport, Wilderswil guards the entrance to the heart of the Bernese Oberland.

Schynige Platte is one of the great vantage points of the Alps. From the hotel terrace most of the route of the TJR can be seen

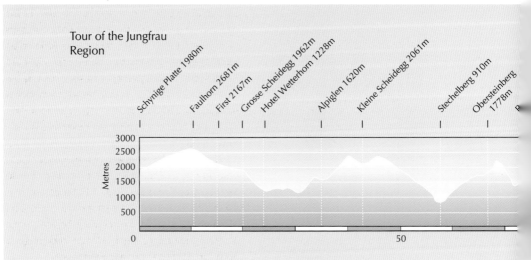

Tour of the Jungfrau
Region

Schynige Platte 1980m
Faulhorn 2681m
First 2167m
Grosse Scheidegg 1962m
Hotel Wetterhorn 1228m
Alpiglen 1620m
Kleine Scheidegg 2061m
Stechelberg 910m
Obersteinberg 1778m

Metres

3000
2500
2000
1500
1000
500

0

50

The glassy Bachsee reflects the Schreckhorn (left) and more distant Finsteraarhorn in its waters

Beyond that modest, unremarkable village a trench of a valley trends southeastward then breaks into two stems. One is the Lutschental, with Grindelwald sprawling across the meadows near its head. The other is the Lauterbrunnental, the most spectacular glacier-carved valley in Europe, from which trains crawl up or along its steep flanks to feed tourists into Wengen, Kleine Scheidegg or Mürren.

These are the main valleys – spokes in a wheel if you like – around and above which the trek makes its circuitous tour over the course of nine days or more, depending on how many diversions you make, or the number of hours spent wandering spellbound by the landscape.

Should your journey to Switzerland bring you to Wilderswil in time, I'd recommend taking the 100-year-old, narrow-gauge cog railway up the 1400m of hillside to **Schynige Platte**, and spend the first night there at the berghotel, which claims a panoramic view of such beauty that it's difficult to believe any improvement could be possible. Much of the route of the Jungfrau tour can be seen (or at least imagined) from that classic vantage point, and when the last train of the day has dragged the most persistent of visitors back down to the valley, those who have taken the precaution of booking a bed for the night are rewarded by hour upon hour of splendour as the light changes and the mountains that form such a dramatic backdrop become detached from their roots and are left floating on mists that fill the lower meadows.

The trek begins here, and before long it climbs onto a ridge that falls away on its northern side to the Brienzer See, more than 1370m below. The south side is a sweep of pasture, and the sound of cowbells drifts in the morning breeze, while across minor ridges Eiger, Mönch and Jungfrau persist in dragging your attention to them.

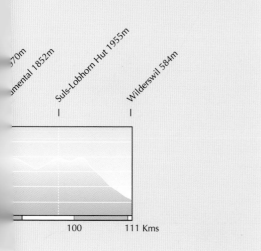

Approaching the tiny Weber Hut on the first day

Most of this first day's stage remains above 2000m. It crosses a saddle, sneaks through a wilderness of limestone blocks and rocks and screes, then eases into a high valley where sheep graze and your boots arouse the fragrance from wild thyme. The echo of choughs is all that disturbs the silence.

At midday (it's always midday when I arrive) the tiny, privately owned Weber Hut springs up in a cleft of rocks and flowers; the perfect excuse to relax with a cold drink, beads of condensation dribbling down the glass, before struggling up a ramp of a path that leads onto a grassy crest from which the stiletto peak of the Finsteraarhorn signals its presence far off to the southeast. There's grave danger in getting a crick in the neck as you make progress up to the **Faulhorn**, for your head is forever being pulled to the right to check that view again and again.

Since 1830 Berghotel Faulhorn has drawn visitors to its lofty perch a few paces below the summit. The composer Mendelssohn was one, but I'm not sure whether he was inspired to compose something stirring (or tranquil) to celebrate what he saw. If not, he should have been, for yet again the panorama is sufficient to warrant any superlative lavished upon it. Sunset or sunrise can be unforgettable, but the Faulhorn is just one option for an overnight stay. My choice is to continue for another couple of hours, downhill almost all the way. Down to the glassy Bachsee in which Wetterhorn, Schreckhorn and Finsteraarhorn are turned on their heads, disturbed only by the ripples of a surfacing fish or a plunging frog. Then beyond and below the lake to a dormitory bed beneath a restaurant at the **First** gondola lift station, with a direct view of the Eiger and an opportunity to return to the Bachsee around the magical hour of daybreak; peaceful and serene and unspeakably lovely.

Next day can be either short and easy, or reasonably long and more challenging. Consider the weather first. If the forecast is settled and you have enough days in hand, take the latter option which strays to the Gleckstein Hut, the climbers' base for the Wetterhorn. But in order to get there, a path known as the Höhenweg 2400 undulates across the pastures of Alp Grindel to the broad saddle of the **Grosse Scheidegg**, across which lies the Rosenlauital flanked by the grey slabs of the Engelhörner, and above which rises the Wetterhorn, one of the symbols of Grindelwald and a buttress of mountaineering's Golden Age. It is from this saddle that a view southwest reveals the Eiger in profile, the north face unseen from here but the Mittellegi ridge appearing razor sharp, and with Kleine Scheidegg beyond marking a future milestone on the Tour of the Jungfrau Region.

If the decision has been made to settle for the short and easy option on this stage, all that is required is a fairly straightforward descent from Grosse Scheidegg to **Hotel Wetterhorn** which stands below the glacier gorge of the Oberer Grindelwaldgletscher – once there, numerous opportunities arise for filling the rest of the day. But if the intention is to make a diversion to the Gleckstein Hut, it's necessary to take the Hotel Wetterhorn path for 30 minutes or so, then break away on an exciting trail that climbs against the lower slabs of the Chrinnenhorn, turns a corner above the deep shaft of the glacier gorge, and works a way along its upper rim towards the icefall of the Oberer Grindelwaldgletscher which hangs below Schreckhorn and Bärglistock. At one point a waterfall sprays onto the trail, and there's no dodging a brisk cold shower.

The Gleckstein Hut occupies a prime site at 2317m with a direct view across the icefall to the

Crevasses of the Oberer Grindelwaldgletscher are on show during the ascent to the Gleckstein Hut

fin-like Schreckhorn and its smaller 'twin'. The Wetterhorn soars above and behind the hut in broken and confused tiers of rock and ice. Tiny pools dazzle the sunlight, and a herd of ibex graze shelves of grass and lichen nearby. The hut guardian puts out salt, and in the morning (if you're lucky) half a dozen of these handsome creatures will be enticed to within a few paces of the door. If the views fail to excite, close proximity to these animals most certainly will.

Wetterhorn to Eigergletscher

There's no way for the trekker to resume the tour from the Gleckstein Hut without backtracking down the glacier gorge to the meadows that spill towards Grindelwald. But from Hotel Wetterhorn the onward route picks its way across the slopes of the Mättenberg – at one point going through a tunnel created to avoid stonefall – which overlook the hotels and chalets of one of Switzerland's busiest resorts. Along this airy trail, however,

The notorious north face of the Eiger, seen from above Kleine Scheidegg

high point with a full-frontal view of the ice-hung Fiescherwand.

Opened in the summer of 2006, Berghaus Bäregg has a dramatic location on a projecting spur about 100m above its predecessor, Restaurant Stieregg, which was destroyed when the moraine meadow on which it stood collapsed – another victim of global warming. Bäregg's view is every bit as majestic and privileged as Stieregg's had been, and a night spent there will endorse that claim and justify straying from the main tour. This is rejoined next day not far from Pfingstegg, and continues by crossing the mouth of the glacier gorge, then climbing through woodland to a path tucked against the lower slopes of the Eiger leading to Alpiglen and another berghaus in which numerous climbers have spent a restless night before setting out to attempt the notorious Nordwand.

The Eiger Trail is taken next day. Crossing grass and scree immediately below the Eiger's north face, it rewards with a succession of highlights, one of which comes when reaching a prominent spur at 2280m, where a fresh panorama is revealed, as well as an opportunity to study climbers at work on the rock face soaring overhead.

The trail ends at Eigergletscher, where the train from **Kleine Scheidegg** enters the mountain on its remarkable journey to the Jungfraujoch at 3454m, making it Europe's highest railway. From Eigergletscher, however, the trekker's focus is no longer up, but down, for it is from this point that the Tour of the Jungfrau begins the long, knee-crunching descent to the Lauterbrunnen valley.

Eigergletscher to Obersteinberg

As with all Alpine ice fields, the Eiger's glacier is shrinking, and its right bank lateral moraine now forms a towering wall that tapers in its descent towards Biglenalp. High above, Mönch and Jungfrau appear immense, stately, graceful. On warm summer days, avalanches pour from

Grindelwald fails to intrude, and the only real link with that town is the Pfingstegg cableway, passed about one and a half hours from Hotel Wetterhorn.

Again there are options to consider. The direct route works its way to **Alpiglen** at the foot of the Eiger, but a recommended diversion strays above another glacier gorge – this one created by the Unterer Grindelwaldgletscher – to gain a remote restaurant (with matratzenlager) on a

the Jungfrau's face to land far below in a cone of powder on the safe side of the Trümmel Bach away from the Biglenalp chalets. Our route picks a way down the crest of this moraine, then through pinewoods to Biglenalp and on to Mettlenalp, from where a fresh perspective is won across the Lauterbrunnen valley.

The way down into that valley is aggressively steep, and several times you gaze directly onto toy-town rooftops hundreds of metres below, before crossing the ravine which sucks all the snowmelt from Eiger, Mönch and Jungfrau into its cavernous depths, then spews it out via the famed Trümmelbach Falls. An hour later you arrive at **Stechelberg**, the tiny village at the Lauterbrunnen roadhead, where there's a choice of accommodation.

The next stage is seduced into the upper reaches of the Lauterbrunnen valley. A short option for bad-weather days takes only two and a half hours to reach the berghotel chosen for an overnight stay, while the recommended route doubles that time by following an old hunter's trail up the east side of the valley, climbing towards the thunderous Schmadribach Falls within a UNESCO World Natural Heritage Site (the first such site designated in the Alps). Above the falls glacier streams gather in a rough stony meadow overshadowed by the Breithorn, Tschingelhorn and curiously turreted Lauterbrunnen Wetterhorn. Nestling among moraine deposits, the unmanned Schmadri Hut provides shelter for those carrying supplies, while the rustic Berghotel **Obersteinberg** on the north slope makes a wonderfully romantic lodging with neither electricity nor hot running water in the rooms, but a truly memorable atmosphere and first-rate views.

Obersteinberg to the Blumental

Now the Tour of the Jungfrau Region begins its northward trend, slanting up the mountainside above Obersteinberg to turn a spur at the end of a long ridge system that began on the summit of the Gspaltenhorn. Another short diversion is tempting here, for a severely steep scramble up the ridge leads to an extraordinary little meadow known as the Tanzbödeli, from which yet another panorama of eye-watering beauty is revealed. Below it, another optional alternative is given which visits a lonely alp farm above the Sefinental, where, from its window, we studied no less than 17 chamois grazing a few metres away.

This stage of the tour swoops into the deep Sefinental by a path as hard on the knees as that from Eigergletscher to the Lauterbrunnen valley, but then eases towards Gspaltenhorn and Bütlasse, before climbing the abrupt north slope to reach the **Rotstock Hut**, built in traditional style on the Poganggen alp. From here the evening alpenglow on the Jungfrau's west flank is another memorable highlight.

The hut faces into a little hanging valley headed by the west ridge of the **Schilthorn**, and it is by this ridge that the next stage is directed. While a lower alternative trail to the Blumental is available in the event of bad weather, the main route is not to be missed unless it's unavoidable.

Thousands reach the Schilthorn's summit every year by cable-car. Many more know it from the James Bond film On Her Majesty's Secret Service that was partly filmed there. But only those who scramble along its west ridge know its full worth, and can properly enjoy its unique situation from which to study the peaks that have become so familiar during the days spent trekking below them. The ridge is not difficult, but it is seriously exposed in places. Safeguards of fixed ropes, rungs and ladders ease the way, and once you've crossed the summit – with its revolving restaurant and souvenir stands – the descent by way of the east ridge is straightforward, albeit briefly despoiled.

But the moment you break away from a piste and drop to the jade green Grauseeli, a wonderland is regained, and every step of the way from the lake to the **Blumental** above Mürren (with two mountain inns to choose from) is sheer delight.

The Soustal is crossed en route to the Suls-Lobhorn Hut

Blumental to Wilderswil

For a week or more the trek has been face-on to the main Oberland wall, but the final two stages lead away from it. That's not to say the big mountains are hidden – far from it – but more intimate scenes dominate. Crossing the Blumental meadows, the path tops the green Allmendhübel ridge, then slopes down into a long shelf of pasture bordered by bilberry, juniper and wild raspberries. There are patches of woodland, natural rock gardens, boulders smothered in moss, tall stands of willow gentian. Alpenroses blaze scarlet in the early summer. Later in the year it's the rosebay willowherb that fires the hillside with its brilliant colouring.

The route enters the Soustal in a symphony of cowbells and rushing streams, then climbs out again, turns a wooded spur and throws Eiger, Mönch and Jungfrau into momentary focus. And at the end of the day you're drawn up a gully of ribbed limestone pitted with flowers to emerge by the timber-built **Suls-Lobhorn Hut**, which has one of the loveliest outlooks of any lodging on the tour: the perfect place in which to spend the last night of the trek.

As for the final day, well, there's not much height to gain to cross the Bällehöchst ridge, but a long and steady descent through the Saxettal via rough pastures, flower meadows and woodland brings you at last to **Wilderswil**, where a sudden view to the right shows the Jungfrau once more, framed by the steep walls of the valley. The undisputed Queen of the Oberland.

Trek 12
Tour of the Matterhorn
by Hilary Sharp

If any one mountain could be taken to symbolise the drama and beauty of the Alps it must surely be the Matterhorn. Like a gigantic maypole it stands at the centre of this anticlockwise tour, and over the course of nine or ten days the route unravels the ribbon-like trails on both the Swiss and Italian slopes to reveal the Alpine icon in all its splendour. Steep paths, broken slopes and the crossing of six passes and two glaciers make this a challenging route, but homely huts and inns at the end of each stage provide opportunities to relax and restore energy for the continuing journey. Zermatt, Zinal, Arolla and Breuil-Cervinia are the main mountaineering centres en route, and a number of small villages and hamlets are also visited to help counterbalance long days in the rugged mountain heartlands.

Straying from the official Tour of the Matterhorn to enjoy more good views near Trift

Route summary

Location	Swiss canton of Valais/Wallis, Italian Valle d'Aosta
Start/Finish	Zermatt
Distance	145km
Duration	8–10 days
Maximum altitude	3301m
Accommodation	Mountain huts and inns
Grade	Demanding
Guidebook	*Tour of the Matterhorn* by Hilary Sharp (Cicerone Press, 2009)

The unmistakable but ever-changing Matterhorn from above Zmutt

Resting after a long climb up to the Colle Superiore delle Cime Bianche on my first time around the Tour of Monte Rosa, my group and I took in the view, dominated to the north by a rocky, rather broken-looking summit. 'Must be the Matterhorn,' said one of them. 'No I don't think so,' I replied, and immediately regretted it. What else could it be? We had to be able to see that most famous of summits from here, didn't we? For the millionth time in my life I regretted that I didn't possess that useful instinct of thinking before speaking. But I'd never seen the Matterhorn from the Italian side and was looking for a similar shape to the soaring, perfectly formed spire of rock which is the face it presents to Zermatt.

The Matterhorn, or Monte Cervino as the Italians call it, has to be the most recognisable mountain in the world. Even if people don't know its name, they've seen its shape replicated on anything from chocolate boxes to corporate adverts. Ask a child to draw a mountain and that's what you'll get – a pointed pyramid reaching to the sky. It's interesting to imagine what the long-ago first inhabitants of the region thought about this summit as they strove to survive in the high Alpine pastures that butt up against its base. Did they ever dream that one day people would stand on its precarious summit? Did they worship it? Believe it to be the source of evil and danger? Even in this age when we are bombarded with extreme

images on a daily basis, the Matterhorn certainly remains an arresting sight, especially when seen from Zermatt and even more, I would venture to suggest, when you have trekked there.

So what could be better than to tackle a hike that circumnavigates it? The Tour of the Matterhorn has been touted as 'the most beautiful trek in the world'. I'm not sure any trek could take this honour, as surely all excursions in the mountains are made special according to the weather, the company and the experiences encountered along the way. However, there are many parts of this trek that are outstanding: delightful footpaths leading out from Alpine valleys and up through flowery meadows to finally emerge at high passes, with the most rewarding, spectacular views; deep valleys and high boulder slopes accessed by audacious trails that have to

On the descent towards Lago Cignana

be protected by cables and rungs; lakes and hamlets where you can spend the night watching the sun cast its final rosy glow as it dips behind the high peaks. As a whole the expedition is varied and incredibly satisfying: not only will you see the Matterhorn from all sides, but also many of the other high summits of the region; two countries, Switzerland and Italy, are visited, and thus two very different cultures; and this is a trek that includes two glacier crossings and the chance at the end to ascend the Breithorn, a summit which surpasses the magical 4000m height by 164m and dominates Zermatt. The only downside is that the tour passes through the major ski areas of Cervinia and Zermatt. If there is plenty of snow cover then these areas will be quite pretty, but be warned – towards the end of the season there are a few places that look more like building sites – notably Trocknersteg above Zermatt, where it's better to concentrate very hard on the fantastic views of

the surrounding peaks and ignore all the mess that surrounds this lift and the ski slopes. This should not put you off – it's a small blip which is more than compensated by the beauty of the rest of the trek and the feeling of achievement as you return to Zermatt having completed the tour.

The Tour of the Matterhorn is regarded as a relatively 'new' trek as it has been documented only in the last few years. The paths it uses, though, are generally anything but new – these are often ancient ways over passes leading from one valley to another and would have been used for centuries for trading, transhumance (seasonal movement of cattle) and people migrating or fleeing from enemies. A part of the tour on the Swiss side shares paths taken by the popular Walker's Haute Route from Chamonix to Zermatt (see Trek 9: Walker's Haute Route). This adds to the social aspect of the trek since if you do the Tour of the Matterhorn in the usual

Tour of the Matterhorn

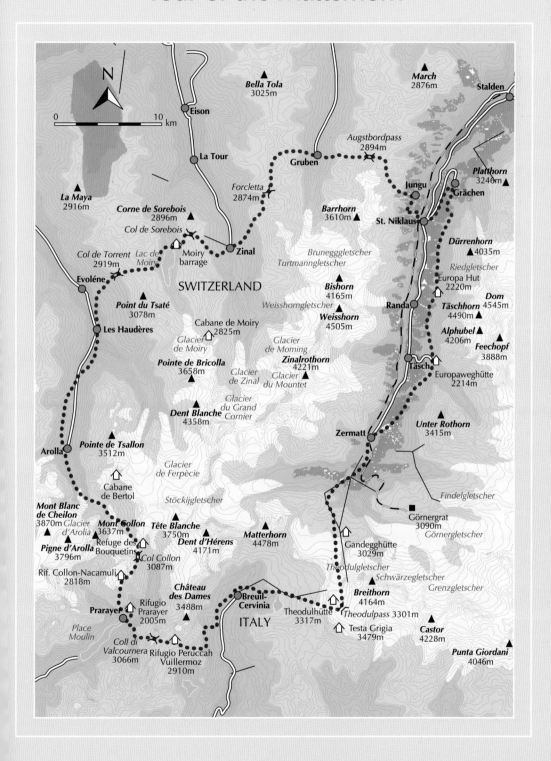

Bicolour goats are traditional in Zermatt

direction you'll be passing Chamonix to Zermatt hikers going the other way, but a quick greeting is all that's necessary.

So, where to start? Since it's a circular tour, theoretically it can be started anywhere along its length, but clearly some places are easier to get to than others. It is usually nice to start and finish in a place which is accessible transport-wise, somewhere you can leave excess gear,

buy picnic food and celebrate at the end, and to my mind it's good to do this tour with views of the Matterhorn at the start and finish since this is what you're walking around, so I'm going to describe it from Zermatt.

Next decision – which direction to go in? It's generally walked anti-clockwise and since I can't think of any reason not to go this way that's what I've described. It seems to work well that way and if you start in Zermatt it means that the highest altitude on the trek comes at the end when you're most acclimatised.

Zermatt to Arolla

The trail leaves the fleshpots of **Zermatt** to head down the Mattertal towards St Niklaus, a delightful town with a characteristic onion-shaped church tower. There are various ways of getting there. One is to take the high-level Europaweg path which leaves from the top of Zermatt's Sunegga lift. This is a spectacular trail, contouring high above the valley with amazing views, notably of the fine-sculpted snowy faces of the Weisshorn. It takes a couple of days from Zermatt, with a night at the well-positioned **Europahütte** at 2220m, to reach the village of Grächen, from where a bus goes down to St Niklaus.

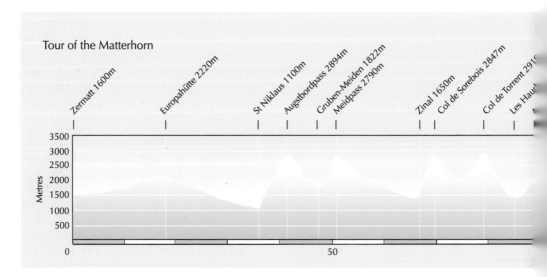

The unforgettable balcony trail from Hotel Weisshorn to Zinal gives great views of the high peaks

A shorter alternative is to take the wooded footpath from Zermatt to Täsch, then carry on down back roads though the villages of Randa (scene of a huge landslide in 1991) and Herbrigg to reach St Niklaus in an easy day. Both ways have their merits. Obviously the Europaweg is longer than the valley alternative and doubtless more spectacular, but it does have its downside. This balcony trail stays high above the valley, crossing hillsides which in winter are raked by avalanches. Much of the terrain above the trail is unstable and rockfall is common. For this reason the path is very high-maintenance and can be subject to sudden closures during or after heavy rain. The Europaweg should not be underestimated – a traverse it may be but it requires two hard days of hiking on very undulating terrain – an adjective that strikes fear into any seasoned Alpine hiker!

Once at **St Niklaus** you'll find a not-to-be-missed spectacular cable-car ride that leads up to the wonderfully positioned hamlet of Jungu (Jungen), with its gleaming white church and flower-filled meadows. You could walk up to here but, not being a purist, I highly recommend you don't. Take the lift, enjoy it, then head for the next pass on fresh legs.

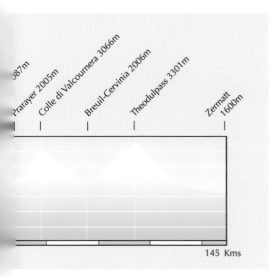

145 Kms

An old trail heads away from the traditional wooden chalets and up into the mountains, quickly leaving the sparse larch and spruce forest above the village. After a short time the trail levels and leads to a huge cairn that marks the best place to stop and view the surrounding peaks, pride of place being taken by the Dom, the Täschhorn and the Weisshorn. Linger here before tiptoeing across the exposed traverse to reach rocky terrain leading up to the 2894m **Augstbordpass**, a crossing used since ancient times to reach the valley of the Turtmanntal. As long as the Tour of the Matterhorn coincides with the Chamonix to Zermatt Walkers' Haute Route you're likely to meet plenty of fellow walkers and this is usually the case here. Haute Route candidates are nearing the end of their route, and this is their last col so they'll either be overjoyed, relieved or sad.

Gruben-Meiden is the next stop and the Hotel Schwarzhorn is directly at the foot of the descent. This is a grand building and unless you choose to pay for a room you'll be toiling up four floors to reach the dormitories at the top – but then this is a walking holiday, right? The Turtmanntal is beautiful and relatively unspoilt and begs to be explored for a couple of days. At least stroll around the small hamlet and pretty church after dinner to get a feel for a valley that is only occupied in the summer and hence has kept its authenticity, unblemished by lifts and bulldozed ski pistes – a rare find these days.

To get to the Val d'Anniviers two options present themselves. If you want to sample the traditional old Victorian Hotel Weisshorn, then the **Meidpass** (2790m) is the col to aim for. Otherwise the 2874m Forcletta is a shorter pass option. Both lead onto an exceptional balcony trail that wanders high above the valley with fantastic views of the glaciated mountains – the Dent Blanche, Zinal Rothorn, Obergabelhorn, Weisshorn and, if you're lucky, the Matterhorn. This trail forms the route for the famous Sierre-Zinal race which takes place mid-August and is one of the classic Alpine fell races. Anytime in the summer you're likely

to see budding racers checking out the route, and testing themselves. Probably best to avoid being on this path on race-day – runners are very single-minded.

After some time the trail plunges down into forest and steepens to quickly deposit you in **Zinal**. The old part of town is a delight and there are also plenty of shops, bars and cake-eating possibilities.

There's a cable-car from town that goes in our direction: it can be taken, or alternatively you can walk. The route onwards from the cable-car up bulldozed ski pistes to the **Col de Sorebois** (2847m) is not a beautiful walk, but the other side of the col provides a great vista – the incredibly blue waters of the artificial Lac de Moiry and, beyond, our next objective, the **Col de Torrent** (2919m). Meadows and gentle pastoral slopes are the order of the day all the way down to the Val d'Herens and the hamlets of Villa and La Sage which lead to **Les Haudères**. Again old larch chalets and flowery window boxes dominate.

Take the bus or walk to **Arolla**? The trail to this tiny village, which enjoys Alpine renown totally out of proportion to its diminutive size, is easy to climb, but you're not missing much if you get on the bus.

Arolla to Breuil-Cervinia

Now we are heading into the high mountains – up the Haut Glacier d'Arolla, a more or less icy, crevassed slope which gains the 3087m **Col Collon**. The scenery is dominated by snowy ice peaks, notably the Evêque and Mont Collon. It's reassuring to have good weather for this ascent; there are blue plastic waymarker poles on the glacier but they shift with the movement of the ice and it can be difficult to see the best route if there is a lot of grit and moraine exposed, or indeed in foggy conditions.

In my experience you need to carry crampons for this section, and when there is snow on the ice you certainly need a rope – it's a glacier and they generally have holes in them. The glacier abruptly ends at the col and at the Swiss–Italian

frontier. Stony ground leads past the Rifugio Collon Nacamuli, perched on rocks, and on down very steep slopes, where the passage is protected by iron rungs and chains, to reach the wild and remote upper Oren combe. An enormous lateral moraine almost pushes the trail into the stream, before the valley suddenly widens out with an abrupt transition from the higher barren Alpine tundra to lovely grassy meadows, which take you all the way to the edge of the larch forest and the startlingly blue waters of the Place Moulin lake. The flat track along this lake provides a perfect day out for young and old, so expect to see plenty of Italian families walking the bambinos and grandparents. **Prarayer** at the far end of the lake is a good place to spend the night.

Although the next hurdle, the **Colle di Valcournera** (3066m) is not glaciated, it can provide the most difficult terrain of the trek. The ascent is steep and rocky and névé may remain well into the season. Both sides of the pass can present difficulties – the southerly ascent tackles an unstable boulder field and rockfall caused by walkers above is common, while the short northeasterly slope on the far side is very steep and conditions vary from day to day. There is usually a fixed rope for the first part of the trail and where the good path ends there is a bolt which could be used for a short abseil. Névé here can be intimidating and again the crampons may come out. Rifugio Perucca e Vuillermoz is very quickly reached just below the pass and this basic hut is a good place to spend the night high up in the mountains. As evening approaches ibex often gather round the hut and the peaks are bathed in the reddish glow of dusk.

The trail towards Lago Cignana is super in the early morning, down steep rocks splashed by waterfalls and through flower-strewn meadows. Once down near the lake the trail heads left for a short climb to the Finestra di Cignana at 2441m. Beyond, the path wends around a grassy rib and, suddenly, there's the Matterhorn dwarfing the resort of **Breuil-Cervinia**. Take time to sit and savour this view, for it's one you'll have been looking forward to for some time. This is where you get to know that rather different Italian face of the peak.

Eventually you must drag yourself away, carrying on down to the dubious joys of the town. It may be a good idea to take the regular year-round bus the last few kilometres from where the trail hits the road at Perrères – there is a low-level footpath that avoids the road but it's not very pleasant. There is a higher variant which stays above the valley but this is getting quite overgrown.

Breuil-Cervinia enjoys two names; the second was given by Mussolini during the war and is one of the few still used from that time – it's association with Monte Cervino is presumably seen as a tourist attraction.

Breuil-Cervinia to Zermatt

There is a triple cable-car ride that goes all the way up to the Testa Grigia at 3480m. Having taken this on many occasions I eventually decided to walk from town up to the neighbouring **Theodulpass** (3301m). This appealed to me, as this pass has been used since time began – artefacts have been found from Roman times attesting to the fact that the climate was indeed considerably warmer then. I was keen to tread in the footsteps of the ancients and to try to imagine how it felt to be toiling up to this lofty pass – I saw on the map that there was even an old chapel (Capelle Bontadini) en route, where the travellers would pray for protection from the elements before embarking on the final stage of their climb. I was disappointed. This area is an example of the worst ravages of winter tourism. Lifts abound, along with the associated junk and destruction of the slopes; even the chapel is almost hidden, squashed between two ski lift buildings and inside I found it used as a storeroom for rescue equipment! So I strongly advise taking the lifts up to the Testa Grigia, from where a short walk down snowy slopes leads to the Theodulhütte next

Going for the Breithorn

to its col. There is also accommodation at Rifugio Guide del Cervino at Testa Grigia itself. Once you raise your eyes above the nearby lifts and summer ski slopes the mountains are stunning – best of all of course the Matterhorn, soon to be seen from its Swiss side again.

An ascent of the Breithorn could be envisaged before descending to Zermatt, and professional guides for this can be hired at either of the two huts. For this summit, and for the descent from here down to the top of the Trocknersteg lift, you will be walking on glaciers. The summit takes about three hours to reach from Testa Grigia and is really a great finale to the trek – in good conditions.

The descent from the Theodulpass and Testa Grigia takes a ski piste, and you will almost certainly see people not only skiing and snow-boarding but also walking unroped. I can attest to the fact that there are crevasses in this slope. Depending on the snow conditions you may or may not see the holes, or even put your leg down one, but best to be protected just in case. Views of the Matterhorn are superb as you descend, and it's worth breaking off the piste lower down to go to Gandegg, where there is a fine restaurant with a terrace facing all the Zermatt peaks – Breithorn, Pollux, Castor, Liskamm and the many summits of Monte Rosa; definitely a place to hang out and enjoy.

Walk or take the lift down to Furi, then definitely walk the last part through larch forest past picture-perfect wooden chalets into the madness of Zermatt's high street.

Trek 13
Tour of Monte Rosa

by Hilary Sharp

Seen from the Gornergrat above Zermatt, Monte Rosa is a vast sprawling mass of ice and snow, with shadows rippling across her slopes to indicate dips and mounds, seracs or crevasses, her supporting rock exposed here and there in a teasing seduction. Viewed from Macugnaga the East Face, fully 10km wide, soars up and up for more than 2000m to create the greatest sheer face in the Alps, beautiful but aloof and dangerous. From whichever direction or angle she appears, Monte Rosa has a distinct presence hard to deny but impossible to define. For the trekker she forms a graceful backdrop, and even when her summit snows are concealed by intervening mountains, her surrounding valleys contain pleasures of their own. This circular trek is a flirtation that could be summarised as romancing Monte Rosa.

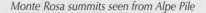

Monte Rosa summits seen from Alpe Pile

Route summary

Location	Swiss canton of Wallis, Italian Valle d'Aosta and Piedmont
Start/Finish	Zermatt
Distance	about 134km
Duration	8–10 days
Maximum altitude	3301m
Accommodation	Mountain huts and inns
Grade	Demanding
Guidebook	*Tour of Monte Rosa* by Hilary Sharp (Cicerone Press, 2007)

Seen from the flatlands of Italy's Po valley near Milan, Monte Rosa presents a surreal far-off hulking mass, often shrouded in mist with occasional glimmers of its icy slopes. Forming the southern extreme of the Pennine Alps, it is the first obstacle encountered when approaching from the south. The Monte Rosa massif has inspired not only mountaineers but also poets, writers and explorers, for the range is a visual bastion, its imposing, characteristic presence dominating viewpoints from valleys on all sides. As Leonardo da Vinci wrote in his Milanese memoirs at the end of the 15th century, Monte Rosa 'is so high that it seems almost to overtake the clouds'.

The Tour of Monte Rosa (TMR) is a journey of dreams, an adventure that goes way beyond a hike or trek; it's a voyage of discovery in one of the most fascinating Alpine regions. To embark on this as a mere walking tour would be to miss out on many of its most alluring aspects: the varied culture of the Swiss and Italian valleys and mountain villages passed through, the gastronomical specialities which change from one valley to the next, the people themselves; the rich history of the area; the

wealth and diversity of the flora and fauna. If you don't have time to do it all in a leisurely fashion, then you may be well advised to tackle a section one year and leave the rest for another visit, rather than miss the chance to fully immerse yourself in the experience.

Monte Rosa itself is far from being one single summit. This is the biggest massif in Western Europe, consisting of 10 defined summits which surpass the magical 4000m height, and its highest peak, the 4634m Dufourspitze, is the third highest in the Alps.

The name conjures up images of rose-tinted rays on glistening snowy summits. While this wonderful spectacle does occur when the first and last light hits the different faces of the massif, the name 'Rosa' is said to come from *roises*, the ancient local name for glaciers. And indeed glaciers there are, many of them.

The Tour of Monte Rosa was established in 1994, linking ancient routes over a series of mountain passes to create a circuit

The huge east face of Monte Rosa dominates the view on the ascent from Macugnaga to the Monte Moro Pass

A splendid morning vista – the Zinalrothorn and Weisshorn, seen from the slopes of the Breithorn

that hugs as closely as possible the glaciated massif. Since then it has grown slowly in popularity, but is still far from being in the league of the well-known classics around the Mont Blanc region.

To walk around the massif is to enjoy all the incredible scenery with none of the dangers and perils of ascending the peak. The tour flirts a little with glaciers as it passes from Italy to Switzerland by the Theodulpass, but although this is glaciated there are far more demanding ascents elsewhere on the tour. However, the pass takes the hiker into the high mountain world of ice and snow with all the associated excitement.

Apart from that short section, the trek is on non-glaciated ground, climbing from valley villages up through meadows past summer farms and grazing cows, onto higher rocky slopes where only the hardiest animals live, and over passes tucked against the slopes of the glaciated mountains, to then descend into new valleys, each one being different in character and scenery. It not only takes you over lofty, impressive mountain passes and among barren and remote hillsides, but through or around major ski areas and tourist resorts, although there's not a huge number of places to stock up on food, and escape from some parts of the route would be long and complicated.

The trek has developed considerably over the last few years, especially on the Italian side where there are now several variants that allow you to more or less avoid the ski areas which, it has to be said, do not look their best in summer, devoid of the thick mantle of snow which disguises the horrors of bull-dozed pistes and the like. Now an informed walker can enjoy all the benefits of an area that caters to tourists and mountain lovers, but is able to escape the downside of overdeveloped ski resorts and heavily cabled hillsides.

As a circumnavigation of the massif the trek can be started anywhere along its length, at any town accessible from the main valleys. Since it's nice to see what you're going around at the start of a trek, we'll set out from Zermatt in a clockwise direction, but bear in mind that you hit the

Tour of Monte Rosa

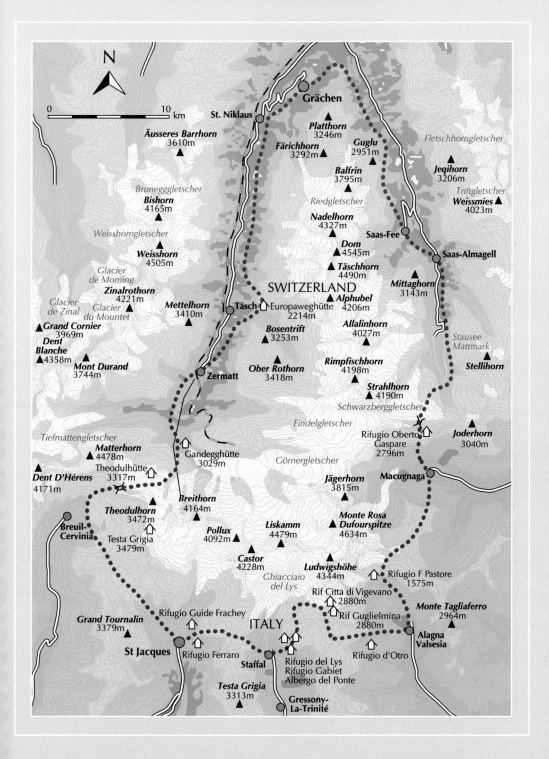

highest altitude on day one. For this reason it is strongly recommended that you take some days beforehand to acclimatise. Or start in Saas Fee and use the Europaweg as a warm up for the arduous ascent out of Zermatt to Italy.

Zermatt to Val d'Ayas

Starting the trek in **Zermatt** allows the Monte Rosa massif to be seen on the very first day. An exciting sight, it's one you'll want to savour as you try to distinguish the different summits of the massif, as well as acquainting yourself with the neighbouring giants of Liskamm, Castor, Pollux and the Breithorn.

Several lifts lead out of Zermatt which could help shorten the first day. You could, for example, take the lifts to Trocknersteg and walk up from there, or ride the Klein Matterhorn lift and walk down from that one. Alternatively, don't take any lifts but have a leisurely start up to Gandegg, then spend an evening admiring the spectacular summit panorama from there.

The Oberere Theodule Glacier leads to the 3301m **Theodulpass**. Although it's a summer ski piste, it's also crevassed, and though you will doubtless see folk in all manner of attire strolling, running and skiing on it, care should be taken. It's

a glacier, it may require crampons, and the use of a rope is advised.

Once at the pass several options present themselves. The Theodulhütte and the Rifugio Guide del Cervino at nearby Testa Grigia are both accommodation possibilities, where an overnight could allow an early morning ascent of the Breithorn. Even though the area is a ski circus, you only have to raise your eyes to be totally distracted by mighty peaks all around.

The route down towards Breuil-Cervinia is more beautiful when snow covered, but this makes it difficult to find the trail. When snow-free the horrors of the ski area are revealed in all their ugliness. There is an option as the first stage of the Testa Grigia (Plateau Rosa) cable-car drops you at the trail heading south to the Colle Superiore delle Cime Bianche (2882m). Pop over this and the ski area is gone, replaced by the fabulously wild Ventina or Rollin valley (the map does not give a precise name). Be sure to look back and enjoy the views of the Matterhorn as you won't see it again until you return to Zermatt.

Take your time as you descend steeply via well-made zigzags to the Gran Lago lake; this is a good place for a break as you acclimatise to the wild and silent surroundings. The way is now fairly

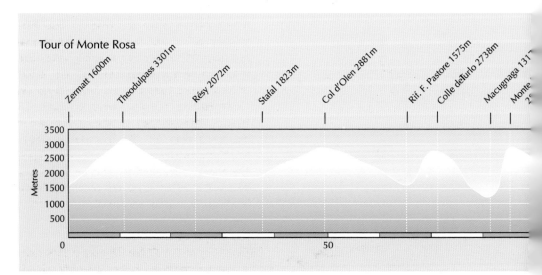

The final slopes leading to Colle Supérieur delle Cime Bianche

gentle and you can enjoy the views. To the west are the impressive multi-coloured cliffs of Monte Roisetta and soon the basic but lived-in summer farm at Alpe Mase is reached. From here the terrain is flowery meadows and grass-bordered streams leading down towards the larch and spruce forest.

The trail splits, one way descending to Val d'Ayas and the village of St Jacques where there are a couple of small hotels; the higher alternative goes left into a neighbouring valley and holds a fairly high contour to reach the hamlet of **Résy** where there are two huts: Rifugio del Guide Frachey and just above it Rifugio GB Ferraro, named after a local alpinist who died in the mountains in 1931. Résy has a fabulous position high above the valley on south-facing slopes. There used to be a thriving farming community here, and at 2072m it was one of the highest villages to be inhabited year-round.

Val d'Ayas to Valsesia

From Résy to Col d'Olen the regular TMR route is basically contained in the Gressoney ski area

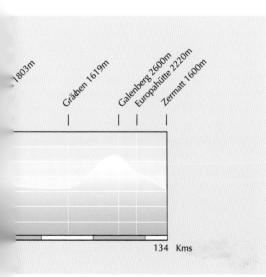

134 Kms

Striding up to the Guglielmina Hut

and could be done almost entirely on lifts. If time is limited this could be the way to do it, walking from Résy up to the Colle di Bettaforca then taking the chairlift down to Ste Anna and the cable-car to **Stafal**. From here two télécabines take you to the ridge above Col d'Olen, then you could continue down to Alagna or Rifugio F Pastore the same day. However, assuming time is not an issue, there's plenty of good walking to be enjoyed on this section to the 2881m **Col d'Olen**, by either the regular route or the variants described below, and it would be a crime to miss out on a night at Rifugio Guglielmina on the col, run by Alberto and his team. Named after the hoteliers who built it, Rifugio Guglielmina is steeped in history. For many years it was Europe's highest hotel perched on the ridge between the Valle della Lys and the Valsesia. After being transformed into a mountain

refuge it was re-opened in 1994, since when it has been run by descendants of the same family. This hut is very special, with its cosy warm interior, regional cuisine and fine selection of local wines, not to mention the superb welcome.

From Résy the normal TMR goes over the Bettaforca, down to Stafal then up to Gabiet and onwards to Col d'Olen. Parts of this route are quite nice, but there are lifts and ski pistes all around.

Taking the variant over Passo di Rothorn is much wilder and more exciting, but it's also a lot longer and more arduous. There's accommodation in the Gressoney valley at Gressoney St Jean, and a regular bus service runs along the valley. An alternative route from the valley to Col d'Olen is a trail that heads out from Gressoney-la-Trinité, up a beautiful pastoral valley to the high dammed Gabiet lake, avoiding signs of the ski area until

Trekkers heading for Passo Foric

you reach the end of the lake. For the last part up to the col you'll just have to keep your eyes on the snowy peaks and ignore the ski trash.

The ski area is quickly forgotten as the joys of this high, barren col are discovered. Often a herd of ibex graze the slopes around the hut and if you're lucky there may be big males right on the trail. As evening draws in you might see the lights of Milan glittering far below as the last pink rays of dusk slip down behind the horizon.

Although Col d'Olen is right in the midst of the Gressoney and Alagna ski areas, the area around it, especially on the Alagna side, is a hiker's paradise and you have the choice of three routes down from the col, all taking beautiful wild valleys to reach the Valsesia. The easiest, most straightforward descent is the trail that goes directly down to the lift station at Alpe Pianalunga, then down to

Alagna in the cable-car. There is a path down from Pianalunga but it's not always well-maintained. The second option takes a fabulous route down to the Diavolo rock then across to Passo Foric which leads into the Valle d'Otro, famous for its Walser hamlets with numerous classic examples of the traditional wooden chalets favoured by these ancient Germanic communities. Rifugio d'Otro offers a tempting place to stop for the night – passing by on a sunny afternoon even the most hardened hiker will surely find it difficult to resist the idea of setting down his heavy pack and hanging out on the grazed slopes in the heat.

The third alternative for the descent is to go over the ridge running east from Col d'Olen and down a steep and cable-protected trail into the aptly named Vallone delle Pisse – the massive vertical waterfall plunging directly down cliffs

A view of Monte Rosa from Colle delle Pisse (photo: John Berry)

Alberto and Franco, guardians of the Guglielmina Hut, once the highest hotel in Europe and still owned by the same family

Valsesia to Saastal

Many people seem to find this ascent an ordeal, but I really like the **Colle del Turlo** and do not consider it a grind at all. It's a good honest mountain day and if you take your eyes off the trail and look around there's plenty to see.

The col has seen traffic since medieval times as it's the only direct way from the Valsesia to the Macugnaga valley. From Rifugio Pastore the route takes a beautifully maintained mule track up to the higher meadows, then continues all the way to the pass. But it's the far side that sees the mother of all trail maintenance, thanks to the Italian Alpini troops: you won't see better than this anywhere in Europe, I promise! Huge rock slabs guide your feet down the most aesthetic winding stairway, past the red Lanti bivouac hut and its neighbour – which can be a godsend in bad weather – along a wide ledge bisected at intervals by gushing streams and into alder bushes which then clear for the summer alpage at La Piana. A more normal trail continues on through forest, down the Valle Quarazza, to eventually emerge at Quarazza itself, where there's a welcome café next to a lake. There follows a not-quite-flat track alongside the Anza torrent and up into **Macugnaga**.

Macugnaga is a buzzing little resort in the high season, but the rest of the year it must be very quiet as it really is in the back of beyond, an almost forgotten, secretive little place, snugly shoehorned into this corner of Italy nestling against the Swiss border. It can be difficult to find accommodation for one night here, and you might prefer to catch the cable-car up to Rifugio Oberto Gaspare just below the 2868m **Monte Moro Pass**.

The trail to the pass has improved a lot these last few years. The first part up through forest follows an ancient mule trail to the higher meadows. After that the path wends up through ski pistes, but is well signed and quite pleasant. If you're lucky enough to hit a clear day the imposing east face of Monte Rosa will keep you well distracted during the climb. Towards the top you'll have to keep half an eye on the waymarks which take you up rocky

in the back of the lower valley was presumably the inspiration. This route is exciting and wild, despite the presence of lift cables overhead and an old disused, but not entirely dismantled, lift further down. However, this way is sometimes not recommended, and can even be closed because of the risk of rockfall in the base of the valley. If you choose to go this way you emerge much higher up the Valsesia, near **Rifugio Pastore** at the Alpe Pile. Pastore is a very convenient place to stay as it leaves you poised for the following day's long ascent to Colle del Turlo (2738m). In good weather you gain the most wonderful views of the mighty east face of Monte Rosa, and in the evening you'll be able to spot the lights of Rifugio Margherita perched 2000m above on the summit of the Signalkuppe – the highest hut in Europe at 4559m.

fins to reach the café at the refuge. Beyond this on any good summer's day there will be lots of people emerging from the cable-car to scramble the last part of the trail (equipped with chains) up to the shining gold Madonna which marks the pass itself.

The Swiss side is nothing short of magical. Rocky slabs equipped for a very short section with cables give way to grassy meadows, woven with gently babbling brooks which take you down to the Mattmark lake. A pleasant track gives some rare flat walking, allowing you to enjoy the views of the Saastal peaks. At the Mattmark dam there's a café and a bus stop, but nowhere to stay so you must either walk or bus down to the Saastal for accommodation.

Saastal to Zermatt

The Saastal is divided from the Mattertal by the Mischabel peaks, extending from the Strahlhorn to Balfrin, whose height puts them up there with the surrounding giants. All passes through this range are glaciated, but the walker can pass from one valley to the next by means of a fabulous high balcony path known as the Höhenweg, which leads to Grächen. This is an old and well-established trail (opened in 1954) which can be accessed from either Saas Grund or **Saas Fee**. After an initial climb the trail stays around the 2100–2200m level the whole way. The terrain is varied, ranging from forest track to open trail bordered by bilberry bushes and juniper, to rocky boulders and short sections of exposed ledge. Animals are often seen grazing the steep slopes below, seemingly unperturbed by the passage of walkers above.

As with all balcony paths views can only be described as stunning – here, the Saastal peaks, notably the Weissmies, Lagginhorn and Fletschhorn. At the end the path turns the Grossi Furgge ridge at Hannigalp, to be greeted by a new panorama, that of the Mattertal peaks dominated by the Weisshorn, a summit you'll have plenty of time to admire in the final part of the trek.

From **Grächen** the mighty Europaweg leads all the way to Zermatt. This trail should not be underestimated! On 6 July 1997 it was officially opened as a two-day hike. Without doubt it's one of the most magnificent high-terrain routes of the Alps and, along with the Saas Fee Höhenweg, is regarded as the show-piece of the Swiss Tour of Monte Rosa.

After climbing from Grächen to reach a statue of St Bernard on the Zum Grat Ridge at around 2300m, the trail stays high above the Mattertal for the next 25km or so. The Europaweg reaches its highest point at **Galenberg** (2600m) and throughout this section views of glaciated peaks such as the Weisshorn, Zinal Rothorn and, as Zermatt is reached, the Matterhorn, are unsurpassed. The **Europahütte** situated about halfway along the route provides an overnight stop to savour these unique vistas.

However, the Europaweg is not the perfect hike it would seem. In fact the authorities have created a monster that requires constant attention and nurturing. The trail traverses steep slopes, which in winter are prone to avalanche and are denuded of trees. The high altitude in any case ensures the trail is above the treeline – great for views but inevitably on unstable ground. Landslides are frequent and it is not uncommon for parts of the Europaweg to be closed due to stonefall. This problem is being dealt with by very careful trail maintenance and the construction of metal tunnels and a remarkable 250m-long suspension bridge on the worst affected slopes, which allow the walker to safely cross gullies raked by falling stones, but closures are not uncommon during the summer when heavy rain can cause rockfall.

As the trail nears its end, it winds through Täschalp and out again, finishing near the Sunnegga lift above **Zermatt**. A final gentle descent down tracks brings you into the back streets of Zermatt.

Rifugio Crespi-Calderini and Monte Rosa

Trek 14
Tour of the Rätikon

by Kev Reynolds

I n early summer the chaos of rock and scree that lies at the foot of the Rätikon's steep south-facing walls is softened, coloured and fragranced by a succession of natural rock gardens. Bonsai-sized trees squeeze out of cracks in weathered boulders; cushions and mattresses of alpenrose edge narrow trails; deep blue gentians expose their trumpets in every direction, and the scent of daphne cneorum lingers in unseen clouds of perfume. And above it all rise the limestone cliffs and spires of mountains that define the Swiss–Austrian frontier, on both sides of which this short circular tour explores the best of its views, passes and huts. Although no Rätikon summit reaches 3000m, the mountains have an undeniable appeal, and every twist in the trail presents a fresh scene to admire.

The Drei Türm, viewed from the Lindauer Hut

Kirchlispitzen, seen from the upper slopes of Schesaplana

Route summary

Location	Rätikon Alps, Switzerland and Austria
Start/Finish	St Antönien
Distance	56km
Duration	6 days
Maximum altitude	2354m (Plasseggenpass) on the basic tour; 2965m (Schesaplana) optional summit
Accommodation	Mountain huts
Grade	Gentle/moderate
Guidebook	*Walking in Austria* by Kev Reynolds (Cicerone Press, 2009) describes the Rätikon Höhenweg Nord; no guidebook as yet describes the full tour.

Carrying the frontiers of Liechtenstein, Austria and Switzerland, the Rätikon group must be one of the most cosmopolitan in all the Alps, and

being oblivious of borders, some of its trails cross from one side to the other at will, linking huts in landscapes of great beauty. There are no border formalities of course, and though a few customs buildings remain on the Austrian flank at the head of tributary glens draining into the Montafon valley, they are mere reminders of another age.

These are limestone mountains. Planed, furrowed and castellated, the main crest runs east then southeast from the River Rhine to the Silvretta Alps, where crystalline rocks and glaciers suddenly take over. But glaciers are virtually non-existent in the Rätikon; the only one to survive is the tiny Brandner Gletscher below the Schesaplana, at 2964m the highest of the group's summits, and that little ice field will surely not last much longer.

The frontier crest is like a knobbly spine. Fortress-like turrets rise above screes invaded by flowering plants. Dwarf pine and tangles of

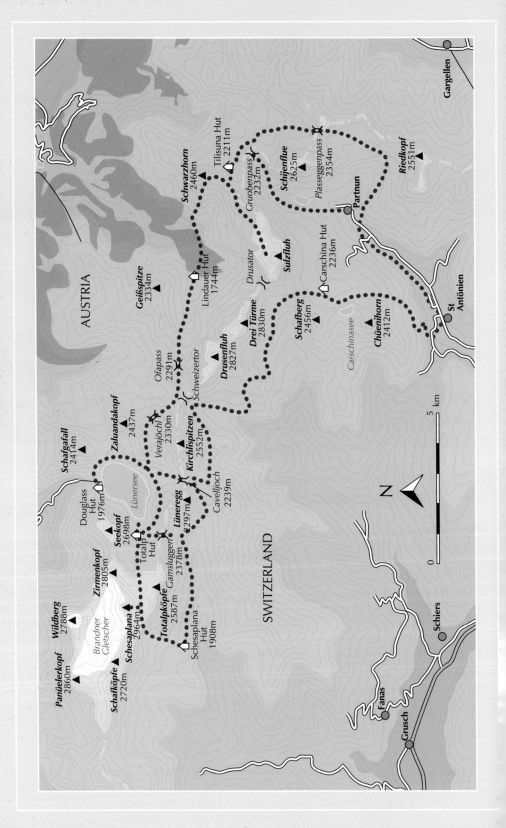

Tour of the Rätikon

AUSTRIA

SWITZERLAND

Gargellen

Riedkopf
2551m

Schwarzhorn
2460m

Tilisuna Hut
2211m

Gruobenpass
2232m

Schijenflue
2625m

Plasseggenpass
2354m

Partnun

Drusator

Sulzfluh
2278m

Carschina Hut
2236m

St
Antönien

Geißspitze
2334m

Lindauer Hut
1744m

Drusenfluh
2827m

Drei Türme
2830m

Schafberg
2456m

Carschinasee

Chüenihorn
2412m

Schafgafall
2414m

Ofapass
2291m

Zaluandakopf
2437m

Verajöchl
2330m

Schweizertor

Kirchlispitzen
2552m

Lünersee

Douglass
Hut
1976m

Seekopf
2698m

Totalp
Hut

Lüneregg
2297m

Gamsluggen
2378m

Cavelljoch
2239m

Wildberg
2788m

Zirmenkopf
2805m

Brandner
Gletscher

Schesaplana
2964m

Totalpköpfe
2587m

Schesaplana
Hut
1908m

Panüelerkopf
2860m

Schafköpfe
2720m

Schiers

Fanas

Grusch

N

5 km

0

St Antönien, built snug into the hillside

scarlet alpenrose make an attempt to soften the debris of rocks that lie at the foot of formidable slabs. From below, intimate details of these slabs on the Austrian flank are too often obscured by shadow, and you have to draw near, clambering over the screes and boulders, before their complex grooves and folds are revealed. On the Swiss side some of the south-facing walls appear impressively smooth, but it's not until you see a mountain hut dwarfed at their base that you realise just how big they are. Not as big as the Eiger Nordwand, of course, nor worth comparing with many of the great walls of the Mont Blanc range, nor as bizarre or precipitous as some of the famed Dolomite rock faces. But for a range of modest proportions, these south-facing Rätikon walls have the wow factor in abundance.

I first came to the district almost as an afterthought. Having spent the summer guiding walking groups around other Alpine regions, I checked my final group of the year onto their homebound plane at Innsbruck, then gave myself a two-week holiday exploring the Silvretta and Rätikon because they were close enough to reach in a half-day's journey by bus and train. The Silvretta was not entirely unknown to me, for many years before as a newly married man I was almost rapidly divorced when I knocked a rock onto my wife's head near the summit of its highest peak, Piz Linard. Forgiven, decades later we had a brief preview of the Austrian side of Piz Buin and the Dreiländerspitz, but now I was back for a solo trip, skirting the glaciers, crossing one pass after another until I found myself in the village of St

Antönien in the Swiss district of Prättigau with the Rätikon wall high above me catching the stain of alpenglow. From that moment on, I realised these really were mountains worth exploring.

Over the following 10 days or so I wandered from hut to hut and from col to col. I went up onto summits and scrambled along ridges alone with the choughs and the minuscule clusters of flowers that filled cracks and crevices. I strayed across borders, passed through Liechtenstein, crossed the Rhine and wandered onto the Alpstein for a close-up and personal view of the Säntis, then scurried away from crowds that swarmed over its summit and headed south across the Churfirsten's wave-like peaks, meandered over beautiful limestone pavements, then found myself irresistibly drawn back to the Rätikon's Austrian flank. And there I squeezed the days dry.

Austria has a popular linear route, the three-day Rätikon Höhenweg Nord, which goes from the Douglass Hut at the head of the Brandnertal to Gargellen at the western end of the Silvretta Alps. The Swiss side of the mountains has a parallel trail that links a couple of huts before continuing into Liechtenstein. What I have done here is join the two routes to create a week-long circular tour. Although there are some scrambling variants, the basic route is not one of the most demanding in this collection of treks, but that could be in

its favour, for this is a tour to walk at ease. Most of the stages are reasonably short, which allows plenty of opportunities to linger among the flowers, to laze upon a sun-warmed pass and, if the urge is there, to divert onto a summit or two.

St Antönien to the Schesaplana Hut

Since access from Zürich is straightforward, begin the tour on the Swiss side of the mountains and tackle it in a clockwise direction. At least one train an hour connects the city with Klosters via Landquart, and from Kübris (midway between Landquart and Klosters) a local postbus heads north into the valley of the Schanielabach to the small village of **St Antönien**, which has both hotel and low-priced dormitory accommodation. The road ends about 5km further upvalley at Partnun, from where the Rätikon Höhenweg Sud makes a direct approach to the Carschina Hut. But a slightly longer approach walk from St Antönien helps to build anticipation and rewards with a succession of fine viewpoints, so this is described here.

It's an 800m climb from St Antönien at 1420m to the Carschina Hut nestling at the foot of the Sulzfluh, and it begins on a minor road looping up the steep hillside between meadows. The road is soon exchanged for a farm track, and this in turn gives way to a footpath banked by a wonderland

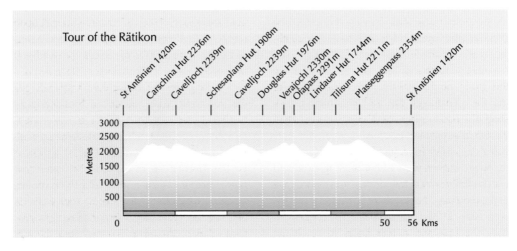

Tour of the Rätikon

The Carschinasee rimmed with cotton grass

of wild flowers. Coming onto a grassy crest the Sulzfluh rises out of the landscape ahead as you wander across a basin in which the lovely Carschinasee is cupped in a shallow depression almost completely ringed with cotton grass. From here the cross on the Sulzfluh's summit is visible on a clear day.

A few minutes after leaving the lake, you cross another grass ridge and have the south-facing wall of the Sulzfluh revealed ahead, with the craggy fingers of the Drusenfluh carrying the group northwestward. Over the saddle of the Carschinafurgga the trail continues a very short distance to reach the **Carschina Hut**, set at 2236m in a splendid location. Having taken only half a day to get there, you'll have plenty of time to lounge outside with a cool drink in hand and watch climbers in action on the stupendous face of the mountain that looms overhead.

A sign at the Carschinafurgga suggests it will take four and a half hours to reach the

Schesaplana Hut, the next stop on the westbound stage of our itinerary, and this is about right – if you can resist delaying and diverting among the wealth of mountain flowers that makes the walk so memorable. But the scenic dimension is no less exciting than the natural rock gardens the trail sneaks through, for the Rätikon gives a passable impression of the Dolomites, with rank upon rank of pale limestone walls, towers and turrets projecting from jumbles of scree. If the weather is favourable, delay is almost impossible to avoid.

Not long after recrossing the Carschinafurgga the trail forks, with one option breaking away to the Drusator, a gash in the frontier mountains between the Drei Türm and Kleine Sulzfluh beyond which lies the Lindauer Hut to be visited on the Austrian leg of the tour. The other trail passes below the Drei Türm and the complete block of the Drusenfluh – soaring rock walls on one side, but green slopes folding down to a pastoral valley on the other. Turning a spur, the way

From the Cavelljoch a view to the north shows the Lünersee reservoir

edges the Drusenfluh's western section to gain a preview of the Kirchlispitzen that looks immense as it stretches beyond another shadowed cleft in the frontier, through which it seems mere nicks of light intrude.

Angling down into a wild rock garden the path twists among alpenrose, juniper and arthritic tangles of dwarf pine whose bent trunks and branches have been bleached by long summers of reflected sun-scorch. There are tongues of scree among which crimson, yellow and iridescent blue patches of flowers demand close study; then an extraordinary group of pinnacles and fingers of limestone directs the way to another junction below the Schweizertor – the 'Swiss gateway'.

The upper path swings round to the very head of the valley that falls from the Schweizertor, crosses the Alplibach stream, then ignoring the Schweizertor's seduction, begins a long ascent of more flowery slopes, and up a narrow groove reminiscent of an ablation trough before emerging to a final climb leading to an obvious saddle. Now the Schesaplana demands attention ahead as an obvious path eases alongside the supporting cliffs of the Kirchlispitzen and makes for the 2239m **Cavelljoch** on the Swiss–Austrian border.

From this point there's a fine view onto the dammed Lünersee and the Douglass Hut on the Austrian flank. One option is to descend to that hut and begin the eastbound trend of the tour next day, but that should be resisted unless you're very short of time, for the Schesaplana Hut, lying a little under two hours ahead, is well worth a visit.

Continuing on the Swiss flank the trail is briefly exposed in places, but it soon gains another grass spur from where a new valley system appears. The Valser Tobel is a splendid pastoral landscape headed by the Schesaplana, and descending into the upper pastures you step lightly around a boggy area, then slant across a hillside ablaze with alpenroses towards scree fans. A succession of minor spurs and bluffs are crossed until at last the hut you've been seeking comes into view.

Perched upon a grass shelf at 1908m, the two buildings that comprise the **Schesaplana Hut** are backed by the grey limestone wall of the mountain after which it is named. Dating from 1898 and owned by the Pfannenstiel section of the Swiss Alpine Club, it's a cosy place to spend a night, with hillsides falling away to the south and the Rätikon wall rising into clouds behind.

Schesaplana Hut to the Lindauer Hut

Faced with many options for continuing a tour of the Rätikon mountains, a decision needs to be made before moving on. You could head north-west to the Pfälzer Hut on the Liechtenstein–Austria border in three and a half hours; make the ascent of the Schesaplana (3hrs) by a blue-and-white waymarked scramble and descend to the Totalp Hut (another 1¼hrs); return towards the Cavelljoch but cross the 2378m Gamsluggen on another blue-and-white 'Alpine' route to reach the Totalp Hut in two and a half hours; or retrace yesterday's trek to the Cavelljoch and descend on the Austrian side to the Douglass Hut for an easy three and a half hour stage.

For those with scrambling experience and a good head for heights, the ascent of the lofty Schesaplana is hard to resist. In truth it is not a particularly difficult ascent by the waymarked route from the hut, but caution is needed. Views from the summit are outstanding, and descent to the Totalp Hut is interesting but rough under foot.

But since this book is about trekking in the Alps, I'll suggest the more straightforward option of crossing the **Cavelljoch** and descending to the busy Douglass Hut set beside the Lünersee, as this is where most treks along the Rätikon Höhenweg Nord begin. And even this route has the option of straying to the Totalp Hut for a more authentic mountain experience, for those who prefer.

It will take perhaps two hours of easy walk-ing to return to the joch. All the way views are very fine and, since you're facing what you had your back to yesterday, they have an added interest. The massive bulk of the Kirchlispitzen, for example, is especially grand; a solid guardian built to defend the international border. The Cavelljoch sad-dle lies at its western end, and it is there that you enter Austria and wander down

into a shallow hanging valley that spills out to the Lünersee Alm and the lake beyond. Since the alm is at the southern end, and the Douglass Hut located at the northern end of the lake, you can take your pick as to which lakeside path to follow to the hut. Alternatively, you could head west from the alm on a higher path making for the Totalp Hut, base for climbs on Schesaplana.

The timber-built Totalp Hut has the ambience of a 'real' mountain hut, while the **Douglass Hut** stands adjacent to a cable-car station and attracts crowds of non-active (and active) visitors by day, although when the last cable-car has returned downvalley, a much more peaceful atmosphere settles on the place. The view along the lake, of course, can be serene. The original hut to stand here in 1872 was the first ever built by the German Alpine Club (DAV) and named after a British mountaineer, but this was flooded when the Lünersee reservoir was created in the late 1950s, and a replacement was opened in 1960.

Working its way between the Douglass and Lindauer huts, the trek

Being the highest in the Rätikon Alps, Schesaplana is a very popular mountain

crosses two passes, neither of which is unduly taxing, and from both of which you gain a proper appreciation of this largely unsung corner of the Alpine chain.

Returning to the Lünersee Alm, wander into the hanging valley by which you came yesterday, skirt a marshy basin, veer left to pass an abandoned customs hut and continue across a region littered with rocks and boulders before gaining the 2330m **Verajöchl**. Looking back to the west the Schesaplana has an elegant, almost distinguished appearance that was missing when studied from a closer vantage point. Ahead the great gash of the Schweizertor cleaves the frontier wall and appears as a much more profound breach than was suggested from the Swiss side, while far

off one ridge after another fades into the haze of distance, teasing with promise.

The trail descends easy grass slopes to another disused customs hut set close to the Schweizertor, after which you romp up through a narrow hanging valley to the second saddle of the day, the **Ofapass** at 2291m, gained just 40 minutes or so after leaving the Verajöchl. Now the Lindauer Hut can be seen tucked among trees at the far end of a pastureland, and you can amble down the Ofental to the pastures of Sporaalpe in the sure knowledge that your destination will soon be reached.

Originally built in 1898, the large shingle-walled **Lindauer Hut** is an atmospheric place belonging to the Lindau section of the DAV. Set among pine trees at the head of the Gauertal,

Crossing the Sporaalpe to the Lindauer Hut gives views ahead to the Sulzfluh

there's an alpine garden nearby, with labelled plants that should help identify some of the flowers you will have seen so far along the trek. To the southwest, across the Sporaalpe pastures and forming a perfect backdrop, the distinctive turrets of the Drei Türm will have a climber's fingers itching, while the Sulzfluh marks a change in direction of the frontier wall like a mighty hinge spreading from the Drusator's cleft.

Lindauer Hut to St Antönien

A morning's walk takes the trek to the **Tilisuna Hut**, which is useful timing for anyone interested in making an ascent of the Sulzfluh. From the Carschina Hut at the start of the Rätikon tour, the Sulzfluh showed itself to be a climber's mountain, its massive south-facing wall a true vertical challenge. When viewed from the Lindauer Hut its appearance is just as formidable. Yet there's an easy, uncomplicated trekker's route to the summit which begins not far from the Tilisuna Hut, and given fair conditions it would be a shame not to take advantage of it.

So set off shortly after breakfast, leaving the Lindauer's pinewoods behind as you wander eastward below the Sulzfluh's big rock walls to reach a trail junction. Surprisingly one route is signed to the Tilisuna Hut via the Sulzfluh itself in a little under four hours, but we take the alternative trail towards the Bilkengrat. This is a steep spur projecting from a transverse ridge dividing the Gauertal and Gampadelstal valleys, across which lies the Tilisuna Hut. The ridge pushes northward from the frontier mountains with its highest summit, the 2460m Schwarzhorn, clearly seen from the Bilkengrat spur.

Climbing this spur, carpeted with heather, bilberry and alpenrose, is probably the most physically demanding section of the whole tour, for the path is unremittingly steep, but with consistently fine views to enjoy along the way. At the top of the Bilkengrat the path cuts along a narrow shelf safeguarded with fixed cable, then brings you onto the 2336m saddle of the Schwarz Scharte with the Tilisunasee tarn seen glinting in its grass basin 200m below. The hut, unseen from this point, is just 20 minutes' walk away.

Have a light lunch at the hut, check in for the night and leave most of your baggage there, then spend a couple of hours or so making the ascent of the Sulzfluh by a well-marked route that takes you across a large and featureless limestone pavement, up a multi-braided path to a ridge, then via rough slopes and snow ramps to gain the summit tower. The summit is marked by a huge wooden cross, and the panoramic view is vast and truly rewarding.

The final stage of the tour returns the trek to the Swiss flank. Leaving the Tilisuna Hut, a short stroll brings you to the Tilisunafürggli at 2226m. Linked with another trail which crosses the 2232m Gruobenpass in less than half an hour from the hut, it offers a short way down into the Swiss valley that leads to St Antönien. Both are perfectly feasible options, but there's a third alternative which continues along the Höhenweg Nord as far as the **Plasseggenpass** (2354m) where the limestone of the Rätikon gives way to the crystalline rock of the Silvretta Alps. This pass is reached in a little under an hour from the Tilsuna Hut, and from it you descend into Switzerland on a path signed to Partnunstafel (1¼hrs) and to St Antönien in two and a half hours. It's a valley walk throughout, and a very pleasant way to conclude the Tour of the Rätikon.

Trek 15

Across the Eastern Alps: E5

by Gillian Price

From the shores of Lake Constance, where Germany, Austria and Switzerland meet, to the unmistakably Italian city of Verona, the month-long trek that follows the trans-Europe E5 trail weaves a course through the ever-varied and scenically uplifting Eastern Alps. First among these is the lush, well-watered Allgäuer group with green valleys and bare rocky ridges, a range shared between Bavaria and Austria. The way then swings south to cross the glacier-girt Ötztaler Alps that spill over the Austro-Italian border, before the lovely Trentino region carries the route towards its final destination. Mountains (but what mountains!) are only part of the appeal of this route, for there's much of cultural as well as gastronomic interest; activity on summer farms to observe, and milestones of European history to decipher along the way, as if to underline the fact that trekking across the Eastern Alps offers a truly multi-dimensional experience.

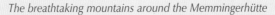

The breathtaking mountains around the Memmingerhütte

Route summary

Location	Eastern Alps, taking in Germany, Switzerland, Austria and Italy
Start	Lake Constance, Germany
Finish	Verona, Italy
Distance	495km
Duration	29 days
Maximum altitude	2995m
Accommodation	Village guesthouses and mountain huts
Grade	Moderate +
Guidebook	*Across the Eastern Alps: E5* by Gillian Price (Cicerone Press, 2007)

It's amazing really: you set out from Germany along the lovely shores of Lake Constance in the country's south, and before you can say *guten Tag*, you've crossed into Switzerland and Austria in quick succession, and even find yourself back in Germany again! This region does get its fair share of visibility-hampering mist, but that doesn't mean you're lost and have gone backwards. Rather, it is a reminder of the crazy international border kinks in this central part of Alpine Europe. Thankfully the Schengen Agreement means you can ignore the multiple border crossings as no passports need to be displayed and customs posts have been dismantled. Oh the beauty of Unified Europe! So all that walkers need to think about is the wonderful scenery that unfolds before their eyes.

And what scenery! In its northern chunks the E5 traverses the superb Allgäuer and Ötztaler Alps with sweeping glaciers and dizzily placed huts. Day after day of high-altitude heaven, interspersed with lower strolls when day-to-day local life is experienced first

hand. Many a village upholds its working traditions – affable bearded men in *lederhosen* and felt hat summon the dairy cows one by one by name, in from the rich pastures to return home for milking. (Yes, there were times when I expected Heidi to come waltzing over the hill too.) Further south come the quieter mountains in Italy. Here you find that cultural diversity that makes me love Europe: my favourite example is a valley in the middle of Italian-speaking Trentino where people continue to use a medieval German dialect on a day-to-day basis in the 21st century.

Along with the European currency the euro, *Apfelstrudel* is a delicious common denominator along the route. That luscious flaky pastry roll containing warm spice-enhanced apple slices is a perfect gap-filler when dinner is still a few hours off. Remember the trick to ordering: *mit Sahn* or *ohne Sahn* – with cream or without. Chances are you'll find yourself compiling your own personal list of favourites en route. Mine is headed by the Hirzerhütte, a rambling family farm dating back to 1873 and located midway along the trek in Italian South Tyrol.

The shores of Lake Constance, shared by Germany, Austria and Switzerland

Wartime remains on the Dente Austriaco, Pasubio

One of the recognised long-distance walking routes that criss-cross the continent, the wonderful trans-Europe E5 is monumental – just over a month to cover just under 500km. One of the many things I loved about it was the sense of travelling it gave me. I'd got off the train in **Konstanz** with rucksack on shoulders and clad in trekking gear and boots, and covered all that distance under my own steam. Poring over the maps afterwards gave me a real thrill and sense of satisfaction as I highlighted the route in marker pen. Looking back on it inevitably brings to mind a kaleidoscope of impressions, places, people and mesmerising mountain ranges, every single one a reason to go back and explore further, as inviting detours popped up all along the way.

From Lake Constance through the Allgäuer Alps
A superb start to the trek, the gentle banks of Lake Constance can be fully savoured on the stroll through picturesque fishing hamlets and nature reserves. Lunchtimes can be eagerly anticipated as you are spoilt for choice – how about a picnic bench on the waterside fringed with reeds? Herons and peregrine falcons take their midday meal in the lake itself, thanks to the fish-rich waters, while you may be lucky to see the storks that nest on dry land. You can always treat yourself to a sit-down al fresco affair at any of the charming inns shaded by trees. Rolling green hills provide the backdrop, cultivated with tidy orchards of apples as well as grapes that go into the region's crisp white wines.

Soon one of the most important rivers in Europe, the massive Rhine, makes its entry into Lake Constance through a double series of reinforced channels to deal with flood overflow. Only a short distance from its source in the Swiss Alps, it was a modest but steady flow when we crossed it by bridge one July, but the overall dimensions are awesome. Just think, in its northern realms, this river is rife with legend – the Lorelei,

Across the Eastern Alps: E5

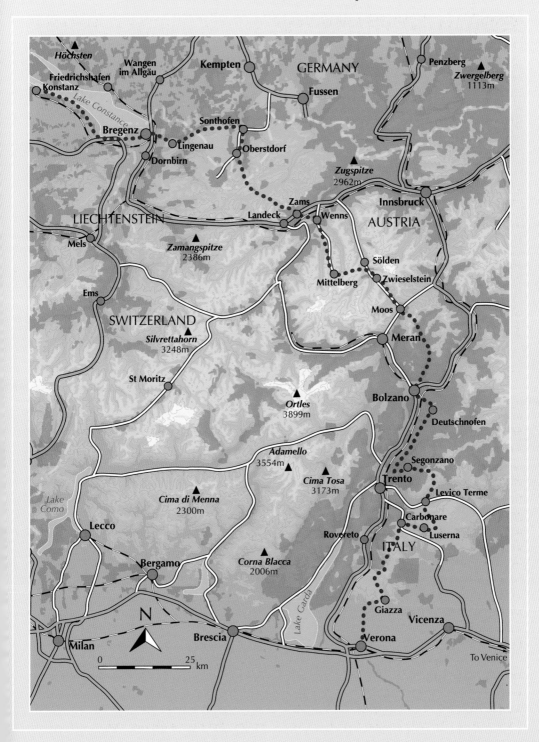

Höchsten ▲

Wangen
im Allgäu

Kempten

GERMANY

Penzberg

Zwergelberg
1113m ▲

Friedrichshafen
Konstanz

Lake Constance

Fussen

Bregenz

Lingenau

Sonthofen

Oberstdorf

Zugspitze
2962m ▲

Innsbruck

Dornbirn

Zams

LIECHTENSTEIN

Landeck

Wenns

AUSTRIA

Mels

Zamangspitze
2386m ▲

Sölden

Zwieselstein

Ems

Mittelberg

Moos

SWITZERLAND

Silvrettahorn
3248m ▲

Meran

St Moritz

Ortles
3899m ▲

Bolzano

Deutschnofen

Adamello
3554m ▲

Cima Tosa
3173m ▲

Segonzano

Lake
Como

Cima di Menna
2300m ▲

Trento

Levico Terme

Carbonare

Lecco

Rovereto

Luserna

Bergamo

Corna Blacca
2006m ▲

ITALY

N

Lake Garda

Giazza

Vicenza

Milan

Brescia

Verona

0   25 km

To Venice

Oberstdorf is left behind as the route leads up the Trettachtal en route to the Kemptnerhütte

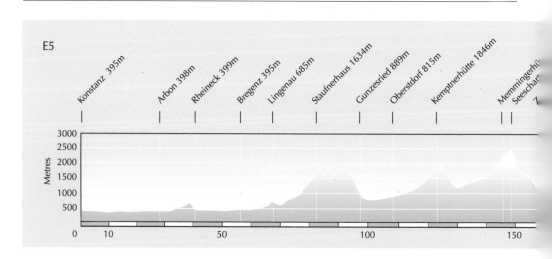

beautiful maidens, treasures and gold that so inspired Wagner.

These opening lakeside days stretch out into a pleasant promenade, worthwhile in its own right. Before moving on to bigger things, one last delight awaits as you wander into the city of **Bregenz** to the mind-boggling sight of a full-scale theatre stage – floating on the water. Without fail it comes to life every single summer to host memorable opera and symphonic performances.

But now the E5 heads for higher ground and the musically sounding Nagelfluhkette, which turns out to be a jagged ridge belonging to the Allgäuer Alps. Stretched-out, airy, slippery and tiring are also suitable adjectives – along with spectacular, panoramic and thick with wild flowers! Never climbing higher than 1800m, it eventually concludes at a scattering of dairy farms where the trail descends gently to a traditional Bavarian village after a spectacular day's walking.

The broad Iller valley has a relaxing shady path along the river to the town of **Oberstdorf**. This lovely spa is the southernmost in Germany, while for trekkers it spells access to the Kemptnerhütte. A clear path leads up an ever-narrowing valley to fork up the Sperrbachtobel gully. Though not excessively high – starting at 1300m – the deep V-shape means it is sheltered from the sun, so the winter snow takes an unusually long time to melt here.

The result is an entertaining obstacle course as deep drifts and icy blocks are detoured. However, it is well trodden by German walkers and the hut staff unfailingly keep the route as clear as possible, and they have even fitted lengths of cable along the edge. The reward – there is always a reward in the Alps for energy expended – is a hidden upper valley of brilliant green pasture fed by waterfalls. And to top it off is the **Kemptnerhütte** at 1846m in which to stay the night. A rambling, bustling establishment, it has a lovely terrace where the sunset can be admired colouring the surrounding peaks with delicate pink-orange hues, rendering them worthy of a watercolour. In non-poetic contrast, it was here that I had one of my linguistic revelations, belated alas. My friends and I had been allotted a spacious dormitory, handy as everyone had bits of washing to hang out. In no time at all it looked like a Chinese laundry with unmentionables draped here and there over ladders and tucked into bunk springs. It wasn't until the following morning that I saw other guests to-ing and fro-ing from what I had taken to be a basement storeroom, but was quite peeved to discover labelled as a *Trockenraum*, which translates as 'drying room'.

Southeast over the next valley, a steady climb across streams and flowered meadows concludes at the memorable **Memmingerhütte**. Standing on a rise at 2242m in a wonderful amphitheatre

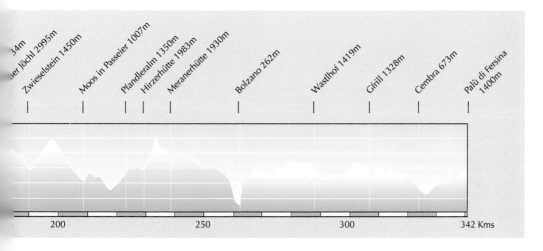

Approaching the Seescharte pass

dotted with tarns, it looks out to a crown of mountains, dominated by the 2412m Seekogel. This modest outcrop offers breathtaking 360° views to anyone who can find the energy to spare for the straightforward ascent. As a delightful alternative, by all means make the most of the hut's ample terrace to catch up on your diary, enjoy a refreshing beer or even take a snooze. Nobody will disapprove.

The ensuing stage is easily one of the highlights of the E5. The path wanders across the pasture basin where livestock grazes freely in Alpine paradise and drinks from the marshy-edged lake with the curious name of Seewi. A broad gully marks the start of a steep ascent, a tough section on crumbly earth, but one that rewards with an outlook of glittering tarns in inaccessible cirques. The direction here is south, and this signifies accumulations of old snow which can hamper progress. But even with patches of ice there are splashes of colour from the hardy blooms that survive on little else but scree. Minuscule pockets of humus invisible to the human eye nourish plants. Scented lilac pennycress and glacier crowfoot, whose white-pink petals contain an anti-freeze liquid. At the top – 2599m Seescharte – tiny violets brighten chinks in the rock face while iridescent blue gentians prefer the sparse grass cover. A lengthy pause is in order here, as close at hand the Schweinrücken stretches out narrow and jagged. The 'hog back', as the ridge name signifies, is the favourite haunt of a herd of majestic ibex that laze on the impossibly precarious rocky terrain – which spells safety for them.

Well below, a lush pastoral basin is traversed, home to a traditional summer alp farm. To reach this spot each summer, the livestock is accompanied by herders from villages on the valley floor. As does the E5, their route passes by way of a dramatic gorge, the Zammer Loch, where a narrow path clings to precipitous limestone flanks hundreds of metres above a tumbling torrent. Very exciting stuff! This wonderful day concludes at a lower altitude this time, in the Austrian village of **Zams** at 775m. This lies in the valley of the River Inn, a key artery for traffic since time immemorial, and a staging post on the ancient Roman way, the Via Claudia Augusta, constructed in 47AD to link the Adriatic plain and ports with provinces on the northern side of the Alps.

The Ötztaler Alps

The Pitztal and the scatter of hotels than go under the name of **Mittelberg** are the gateway to the

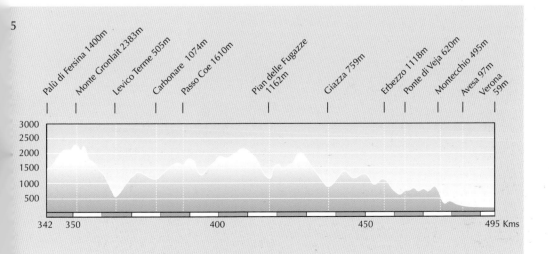

Huge glacier spills below the Wildspitze are skirted during the climb to the Braunschweiger Hut

Ötztaler Alps. Where the motorable road ends, streams of glacier melt clatter down a broad valley with a perfect textbook U-shape, a clear giveaway of its glacial origin. It's an exciting walk, for with every step taken the huge ice spread ahead is revealed little by little, its run-off feeding impressive waterfalls that swell as the day goes by. Huge mountains loom beyond, Wildspitze dominating. A good three hours up stands the Braunschweiger Hütte, its welcoming terrace an unmatchable belvedere. View notwithstanding, I distinctly remember a chilly wind blowing in from the glaciers and driving us inside for a hot chocolate treat, huddling around a sturdy stove coated with ceramic tiles in the Stube room, a long-standing tradition for the Tyrol.

The route continues climbing with scenic rewards of great magnificence, and crosses the **Pitztaler Jöchl**, the highest point on the whole of the E5 trek, at 2995m. Phew! Only a crow's flight away are the extensive world-famous ski fields and lifts of the Ötztal, year-round snow bliss. However, trekkers now need to brace their knees for an initially steep descent that takes the good part of a day to reach the floor of the Ötztal itself. Here of course, it's heaven to collapse in a spotless B&B at **Zwieselstein**, your last night in Austria. As of tomorrow, it's Italy for the rest of the trek.

The vast outlook from well-signed Missensteinjoch, not far from the Meranerhütte

South Tyrolean
Landscapes around Bolzano

Quiet valleys and paths leading through scattered pastoral settlements characterise the following days. And seeing as this was all part of Tyrol for centuries, the local lingo is still German, or at least that was what I had been led to believe. But one day we were stopped in a Passeiertal hamlet by an elderly farmer, well on the way to marking a century. Surprise, surprise when she proudly showed off her fluent Italian, an absolute rarity. She considered herself lucky; when the region became part of Italy in the aftermath of the First World War, all schooling under Mussolini was in compulsory Italian, whereas nowadays 80% of day-to-day affairs, schooling and business dealings are conducted in German. It was like walking into a history book. And the history lessons continued across the ensuing ranges with monuments to Andreas Hofer, great Tyrolean patriot from the early 1800s.

Accompanied by magnificent views of the Dolomites and grazing herds of the handsome blond-maned native Haflinger horses, the route wanders over a broad plateau, finally dropping down to the delightful regional capital of **Bolzano**, or Bozen. This is the lowest point on the E5 as well as the halfway mark. It nestles at a mere 262m in the Adige river valley, whose abrupt flanks are dotted with castles and smothered in terraces bearing grapevines. Here it's tempting to take time out to sip a glass of local wine at any of the welcoming al fresco cafés. Bolzano is also a good place to stock up on tasty picnic goodies, such as Speck (smoked ham) and all manner of crusty cereal breads, at inviting shops in its porticoed streets where frescoed merchant buildings date from the Middle Ages. And do remember that it is also home to Ötzi, the fascinating Copper Age mummy that is a must-see in a bespoke museum. This highlight is a perfect way to round off a holiday after two weeks on the hoof, and Bolzano is a handy place to leave – or join – the trek, thanks to its excellent rail and road links.

But move on we must. On the far side of town a cable-car used by the local people to access upland villages means you can be whisked effortlessly up 1000m to a superb watchtower for unbeatable views o'er mountain and vale, glacier, and meadow.

Our trail now sets a course southwards parallel to the broad river valley through cool woodland and rural landscapes, keeping around the 1500m altitude mark.

The next highlight is Bletterbach, or 'stream of leaves', a very tame tag that gives no hint of the dramatic canyon that gashes open at your feet. Running water was responsible for excavating 400m below ground level, a yawning ravine exposing remarkable layers of geological time as ancient as the Triassic (280 million years ago). Recently recognised by UNESCO as a World Heritage Site, it is a treasure trove of fossilised dinosaur footprints, intricate shells and all sorts of geological marvels, though you need to detour downhill to the museum to admire them at close quarters.

Through the
Trentino and Veneto to Verona

Tramping via pretty farming villages where window boxes overflow with geraniums, the way leads across the Val dei Mocheni past the old mines that brought prosperity in medieval times, along with foreign workers and their curious Germanic dialect that is still spoken and is completely incomprehensible to outsiders. Pretty Lago Erdemolo and its tiny hut nestle at the foot of the soaring rugged Lagorai range, where the going starts to get rougher, solitary – and breathtakingly magnificent at the same time. A superb if punishing day is spent negotiating 2382m Monte Gronlait and 2347m Cima Fravort accompanied by 360° views that take in the Dolomites to the northeast and the glaciated Ortles-Cevedale group to the west. As the edge of the Trentino region, erstwhile border of the Hapsburg Empire, is approached there are abundant reminders of the First World War that led to the empire's

It's a long climb up Monte Gronlait in the rugged Lagorai range

demise. Trenches and fortified lookouts can be observed on many a prominent ridge.

Well and truly in Italian-speaking territory is the charming spa resort of **Levico Terme**, where all manner of watery cures can be indulged in. Here the Valsugana, the Brenta river and the railway line are crossed amidst apple orchards. A good part of a day is spent ascending to the lofty Altopiano di Folgaria-Lavarone. This turns out to be a vast, rolling limestone plateau carpeted with lush pastureland where creamy cheeses like Vezzena and Asiago are produced (delicious for sandwich fillings, believe me). Dotted here and there on this pastoral idyll are crumbling monumental forts from the 1914–18 conflict. If you only visit one, make it Forte Cherle, a labyrinthal structure, its old cannon placements invaded in this day and age by harmless ornamental carline thistles.

Passo Coe and its cosy guesthouse mark the start of two fascinating days traversing the Pasubio mountain range, where ridges and summits are riddled with war-inflicted injuries and long, manmade tunnels gouged through solid rock. Such beautiful surrounds amidst such poignancy. I left the area with a striking sense of desolation and silence – peaceful in a way, but also strangely devoid of the usual riot of flowers and roaming wildlife. Two *rifugi* provide accommodation and meals for walkers and for adventurous cyclists with a penchant for long, winding unsurfaced tracks with abrupt exposed corners shrouded in swirling atmospheric mist.

Beyond the road pass and **Pian delle Fugazze** lie the final mountainous sections of the E5. Wild and wonderful, the Carega massif is like Dolomite landscapes, tumbles of scree and stark white

Rifugio Papa on the Pasubio was named after an Italian general

rock studded with pretty bright blooms. A long wooded valley meanders south to terminate at the sleepy hamlet of **Giazza**. That name ring a bell? Funnily enough, it is related to the production of ice, once a big commercial endeavour here. It would be stored in deep caves and transported to the homes of the Verona nobility at night when conditions were cooler. Of course the arrival of modern refrigeration techniques in the 1950s put an end to all that.

Geology enthusiasts will have a field day in the Monti Lessini. Chunky slabs of *rosso ammonitico*

rock studded with coiled shell fossils line many a rural lane and act as roofing for the squashed stone houses in the quiet farming villages. A final highlight is the amazing arched rock bridge of **Ponte di Veja** spanning a gully, and it comes as quite a surprise as it emerges from jungle-like vegetation cover.

It's not far now to the beautiful Italian city of **Verona** and the trek's conclusion, a real treat well deserved! As well as a good rest, a 'must' is a magical night at an opera performance in the open-air Roman arena.

Trek 16
Stubai High-Level Route

by Allan Hartley

*M*aking a circular 9–10 day tour of the much-loved Stubai Alps, this is the quintessential Alpine hut-to-hut trek. Crossing rock ribs and ridges, skirting tarns and scuffing old moraines, the route studiously avoids roads and villages to concentrate on some of Austria's finest wild landscapes. Shapely rock peaks like those of the Tribulaun on show from the Innsbrucker Hut, or draped with glaciers like the Wilder Freiger, Wilder Pfaff and Zuckerhütl, or the mirror image of the Seespitze captured in the clear waters of the Rinnensee – all these become familiar background features on the journey. As for the huts, they may differ from one another in architecture, décor and outlook, but each one welcomes with a cosy ambience to create a near-perfect introduction to the hutting experience.

The Grosser Trögler is a magnificent viewpoint, with the Zuckerhütl the main focus of attention

An airy view onto the Innsbrucker Hut with the Serleskamm Group behind

Route summary

Location	Stubai Alps, southwest of Innsbruck, Austria
Start	Neder
Finish	Neustift
Distance	80km
Duration	9–10 days
Maximum altitude	2888m on the standard route; 3277m (Habicht) optional ascent
Accommodation	Mountain huts of the Austrian and German Alpine Clubs
Grade	Strenuous
Guidebook	*Trekking in the Stubai Alps* by Allan Hartley (Cicerone Press, 3rd edition, 2011)

Situated southwest of the old medieval city of Innsbruck in the Austrian province of Tyrol, the Stubai Alps are easily reached by postbus in about one hour. Having first discovered the area many years ago while trying to escape atrocious weather in the higher mountains of the Western Alps, I have returned many times and taken a number of groups there, and more recently have been rediscovering its mountains on a pair of snowshoes.

The boundaries of the Stubai are generally recognised as the Brenner Pass to the east, the Sölden valley in the Ötztal district to the west, the mountains of the Italian South Tyrol to the south, and the Inn valley to the north. Its highest mountain is the 3505m Zuckerhütl, with many other peaks over 3000m, some of which have glaciers and permanent snow cover. Generally, the main peaks follow the Wilder Freiger/Zuckerhütl chain that straddles the border with Italy and embrace the area known as the South Tyrol, referring to previous Austrian territory annexed to Italy after the First World War.

Known in German as the Stubaier Runde Tour, and more recently as the Stubaier Höhenweg, the Stubai High-Level Route is a multi-day trek linking eight huts, and by definition requires nothing more than the ubiquitous rucksack and a pair of boots to undertake. Beginning at the small village of Neder, a few kilometres before Neustift, it first goes to the Innsbrucker Hut, then to each of the following huts in turn: Bremer, Nürnberger, Sulzenau, Dresdner, Neue Regensburger, Franz Senn and Starkenburger, to end back in the Stubaital at Neustift.

Whatever your aspirations the Stubai is a splendid area for all mountain enthusiasts to explore, and whatever your wishes you will not be disappointed, so *grüss Gott und gute Bergtouren*!

Neder to the Bremer Hut

Taking the regular Stubaital bus from Innsbruck Bahnhof, the journey to **Neder** is a pleasant ride that includes crossing the famous Europa Bridge

near the Italian border on the Brenner Pass. From its entrance at Schönberg to its head at Mutterberg Alm, the valley is quintessentially Tyrolean, with pretty chalet-style houses and an organised charm that embraces the villages of Telfes, Mieders, Fulpmes and lastly Neustift, the Stubaital's main village and centre.

At Neder signposts point the way up the Pinnistal, with the Serleskamm's towering rock spires and the impressive rock walls of the Kirchdach Spitze that are more akin to the Dolomites than the snow-capped peaks of the Stubai Alps. Beyond Pinnis Alm, the great bulk of the 3277m Habicht dominates the scene and ensures that nothing else gets looked at until the Pinnisjoch is reached. Nearby, but just out of sight, sits the very pleasant **Innsbrucker Hut**.

While at this hut it is worth considering an ascent of the Habicht, the superb 'Hawk Mountain' and the highest in the eastern Stubai. First climbed in 1836, it is best seen from the Tribulaun and Starkenburger huts. The ordinary route via the eastern flank is a popular outing from the Innsbrucker Hut, and in summer the climb is up a well-beaten trail. Signposts and red waymarks indicate the way over broken rocky slabs to the edge of what remains of the Habicht glacier.

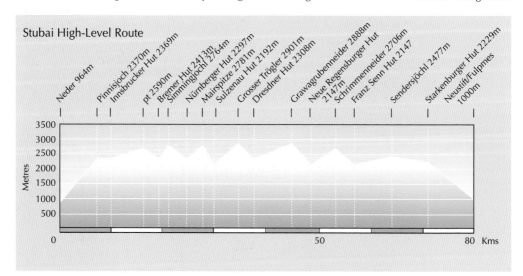

Stubai High-Level Route

Stubai High-Level Route

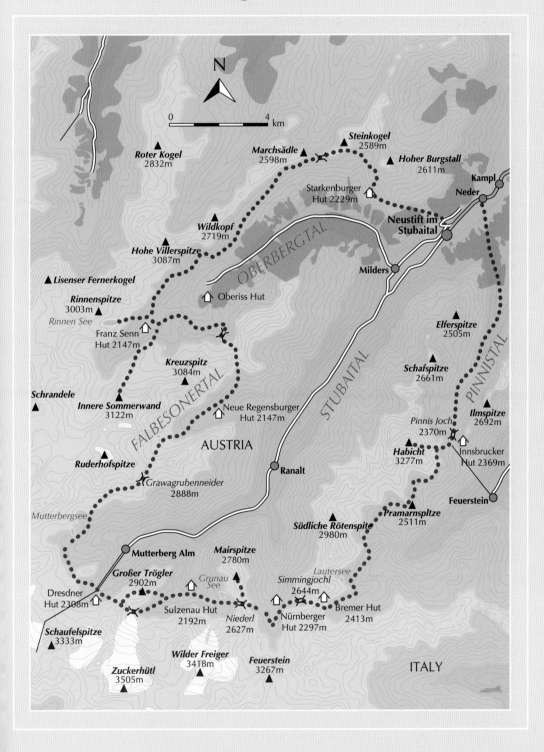

N

0   4 km

▲ Roter Kogel
2832m

▲ Marchsädle
2598m

▲ Steinkogel
2589m

▲ Hoher Burgstall
2611m

Kampl

Starkenburger
Hut 2229m

Neder

Neustift im
Stubaital

▲ Wildkopf
2719m

OBERBERGTAL

Milders

▲ Hohe Villerspitze
3087m

▲ Lisenser Fernerkogel

▲ Elferspitze
2505m

Rinnenspitze
3003m ▲

Oberiss Hut

Rinnen See

▲ Schafspitze
2661m

Franz Senn
Hut 2147m

PINNISTAL

Kreuzspitz
3084m

STUBAITAL

Ilmspitze
2692m

▲ Schrandele

▲ Innere Sommerwand
3122m

Neue Regensburger
Hut 2147m

Pinnis Joch
2370m

AUSTRIA

FALBESONERTAL

Habicht
3277m

Innsbrucker
Hut 2369m

▲ Ruderhofspitze

Ranalt

Grawagrubenneider
2888m

Feuerstein

Mutterbergsee

Pramarnspltze
2511m

▲ Südliche Rötenspite
2980m

Mutterberg Alm

Mairspitze
2780m

Lautersee

Großer Trögler
2902m

Grunau
See

Simmingjochl
2644m

Dresdner
Hut 2308m

Sulzenau Hut
2192m

Niederl
2627m

Nürnberger
Hut 2297m

Bremer Hut
2413m

▲ Schaufelspitze
3333m

▲ Wilder Freiger
3418m

▲ Feuerstein
3267m

ITALY

▲ Zuckerhütl
3505m

The Tribulaun mountains, just one of the spectacular sights to be enjoyed from the Innsbrucker Hut

Crossing these snowy remnants and climbing shattered rocks eventually leads over easier ground to the large summit cross, complemented by excellent views in all directions, particularly the main peaks of the central Stubai, Tribulaun and Serleskamm groups, plus the distant peaks of the Dolomites, Zillertal and Ötztal.

Having spent the night at the Innsbrucker Hut it's time to move on to the Bremer Hut, a trek that will take most of the day and quite a lot of up and down, but in return it embraces some of the Stubai's finest scenery.

With unrivalled views of the Tribulaun in front and the spectacular limestone cliffs of the Kirchdach Spitze behind, leave the hut and contour across the hillside of the Alfeirkamm high above the pastoral alms of Pfannalm and Glattealm for a couple of hours, before being stopped in your tracks to make a steep descent into the broad couloir of Beilgrube.

Crossing broken rocky ground, you then curse at having to climb back up once again to gain the east ridge of the Aussere Wetter Spitze from where, as if by magic, the Bremer Hut suddenly appears as a distant speck across the Simminger Alm, along with a welcome sight of the snow-capped peaks of the Pflerscher Hochjoch, and a fabulous view down the Gschnitztal. Having huffed and puffed back up onto the ridge, another reluctant descent has to be made to cross the Simminger Alm basin to the delightful tarn of the Lautersee. Everyone says 'not again' for one last time on today's trek, as effort and willpower are needed to climb through steep but broken rocky buttresses with some good scrambling aided by fixed ropes, to emerge on the broad plateau with a sigh of relief just below the magnificently sited **Bremer Hut**.

Bremer Hut to the Dresdner Hut

Having rested at the Bremer Hut, pick up the trail once more following an obvious path with the wonderful snow-capped peaks of the Pflerscher Hochjoch for scenic entertainment. Lulled into a sense of false security the track climbs steadily, then just below the Simmingsjöchl it rises abruptly to get the heart rate going before easing back to emerge at the tiny customs hut used by the border police. While you enjoy a short break at the col it will be the snowy mantel of the Wilder Freiger that vies for attention, for it is possible to see the dawn patrol of climbers crossing the upper snows of the Freiger glacier on their way up the mountain. Or maybe it's the adjacent rock peak of the 2965m Aperer Feuerstein that's caught your eye? At just a tad short of the magic 3000m contour, this satellite peak can be climbed as a short one-hour detour from the police hut by way of the Nürnberger Scharte. The reward will not only be excellent views of the Wilder Freiger, but also the peaks of the Feuerstein. Sharp eyes will also be able to locate the Becher Haus, better known on the Austrian side of the border as Elisabeth Haus, perched on a tiny knoll in South Tyrol.

Resuming the walk to the Nürnberger Hut, which is now in sight, take a moment to recce the route to the Sulzenau Hut which goes by way of the Mairspitze, clearly seen across the void. Meanwhile descend over rocks and boulders of varying size through the glacial debris that makes up the Grübl Cirque, then skip over easier ground until the raging torrents of the Langtal river are reached and crossed by a rickety bridge, followed by a short scramble to the very substantial four-storey **Nürnberger Hut**.

At this stage of the tour I would normally recommend a climb to the snowy heights of the Wilder Freiger en route to the Sulzenau Hut, but that's the domain of the aspirant Alpinist, so my recommendation is to climb the very respectable Mairspitze (2780m) and enjoy one of the finest walks in the Stubai.

By now Route 102, better known as the Central Alpine Way, has become familiar. This is followed for a short time before the track splits off to climb a gradually steepening path over rocky slabs, leading without too much effort to a ridge and a col. The ridge itself provides some excellent scrambling all the way to the craggy top of the Mairspitze, complete with bench seat and large summit cross.

Having relaxed and enjoyed the tremendous view of the Wilder Freiger and its tumbling glacier, backtrack to the col then descend steep, challenging rocks into the old glacial basin at Schafgrübel, brightened by several ponds, and eventually reach the delightful tarn of the Grunausee. This is an ideal lunch stop to enjoy the splendid view of the Wilder Freiger mirrored on its surface; all the more satisfying if you remembered to purchase tasty provisions of apfelstrudel and filled your water bottle with a little wine. Absolutely wonderful! Then continue the journey to the newish **Sulzenau Hut**, whose predecessor was totally destroyed by an avalanche in 1975.

Leaving the conviviality of the Sulzenau Hut behind, a choice of two routes to the Dresdner Hut present themselves. There's the easier route via the Peiljoch, or the more challenging and vastly more rewarding option over the Grosser Trögler, and it is this last route that is described here. I should say that the only reason for undertaking this route is that, apart from being one of the best in the district, it provides a classic view of the Zuckerhütl, the Stubai's highest peak.

Crossing pleasant grassy slopes, the path soon leaves the familiar Route 102 and starts to ramp up and over the broken rocky ground of the Hohe Salze. Gradually steepening to get the heart rate pounding, the path zigzags through a rock barrier until the broad ridge of the Kleine Trögler is reached, when suddenly the scenery opens up to

The 3505m Zuckerhütl, highest of the Stubai Alps, as seen from the Grosser Trögler en route to the Dresdner Hut

be appropriately complemented by a wonderful display of alpine flowers: particularly the vivid blue gentian and elusive edelweiss.

Having made a short break to enjoy the view and the flowers, all that's required is to progress along the obvious ridge, negotiate a few rock scrambles here and there, and stride happily to the summit with its large wooden cross in memory of Peter Hofer, a professional guide who was killed on the mountain in a climbing accident many years ago. Once on the summit it is obvious why this is a justifiably popular route, with its truly magnificent view of the Zuckerhütl, whose nickname 'sugarloaf' now makes sense.

The descent heads down a narrow couloir over steep rocky slabs with fixed wires in place, to eventually meet up with the path from the Peiljoch, then very matter-of-factly leads over easy ground to the collection of buildings that comprise the **Dresdner Hut** and the Stubai Glacier Company's cable-car station.

Many years ago when I first visited the Stubai, the Dresdner had the reputation of being among the top three Stubai huts, and was a fine base from which to climb several peaks. Then the adjacent land was purchased by the Stubai Glacier Company, building work started in earnest to tame the Schaufelspitze and develop the area as a ski-resort, and the installation and proliferation of ski-tow pylons commenced.

Despite my quip, do use the lifts to make an ascent of the 3333m Schaufelspitze that can be accomplished as an afternoon excursion. This is a pleasant, popular mountain nicknamed the 'shovel peak' because of its broad summit that dominates the head of the Stubaital above the Dresdner Hut. Sadly much of the route and panoramic vista is now spoiled by the many ski-tow pylons dotted across the Daunkogel and Schaufel glaciers. All that's required is to make your way to the cable-car station and take the 10-minute ride to the top station at Schaufeljoch complete with *Imbiss* refreshment kiosks and a full-blown restaurant that boasts of being the highest in the Tyrol.

Then get onto the snow and mingle with all the other folk to cross what remains of the Gaisskar glacier to another small but obvious col, the 3158m Isidorneider, named after St Isidor, who no doubt would turn in her grave if she could see what they have done to her wonderful glacial plateau. Thereafter, simply climb the obvious ridge to the summit with its large wooden cross and compelling views across the whole of the Ötztal mountains, including the Wildspitze, Austria's second highest mountain, and a very unusual but rewarding view over the Zuckerhütl's north face.

Dresdner Hut to Neustift

Deserting the Central Alpine Way and the enormous Dresdner Hut for the peace and quiet of the mountains, today's trek is the most demanding of the Stubaier Höhenweg, for while the scenery is excellent it involves crossing the lofty Grawagrubenneider, and to do that you need to be on your way early!

Trudging up the broad track, a col on the west ridge of the Egesengrat is soon reached that overlooks the Wilde Grube and snow-capped peaks of the Daunkogel. Once over the col (home to a family of furry marmots), trudge down the road then across scree and rocky slopes into the aptly named Wilde Grube basin. Not so many years ago this was a very wild brooding place indeed, comprising a large open area where many glacial streams congregated, but because of road construction by the Stubai Glacier Company, many of the previous raging torrents have now been tamed and can be crossed more easily.

Across the Wilde Grube the trail contours round the open couloir of the Glamergrube, crossing pleasant high-alpine pasture with a slight detour to the Mutterbergsee, a tiny alpine lake at Höhe Grube. Here rucksacks can be dumped for a short time to rest at this idyllic place for a second breakfast, and to enjoy the best view there is of the Schaufelspitze.

Now make an ascending traverse across the southern flank of the majestic Ruderhofspitze

Named after the so-called 'Glacier Priest', the Franz Senn Hut is one of the busiest in the Stubai

to the left, with fine views of the snow-covered peaks of the Wilder Freiger, Wilder Pfaff, and Zuckerhütl to the right, gradually progressing up and down, zigzagging to and fro, huffing and puffing over rocky spurs at Schaufelspitze and, a little later, the Gamsspitzl, until the 2888m Grawagrubenneider is reached. This is the highest pass on the Stubaier Höhenweg.

From the col, with its wonderful view of the Ruderhofspitze icefall in front, descend steep and difficult terrain over loose, shattered rocks and other dubious ground, to reach the foot of what was once the Hochmoos Ferner glacier. Carefully cross the glacier's scrapyard, step by step over rocky ground strewn with large boulders and other glacial debris, until the trail gradually eases for a final stroll along the Falbersonertal valley to the picturesque Falbesoner See tarn, beautifully fringed with cotton grass. There follows a final easy stroll along the Falbesonertal to the **Neue Regensburger Hut**.

The next stage is perhaps the most straightforward of all, and after the long walk from the Dresdner Hut some may even consider this to be a rest day of sorts with few difficulties.

From the Neue Regensburger Hut, stroll along the delightful level path of the Windtratten for a short distance before turning to climb over rock and scree to the broad col of the Schrimmenneider (2706m). Descending the col by a particularly fine rocky staircase that has been painstakingly laid out leads eventually to the foot of the Platzengrube couloir. Following the now flattish path across rocky spurs created by the Östliche Knotenspitze, a corner is quickly turned to reveal the snow-capped peaks of the Alpeiner and the impressive **Franz Senn Hut**, named after the one-time village priest of Neustift, a founding member of the Austrian Alpine Club.

While at the hut consider taking one of the short excursions to the delightful lake of the Rinnensee, with its magnificent views of the Ruderhofspitze and Seespitze mirrored on its surface. Alternatively, being just a tad longer, wander up the Sommerwand with its particularly fine views of the Seespitze, but more specifically for its profusion of alpine flowers, including the shy edelweiss that grows on its south-facing slopes.

Having had a rest day of sorts, the walk to the Starkenburger Hut is the longest of the Stubai High-Level Route, but being full of scenic interest and the last day of the tour, it is also a very fitting way to end the Höhenweg.

Leaving the Franz Senn Hut and the Alpeiner peaks behind, signposts point the way along the Franz Senn Weg on a good path across the southern flank of the Schalder Spitze to a small hut at Sedugg Hochalm. Located a little before the halfway stage, this tiny chamois hunter's hut has a carved motto which reads: 'My Kingdom is a flock of white sheep and my little hut is my Castle'. If the *jäger* is in residence, the hut provides an ideal opportunity for some interesting refreshments. Meanwhile, as the snow-capped peaks of the Alpeiner recede to merge into the distant horizon, the jagged limestone peaks of the Kalkkögel beckon and become more evident. The excellent flower-fringed path continues contouring high above the Oberbergtal, climbing steadily step by step until you gain the Sendersjöchl, which overlooks the valley of the Senderstal and the whole of the Stubai. Magnificent!

After traversing a broad ridge, the small peak of Steinkogel is soon reached to reveal excellent broadside views of the Kalkkögel. With the geology now changed to limestone, the trail descends slightly over white scree slopes to the Seejöchl col. A further short hop and a skip over more screes below the rocky bastion of the Schlicker Seespitze and Hoher Burgstall on a good but slightly exposed path, leads to the very picturesque **Starkenburger Hut**.

While the panorama from the terrace is dominated by a very fine view of the Habicht, perhaps the most spectacular scene occurs once the sun has gone down; then, if you are blessed with a clear sky, the sunset and night sky are truly memorable and make a fitting conclusion to the Stubai High-Level Route.

The trek all but ended, the journey back into the valley descends through pine-scented trees and flower-covered alpine meadows, following a steep but well-marked path to the outskirts of **Neustift** and the inevitable postbus back to Innsbruck.

At the Rinnensee, easily reached from the Franz Senn Hut

Trek 17
Zillertal High-Level Route

by Allan Hartley

Mayrhofen pulses with life. Nestling deep within the trim Zillertal valley with mountains on three sides and a wealth of tributary valleys to explore nearby, it is understandably popular with walkers, climbers and skiers, for there's something close by for anyone with an active interest in the mountain scene. More than a dozen huts dotted around the Zillertal Alps extend Mayrhofen's scope for outdoor adventure with the opportunity to spend a night in a spectacular location, and linking eight of these huts in a continuous tour makes the Zillertal High-Level Route a hard-to-resist option. It's a tough and challenging route in places, with a whole series of rugged passes to cross, but it avoids glaciers and has a few tempting diversions to summits accessible to walkers with a modicum of scrambling ability.

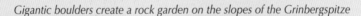

Gigantic boulders create a rock garden on the slopes of the Grinbergspitze

Route summary

Location	Zillertal Alps, Tyrol province, Austria
Start/Finish	Mayrhofen
Distance	70km
Duration	9–10 days
Maximum altitude	3081m on the standard route; 3134m (Schönbichler Horn) optional ascent
Accommodation	Mountain huts of the Austrian and German Alpine Clubs
Grade	Strenuous +
Guidebook	*Trekking in the Zillertal* by Allan Hartley (Cicerone Press, 2003)

If someone asked me to recommend a multi-day trek in the Alps that embraced a constant challenge with each day passing through stunning scenery of peaks, passes and glaciers, then the Zillertal would definitely be on my list. Located entirely within the province of Tyrol, it borders with the mountains of the Venediger to the east, the Brenner Pass and Stubai Alps to the west, the main watershed and Inn valley to the north and the border with Italy to the south – the province of South Tyrol annexed to Italy after the First World War.

The Zillertal is the longest of all subsidiary valleys in the Tyrol, stretching for some 48km, with the picturesque holiday resort of Mayrhofen at its head. Standing guard over this resort are the three peaks of the Ahornspitze, Dristna and Grinbergspitze. Beyond those lie the main snow-capped peaks that straddle

the border with Italy stretching round from the Wollbachspitze across the challenging Grosser Löffler and Schwarzenstein glacier, over the impressive Turnerkamp and Grosser Möseler, ending at the highest summit in the range, the 3510m Hochfeiler, and then down to the Pfitscher Joch, the main border crossing into Italy.

Originally known in German as the Berliner Höhenweg and more recently as the Zillertal Runde–Berliner Höhenweg, the Zillertal High-Level Route starts from Mayrhofen by climbing out of the valley heading first to the Karl von Edel Hut, then in turn to each of the following huts: Kasseler, Greizer, Berliner, Furtschaglhaus, Olperer, Friesenberghaus, and finally to the Gams Hut before descending to the pretty village of Ginzling, where a bus carries you down the valley into Mayrhofen.

This gives a continuous tour of 10 days across exceptionally

The Olperer Hut has a direct view over the Schlegeisspeicher reservoir to the Grosser Möseler and Hochfeiler

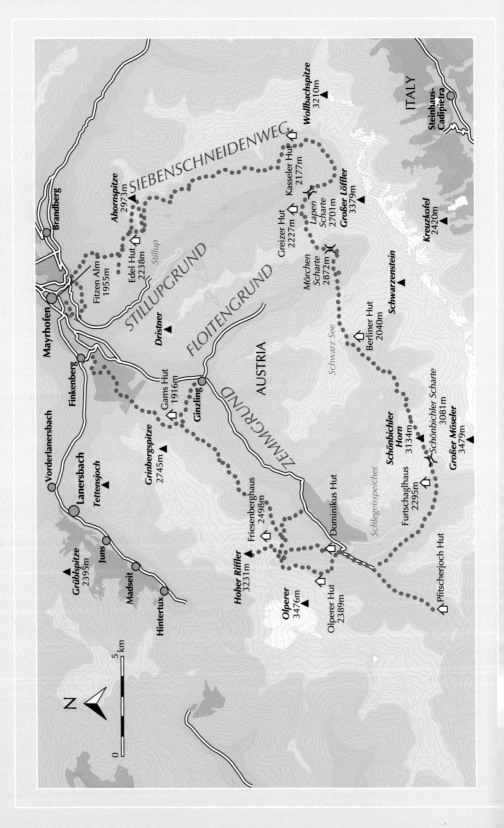

Zillertal High-Level Route

SIEBENSCHNEIDENWEG

STILLUPGRUND

FLOITENGRUND

ZEMMGRUND

AUSTRIA

ITALY

Steinhaus-Cadipietra

Wollbachspitze 3210m

Kreuzkofel 2420m

Kasseler Hut 2177m

Großer Löffler 3379m

Lapen Scharte 2701m

Greizer Hut 2227m

Mörchen Scharte 2872m

Schwarzenstein 2040m

Berliner Hut 2040m

Schwarz See

Schönbichler Scharte 3081m

Schönbichler Horn 3134m

Großer Möseler 3479m

Furtschaglhaus 2295m

Schlegeisspeicher

Pfitscherjoch Hut

Dominikus Hut

Friesenberghaus 2498m

Hoher Riffler 3231m

Olperer 3476m

Olperer Hut 2389m

Ginzling

Gams Hut 1916m

Dristner

Ahornspitze 2973m

Edel Hut 2238m

Fitzen Alm 1955m

Stillup

Mayrhofen

Brandberg

Finkenberg

Vorderlanersbach

Lanersbach

Tettensjoch

Grinbergspitze 2745m

Grüblspitze 2395m

Juns

Madseit

Hintertux

N

5 km

0

Above the Schwarzsee on the stage leading to the Berliner Hut

diverse terrain, without the need to cross glaciers, and requiring little more gear than a rucksack and a pair of boots. However, that is not to suggest it's an altogether easy route, for you will have to negotiate very steep ground, cross patches of late summer snow and make use of fixed wires and the odd ladder installed to aid stability.

The Zillertal Alps is an inspirational area of snow-capped peaks and deep valleys served by some of the very best huts in the Alps, making it ideal for all mountain enthusiasts to explore, and no matter what your ambitions you will not be disappointed. *Grüss Gott und gute Zillerbergtouren!*

Mayrhofen to the Berliner Hut

The adventure starts at the Zillertalbahn railway station, first heading up the road into **Mayrhofen**, passing the post office, various tourist shops and the office for the Alpine Climbing School and Mountain Guides Bureau. This is owned by

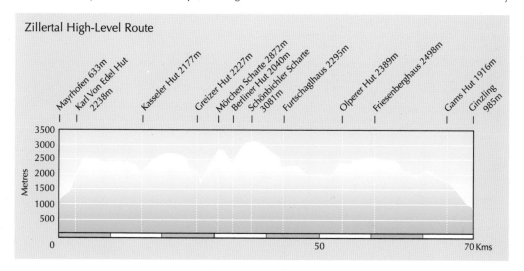

legendary Austrian mountaineer Peter Habeler who, not long ago, with Reinhold Messner from the South Tyrol, took the mountaineering world by storm with many audacious ascents, including the first oxygen-free ascent of Mount Everest. However, their climbing skill was summed up in a ten-hour ascent of the north face of the Eiger, at a time when even the most competent of climbers would take at least one full day. Habeler's companion went on to do greater things, eventually becoming the first person to climb all 14 of the world's 8000m peaks.

Meanwhile at our more modest level, the Ahornbahn cable-car is taken for the five-minute ride to Filzen Alm at 1955m, and you are rewarded on arrival by excellent views across the whole of the Zillertal, including Mayrhofen. Thereafter an easy path leads across a grassy terrace following signs for the Edel Hut, progressing along an obvious trail around the jagged ridge of the Filzenschneide, passing through a delightful rock garden of scattered boulders of car-sized proportions until, after a short two hours, the **Edel Hut** is reached at the base of the west ridge of the Ahornspitze.

While at the Edel Hut it is worth undertaking the two-hour excursion to climb the 2973m Ahornspitze by following the well-marked rocky trail through the mountain's west flank via the Follenbergkar, which roughly translated means 'rocks having fallen off the mountain'! Views from the summit are exceptionally fine, particularly the near mountains of the Zillertal and those in the far distance of the Stubai and Venediger ranges.

The next section of the Höhenweg to the Kasseler Hut is an Alpine treat and outstanding trek, being some 14km long and involving lots of ups and downs, with the gauntlet being thrown down as a challenge that this route is *Nur für Geübte* – and only for the experienced who are also prepared to walk for eight to ten hours. Once you embark on this stage the only way is forwards, or to retreat defeated.

First established during the 1970s by members of the DAV's Würzburg and Aschaffenberger

Sections, the route is now more popularly known as the 'seven ridges way' – the Siebenschneiden Weg. Traversing the hillside high above the Stillupgrund valley, roughly on the 2300m contour level, it crosses the ridges of Popbergschneide, Krummschnabelschneide, Norfertenschneide, Hennsteigenschneide, Weisskarjöchl, Samerjöchl, and finally the Sonntagkarkanzel, before making the steep descent to the **Kasseler Hut** after many hours on the move, during which time you will have crossed endless boulder fields, undertaken difficult scrambles, swung around on gymnasium-style fixed ropes, and gazed endlessly, soaking up the excellent scenery toward the triangular wedge of the 3379m Grosser Löffler.

By contrast the route to the Greizer Hut across the Lapen Scharte is more relaxed and less demanding than the Siebenschneiden Weg, but it remains a fine outing in its own right, taking most of the day to complete. It starts by making a traverse of the extensive boulder fields of the Eiskar with scenic entertainment being provided by the Grosser Löffler, fine views down the Stillupgrund valley and across the seven ridges that make up the Siebenschneiden Weg.

Not to be outdone by the odd challenge, the trail traverses gingerly across the very steep slopes of the Löfflerkar aided by a gangway of fixed ropes. Once across the Lapen Scharte the extensive glacier systems of the Floitenkees and Schwarzenstein glaciers come into view to dominate all the scenery. The best scene of the day is saved to the last, however, when at the turn of an insignificant zigzag and crossing of a small ridge the excellent **Greizer Hut** comes into view.

While sitting on the terrace with tea and cake, try to work out a passage through the contorted maze of crevasses on the Schwarzenstein glacier that guard the border crossing into Italy and the South Tyrol.

It is not often on the Zillertal High-Level Route that you will start the day by walking downhill, but this is how the next stage begins to the Berliner Hut, and sadly well over 300m are lost in the initial stages which will have to be regained on the steep muscle-tugging climb to the **Mörchen Scharte**.

On leaving the Greizer Hut, signposts point the way down the valley toward the lovely village of Ginzling where, after about an hour, the trail turns and crosses open ground through boulders, and streams to a rickety footbridge that spans the raging torrents that drain the Floitenkees glacier. By now the foot of a buttress and ridge coming down from the Mörchen Scharte looms large and obvious, then as the ground rises steeply a 6m high ladder is climbed, followed by a gangway of fixed ropes that lead around the buttress and eventually onto more easy ground.

Hereon the track wends steeply to and fro up the edge of the ridge, pulling tight on the legs, generating much heart-pounding, thought-provoking reticence, as you climb step by step through a narrow couloir until the Mörchen Scharte is eventually reached at 2872m, formed by a gap in the south ridge of the 3285m Grosser Mörchner.

While at the Mörchen Scharte take a moment to relax and enjoy the panorama back to the Greizer Hut, which is now isolated in an expanse of mountains that form the frontier ridge in a wide arc, from the Grosser Löffler round to the Schwarzenstein and Floitenkees glaciers. Also in the opposite direction the route to the Furtschaglhaus across the Schönbichler Scharte can be seen. This marks the highest pass on the Zillertal Runde–Berliner Höhenweg.

Descending from the Scharte, a steep rocky trail leads through the Rosskar boulder field to the delightful Alpine lake that is the Schwarzsee. If the weather is good take time out for an excellent photo opportunity to get those magical pictures of the Berliner Spitze mirrored on its surface. The trail, expanding into a well-worn tourist track, progresses over easy ground to the pride of the German Alpine Club, the spectacular and very grand **Berliner Hut**.

The hut has the distinction of being the first to be opened in the Zillertal in July 1879. Thereafter from 1900 onwards when it became more palatial, the hut was much used by the Austrian royal family, gentry and military elite, as a hunting lodge and for hosting regal entertainment in the main dining room that doubled as a ballroom after feasting.

Berliner Hut to the Olperer Hut

Leaving the Teutonic pride of the Berliner Hut behind, the stage leading to the Furtschaglhaus includes the ascent of the highest pass on the Höhenweg, and the only one to cross the magical 3000m contour.

Crossing the footbridge a little way below the hut, the trail heads up gradually steepening slopes of grass and rocky outcrops, then ramps up significantly, climbing more steeply over glacial debris of the Garbenkar couloir on the approach to the Waxegg Kees glacier, where sharp eyes will be able to pick out the track across the glacier to the Möseler Scharte on the north flank of the Grosser Möseler. Mountain scenery does not come much better than this.

Huffing and puffing up the ridge over difficult ground of contorted rocks and loose scree, patches of snow, tugging on the fixed wires here and there, the ground finally relents on the small rocky pass that is the **Schönbichler Scharte** at 3081m. Suddenly a whole new set of mountains appear to delight you, particularly the glaciated north face of the Hochfeiler, the highest mountain in the Zillertal, first climbed over three days in 1887.

From the col, try to find the effort for a short scramble up the final slopes of the 3134m Schönbichler Horn to obtain excellent views of the Grosser Möseler and Hochfeiler, then across the void to the Olperer and a retrospective view of the route so far back towards the Grosser Löffler. Leaving such an airy perch, the descent from the Schönbichler Scharte is exceedingly steep, zigzagging down tight hairpin bends until the ground gradually eases at the head of an old glacial moraine that leads over easy ground to the **Furtschaglhaus**.

Trekkers on the Hoher Riffler, with the Hoch Feiler in the distance

Turning away from the Grosser Möseler and the Hochfeiler's huge north face, the trek to the Olperer Hut is relatively easy compared to the rigours of the last few days, and statistically is the second on the Höhenweg to start off downhill. However, despite this relative ease it is still quite a long way, taking around five hours to get from hut to hut.

Leaving the Furtschaglhaus the rocky trail descends quickly to the tip of the man-made lake that is the Schlegeisspeicher reservoir. While enjoying the gentle amble along the edge of the lake, take time to recce the route to the Olperer Hut and subsequent traverse to the Friesenberghaus, with the spectacular backdrop of the Olperer and Hoher Riffler to enjoy. While strolling beside the lake remember that various buildings and alms were lost during the flooding of the valley. One such place was the Dominikus Hut, which was privately owned and built by members of the Prague section of the Austrian Alpine Club in 1883. The hut was named after Herr Dominikus who was the hut warden at that time, and it provided much-needed accommodation before the Schlegeis hydroelectric project was completed in 1971, when the valley was flooded and the hut lost for ever. In compensation a new hut was built, whose brightly painted gable can be seen across the lake as you meander along the track.

Once at the dam wall and tourist facility at Jausenstat, the trail quickly aims for loftier places through sweet-smelling juniper bushes to the splendid **Olperer Hut**, with its delightful little terrace and extensive panoramic view back across the Schlegeisspeicher reservoir to the grand peaks of the Grosser Möseler and Hochfeiler. What

At the Gams Leiten on the trail to the Friesenberghaus with the snowy Hoher Riffler in the background

better way to rest and relax after a day's walk than to have a pleasant meal with beer and wine overlooking such a fine scene? Excellent indeed!

Olperer Hut to Mayrhofen

Leaving the friendly Olperer Hut behind, the journey to the **Friesenberghaus** is a very pleasant trek, traversing the eastern flank of the Gefrorene Wand Spitze over rocks and flower-fringed grassy slopes, with excellent, entertaining views across the whole of the Schlegeis valley, and eventually towards the triangular wedge of the Hoher Riffler.

you into thinking it's all downhill. While not as demanding as the Edel to Kasseler Hut connection crossed earlier in the tour by traversing the very demanding seven ridges of the Siebenschneiden Weg, the route to the Gams Hut is equally challenging, being some 14km long, a walk almost the entire length of the Zemmgrund valley that will take eight or nine hours to complete. It's a route that along with the Siebenschneiden Weg took many years to construct, and while scenically stunning with paths decorated throughout with lots of alpine flowers, it is a trek with a sting in its tail that throws up all types of terrain, from familiar tracks over boulder fields and grassy slopes, to the unfamiliar overgrown vegetated slopes of alpenrose, dwarf birch and pine that lead after many hours on the trail to the very pleasant **Gams Hut**, complete with a wonderful bright copper roof.

The hut is soon reached after a few hours, leaving the whole afternoon to be filled with excursions, or by just sitting around relaxing before the finale of the Zillertal High-Level Route. But whatever your choice, do make the effort to climb the little peak of Petersköpfl, where you will find scattered across the summit plateau hundreds of stone cairns that are said to represent those souls lost to the holocaust during the Second World War. Once back at the hut, a plaque in the porch is a reminder of those sad times in the mountains when the hut was a victim of warfare, occupied by the military who needlessly smashed the place up, abandoned it and left it derelict.

On a happier note, picking up the trail once more for the final stage of the route, the journey starts from the highest hut on the Höhenweg and ends at the lowest, but don't let that statement fool

From the hut it is essential to find time and energy to climb the Grindberg Spitze before descending into the valley. This first-class excursion climbs through some amazing rock scenery of gigantic boulders left scattered by nature into a veritable rock garden, finally culminating in a fine summit that will be unmistakable when viewed from Mayrhofen, along with the Gams Hut's gleaming copper roof. You will not be disappointed!

Meanwhile the actual finale will be made by a simple descent to the Zemmgrund valley and into the delightful Tyrolean village of **Ginzling**. Whatever you do, do not rush off but make an appropriate end-of-tour lunch stop at the Alte Ginzling Hotel for a meal of fresh trout and boiled potatoes, before getting the bus to end the Zillertal Runde Berliner Höhenweg in Mayrhofen.

Trek 18

Dolomites Alta Via 1

by Gillian Price

The Dolomites are surely the most colourful, bizarre and other-worldly of all mountains. By standards set by the Western Alps the peaks are of modest stature, for only 50 or so top the 3000m mark. Yet what they lack in altitude, they certainly make up for in terms of surreal beauty. Abrupt, rugged and eccentric in character, their ruined masonry is washed with every pastel shade imaginable as the sun makes its progress from dawn to dusk. Through the heart of this landscape, which mountaineering pioneer Leslie Stephen called 'the fairyland of the Alps', Alta Via 1 journeys south from Val Pusteria to the fringe of the Venetian plain in a gallery of breathtaking summits: Croda del Becco, Tofane, Monte Pelmo, Cinque Torri, Marmarole and the mighty Civetta, likened by Samuel H Hamer to a 'lady of great distinction, she…arrays herself in the golden beams of the setting sun'.

High up near Forcella de Zita Sud

Heading towards the Tofana giants

Route summary

Location	Dolomites, Italy
Start	Lago di Braies off Val Pusteria
Finish	La Pissa in Val Cordevole near Belluno
Distance	120km
Duration	11 days
Maximum altitude	2752m
Accommodation	Mountain huts and guesthouses
Grade	Moderate to strenuous
Guidebook	*Trekking in the Dolomites* by Gillian Price (Cicerone Press, 2011)

It was 1981. I'd arrived in Venice fresh from an extended trek in Nepal and was in the grips of an acute case of 'mountainitis'. So it seemed quite natural to make enquiries as to the whereabouts of the nearest high ground. Bemused acquaintances smiled politely, nodding and muttering about boats and messing about on the water. But luck was with me and I soon struck gold – the work colleagues of a new friend were dedicated mountaineers to a man. Before I knew it, I had signed up to become a member of the Italian Alpine Club, bought myself a pair of sturdy boots and, seeing as funds didn't stretch that far, borrowed a rucksack. Thrilled to bits and clutching a painstakingly detailed diagram complete with profiles, red/blue symbols to denote food quality, comfort levels and mustn't-miss detours, I set off for the railway station in the company of my husband-to-be. We'd been sent to trek the long-distance Alta Via 1 that traverses the Italian Dolomites from north to south – and I've since been back time and time again.

Located in the top right-hand corner of Italy, the region accounts for but a tiny piece of the

Alpine chain, on a decidedly smaller scale than the Himalaya. A world unto themselves, the Dolomites mean delicately pale rock formations of ancient coral reefs that shoot up, sheer and majestic, in weird and wonderful shapes. Every single one is unique and recognisable from afar – there's a fortress, organ, needles and even shark's teeth! Showcase route Alta Via 1 – along with its tougher twin Alta Via 2 – spends day after glorious day wandering through this wonder-land, which was recently recognised as a World Heritage Site by UNESCO, a timely recognition.

Across the Fanes upland to the Lagazuoi
Tucked in a corner off Val Pusteria, the north-ern edge of the Dolomites, the starting point for this memorable adventure is a simply enchanting spot. **Lago di Braies** is the sort of emerald-green lake that you usually see in photos in glossy tour-ist brochures – and you'd almost swear it had undergone a bit of tweaking with Photoshop to bring out those dazzling hues. Yet when the bus deposits you on its shore, you can see its true col-ours for yourself, unadulterated and picture-per-fect. In its own valley enclosed within tall cliffs, it lies ringed by cool forest and overshadowed by the imposing pyramid of Croda del Becco. A stately Grand Hotel occupies the northern shore, an oasis to generations seeking the peace, quiet and inspiration of Alpine resorts. In the 1960s and '70s it even hosted meditation sessions under the guidance of that iconic figure Maharishi Mahesh, guru to none other than the Beatles. And it's perfectly suited for walkers to overcome travel fatigue in an old-world ambience. The waters of the lake itself are deep and bone-chillingly cold, so there's little temptation to indulge in a dip.

A delightful stroll along the shores gives way to the first long ascent of the trek, a resolute 900m in one fell slog. Passing over vast rivers of scree it puffs up to a sequence of rock terraces

Boating on Lago di Braies

Dolomites Alta Via 1

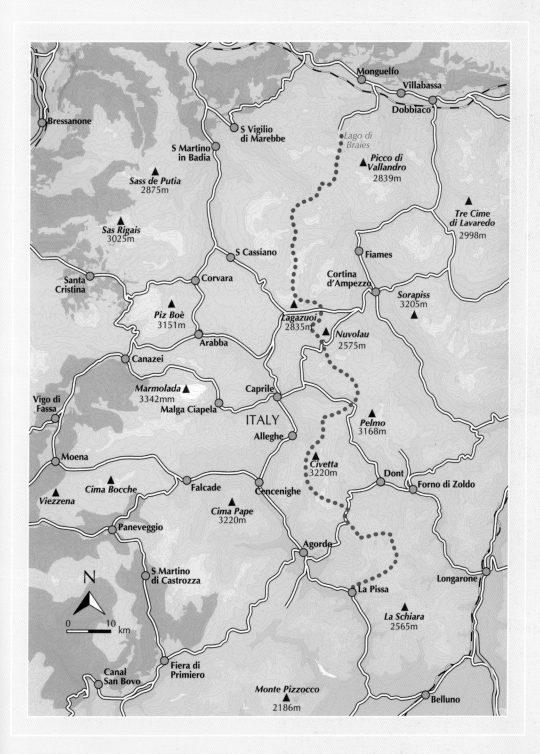

Monguelfo
Villabassa
Dobbiaco
Bressanone
S Vigilio
di Marebbe
Lago di
Braies
S Martino
in Badia
Picco di
Vallandro
2839m
Sass de Putia
2875m
Tre Cime
di Lavaredo
2998m
Sas Rigais
3025m
S Cassiano
Fiames
Corvara
Cortina
d'Ampezzo
Sorapiss
3205m
Santa
Cristina
Piz Boè
3151m
Lagazuoi
2835m
Arabba
Nuvolau
2575m
Canazei
Marmolada
3342mm
Caprile
Vigo di
Fassa
Malga Ciapela
Pelmo
3168m
ITALY
Alleghe
Moena
Civetta
3220m
Dont
Cima Bocche
Falcade
Forno di Zoldo
Viezzena
Cencenighe
Cima Pape
3220m
Paneveggio
Agorde
S Martino
di Castrozza
Longarone
N
La Pissa
0   10 km
La Schiara
2565m
Canal
San Bovo
Fiera di
Primiero
Monte Pizzocco
2186m
Belluno

that give you a chance to get your breath back and begin acclimatising to the 2000-plus-metre altitudes that characterise the coming days.

The path emerges onto a vast rolling upland, the Fanes-Senes Altopiano, under the shared responsibility of two regional nature parks. The reward for the effort of the climb becomes immediately obvious as an astonishingly uncluttered panorama unrolls. Topping the list is the glaciated Marmolada, the highest of all the Dolomites, along with the pyramidal Tofane and giant Pelmo, which shall be admired at closer quarters in the near future. And this is only the first day! But it is not yet time for a rest as a summit accessible to walkers is close at hand and beckoning. Croda del Becco demands an initially steep but contained scramble and is comfortingly aided by cable fixed to the rock. The top is a gently sloping slab that culminates in a brilliant 2810m lookout directly over Lago di Braies, a dizzy 1316m below. The first time I ventured up I was honoured by the discreet company of Gianni, a remarkably tame ibex that lounges around up here, his long curving horns a giveaway in these tree-less surrounds.

After a restorative night at the 2300m **Rifugio Biella**, the route dips via a roadhead before

climbing into a pretty pasture basin with two hospitable mountain huts, Rifugio Lavarella and **Rifugio Fanes**, and edged with horizontal rock strata dotted with Arolla pines. The spot continues to be known as the 'Marmots' Parliament' from a long-gone legendary era when the Dolomites were the Kingdom of Fanes and princesses, treasure and wicked kings were the order of the day. In contrast, reminders of a much more recent empire ruled by the Hapsburgs are soon encountered as Alta Via 1 heads for the Lagazuoi area along trails used by supply mules and troops during the First World War. A pasture trough alongside the huge Cunturines massif leads to the former border between Austria and Italy, with airy **Forcella del Lago** on a jagged crest. From there a roller-coaster route heads into the midst of an open-air museum that bears witness to the folly of man, with ruins of barracks, goods lifts, trenches and even fortified caves. The long uphill route is a fascinating if poignant affair.

To be frank, we noticed none of this on our first trek because of drenching rain and low swirling cloud. More banal things such as keeping warm and dry were on our minds. This turned out to be a landmark day, when we made two discoveries that would set the stage for all our subsequent Alpine experiences: firstly, that bin liners

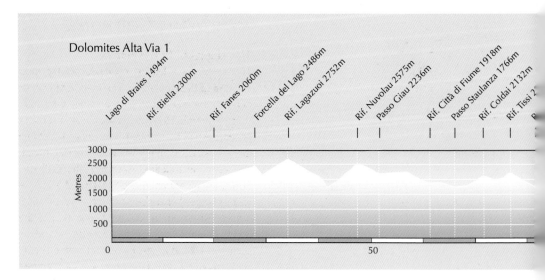

The long climb to Rifugio Lagazuoi backed by Forcella del Lago and the Cunturines

do not make suitable rain skirts and secondly, that rucksack contents should be kept in plastic bags!

The stage's conclusion is **Rifugio Lagazuoi** with a breathtaking viewing terrace at 2752m.

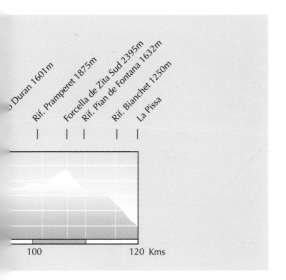

This is the highest the Alta Via 1 climbs and if your luck's in and it's cloud-free, the spectacular views extend over the Cortina basin. Almost at your feet lie curious rock formations – the 'broken teeth' of the Cinque Torri in grassy gums, and the dinosaur backbone of Croda dal Lago.

The Lagazuoi to the Pelmo

This section is a leading contender for the most exciting of the whole trek. The main route coasts beneath the marvellous Tofana giants, a magnificent easy stroll. However, anyone with a sense of adventure and no problem with vertigo should let themselves be tempted by the unforgettable variant, a once-in-a-lifetime experience, the 'Galleria'. Down the sheer front of the Lagazuoi, this unique route plunges helter-skelter inside a near-vertical tunnel excavated by Alpine troops during the 1914–18 conflict. Such passageways served as shelter as well as access for teams to mine enemy positions and is one of the wartime routes secured

The Averau Fortress

and restored by volunteers. Nowadays it's a good idea to don a headlamp, as pitch-black stretches are encountered. The descent is thankfully aided by both steps and a hand cable as the going can be quite slippery. Through the occasional rock window are giddy glimpses of the motorable road snaking hundreds of metres below. Afterwards it's almost a shock to stagger back into sunshine and reach trafficked Passo Falzarego.

Uphill again a path circles the Averau, a fortress-like block of rock that attracts climbers to its acrobatic routes, as do the nearby Cinque Torri. But press on to rejoin the main route on the Nuvolau, an elegant, sloping mount culminating in a 2575m point occupied by **Rifugio Nuvolau**. It's well worth it. Set well apart from its neighbours, this belvedere extraordinaire is a hard place to leave. An overnight stay is a must, as is waking early for the amazing spectacle of sunrise over the Cortina basin.

A short, exciting scramble awaits to **Passo Giau** and its hotel. Now considerably different landscapes come into play with the crossing of the immense undulating Mondeval pasture basin.

Pure delight is guaranteed for a wander across the lush green carpet, thick with gorgeous iridescent blue trumpet gentians and delicate felty pale edelweiss blooms. It is enclosed on three sides by the rocky barriers of Lastoni di Formin which resembles a huge slab, and elegant, pointed Becco di Mezzodì on the far side; an atmospheric setting transformed into a massive hunting ground 4000 years ago by Mesolithic people who would block off the passes feeding into the basin, thus trapping elk, ibex and deer. It's not at all hard to imagine, though modern-day walkers should limit their expectations to marmots, playful chubby herbivores that live in underground colonies here.

Ahead, the eye is drawn towards the solid rock shape of the Pelmo, which from this angle lives up to its nickname 'throne of the Almighty' for its armchair configuration. It towers over **Rifugio Città di Fiume**, a couple of rambling hours away. You will probably spend a night here, unless creature comforts call and you decide to press on for the guesthouse at **Passo Staulanza**.

The Pelmo to the Civetta

First off there's an important choice to be made concerning the opening section – the short and relaxing main route or the long, tiring and spectacular variant. If the weather is on your side and you feel up to a dose of scrambling that verges on vertical, take time out for the second option and the Sentiero Flaibani. It clambers up to the head of Val d'Arcia, the perfect spot to take a breather and admire the Pelmo 'stone throne' at dizzily close quarters. Over the valley is the immense line-up of the rugged Marmarole with triangular Antelao standing apart. The wonderful circuit continues with a plunge over loose scree, finally slowing down at Rifugio Venezia. An excellent place for a lunch break while admiring the elegant Marmarole, this well-run establishment has been operating since 1892, when pioneer mountaineers from the historic Venice branch of CAI (the Italian Alpine Club) laid the foundation stones for what was to be the very first Alpine hut to be constructed in the whole of the Dolomites. It came some time after the first ascent of the Pelmo in 1857 by John Ball, one of the founders of the British Alpine Club.

The ramble around the soaring southern bastions passes the Pelmetto, the second peak, though by now the immensely impressive Civetta has come into view, dominating the Val Zoldana. Remarkably slender, it extends north–south for 6km, and is all but circumnavigated over the next few days. An old mule track climbs to where the variant rejoins the main route at another landmark hut, **Rifugio Coldai**, where you need to bid farewell to the Pelmo.

Over a rise is Lago di Coldai, a pretty tarn that attracts summer picnickers to its shores. However, the best advice is to press on as very soon Alta Via 1 reaches the superb 'wall of walls', the breathtaking western face of the Civetta that soars to 3222m. Its vast vertical grooves and fissures were aptly likened to an 'organ front' by intrepid late-19th-century traveller Amelia Edwards. And the best place to admire this spectacle? **Rifugio Tissi**, perched on a ridge at 2250m, the place to be to enjoy an awesome summer sunset when the entire wall turns a dreamy orangey-pink. The evening quiet is disturbed only by the persistent click of

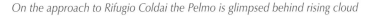

On the approach to Rifugio Coldai the Pelmo is glimpsed behind rising cloud

camera shutters as everyone is inevitably over-awed by the spectacle.

The Civetta to Pramperet

At the far end of this natural monument a track proceeds beneath twin stone pillar guardians, Torre Venezia and Torre Trieste, which vie with each other as magnets for climbers. Below stands **Rifugio Vazzoler** in a lovely woodland setting. An overnight stay is very enjoyable in this spacious, old-style hut where dinner is served around an open log fire on cool evenings. An added attraction is a wander through the well-tended alpine botanical garden, with hundreds of helpfully labelled flowering species. When your back's had enough, straighten up and take a good look at the backdrop – the amazing Moiazza massif, which is to be admired from close quarters in the following section. Walkers thin out considerably from here on, now that Alta Via 1 has distanced

itself from the popular resorts of Cortina and Val Zoldana.

The following hours are spent negotiating eroded gullies and traversing thickets of dwarf mountain pine, remarkably resistant and springy. In the vicinity of Forcella Col dell'Orso, the path hugs the cliffs, a great opportunity for wildflower buffs as a multitude of rock plants such as delightful devils' claw grow here throughout the summer.

The path runs parallel to the Cordevole river valley, whose depths are rarely glimpsed. However, rising to dizzy heights on the opposite side are the pale towers and extensive platform of the Altopiano di San Martino, where Alta Via 2 spends marvellous days. Not far along, Forcella del Camp is gained for the start of the dazzling realm of the Moiazza Sud, a veritable jungle of rock spires. Mere walkers are dwarfed by its sheer walls and buttresses, which are explored with the aid of a host of via ferratas by the mountaineers,

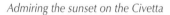

Admiring the sunset on the Civetta

loaded with jangling equipment, with whom the path is shared. Together you reach beautifully redesigned Rifugio Carestiato. Thanks to its lovely terrace and panoramic windows the views can be enjoyed constantly.

A short stroll away is quiet **Passo Duran**, with more accommodation options. Here you need to follow the road, useful for giving your mind time to prepare for the new sights and experiences in store, as you are about to enter the Parco Nazionale delle Dolomiti Bellunesi. A path resumes for a stiff climb through wood. This emerges on blinding white scree to begin a fantastic stretch skirting the interlinked Tamer and San Sebastiano groups, amidst a chaos of fallen blocks and tall dizzy towers such as Castello di Moschesin. Through to a saddle surrounded by banks of pretty alpenrose shrubs, then there's a stretch cutting high over Pian de la Fopa and a pasture amphitheatre. A warm welcome always awaits from the staff at **Rifugio Pramperet**, who are helped by a team of volunteers. A series of simple cabins around a central dining facility, it is an essential stopover in this rugged part of the Dolomites.

Over the Cime di Zita with the Schiara

Clear weather is a must for these concluding sections of Alta Via 1; rugged, mountainous terrain is covered, calling for a little scrambling and difficulty. So if conditions don't warrant it, stay put and wait it out. It's well worth it as otherwise you risk missing memorable landscapes. Views improve step by step on the drawn-out ascent to the Cime di Zita, where huge chunks of the southern Dolomites can be admired as the horizon opens out. Straightforward paths are shared with herds of chamois that skitter over impossibly steep terrain to keep their distance. Take care and go single file on the exposed shoulder and narrow path leading to **Forcella de Zita Sud**. More wonders await as a beautiful valley opens up below, Van de Zita de Fora. In local dialect 'Van' refers to a glacially shaped feature, in this case an ancient cirque which once hosted a hanging glacier.

Many mountains here kept their heads above the ice, thus saving a number of plants, with the result that even today Mediterranean-type plants such as dwarf broom grow up here. The path lopes downhill through pretty terraces and depressions left by the dissolving effect of rainwater on limestone – the phenomenon of karstification is rife here. Earth accumulates in the dolinas and flowers take root – rare species in this case, protected under the auspices of a special reserve of great scientific interest centred on nearby Monte Talvena; walkers must stay on marked paths. But don't let the flowers distract you too much otherwise you'll miss the views to the monumental Schiara alongside the Pelf. Look out for the solitary rock spike known as the Gusela del Vescovà, the 'bishop's needle'. Noah is said to have used it for mooring his ark when the floodwater rose!

Take special care on the final knee-jarring drop, for it's easy to lose your step on the approach to **Rifugio Pian de Fontana**. This converted herders' hut serves local dairy products such as tasty cheese melted over *polenta*, hot corn meal.

Should you be in a hurry, consider pushing on as a little over two hours away is another refuge – admittedly by way of a sequence of stiff ups and downs. Thickly wooded slopes are crossed, then after Forcella La Varetta a veritable rock garden accompanies the path into Val Vescovà. A long rock staircase, the 'Scalon', concludes in a clearing with more opportunities to admire the Schiara and make the most of the facilities at this final hut, **Rifugio Bianchet**.

Don't underestimate the last leg: although it mostly follows a jeep track, it's a long, long way in constant descent through forest to the floor of the Val Cordevole. At a chasm and gushing **La Pissa** waterfall, the trek comes to an abrupt end on the roadside. Take stock of your precious memories as you board the bus to the stately town of Belluno. There, remember to pop by the Tourist Office and present the ink stamps collected in the refuges along the way so you can be awarded with your well-earned commemorative badge of Alta Via 1.

Trek 19
Dolomites Alta Via 2
by Gillian Price

Roughly midway along Alta Via 2, the so-called Queen of the Dolomites shows herself in regal splendour, as the white-capped Marmolada, wearing a glacial shawl, towers over Lago di Fedaia. Unique in a land of bleached towers and skeletons of rock, the Marmolada's glacier draws crowds of tourists who gain the summit snowfield by cable-car to enjoy a spectacular panorama that includes sections of Alta Via 2. The northern half of this trek, an altogether tougher proposition than AV1, begins close to the border with Austria's Tyrol and soon works its way amongst the Puez-Odle group before reaching Passo Gardena and the citadel-like Sella massif. From Passo Pordoi the route curves round the Marmolada to focus on the peaks and pinnacles of Pale di San Martino, and these in turn lead to rugged Vette Feltrine and the end of the journey. Alta Via 2 is without question one of the great treks of Italy's Dolomite region.

The magnificent Sella massif and Passo Gardena

Route summary

Location	Dolomites, Italy
Start	Bressanone
Finish	Croce d'Aune near Feltre
Distance	150km
Duration	13 days
Maximum altitude	2900m
Accommodation	Mountain huts and guesthouses
Grade	Demanding
Guidebook	*Trekking in the Dolomites* by Gillian Price (Cicerone Press, 2011)

We're up in the top northeastern corner of Italy, the country's Alpine region just before it merges into Tyrolean Austria. Here is the start of the Alta Via 2 long-distance trek which runs parallel to the more popular and well-trodden Alta Via 1. This is big brother, and he's a tough one. But also one that guarantees two utterly exhilarating weeks as walkers are immersed in the breathtaking landscapes that account for the entire north–south run of the spectacular Dolomites, a magnificent procession of immense mountains that soar to weird and wonderful heights. Slabbed peaks, breathtaking campanile pinnacles, fortress-like massifs, and even immense high-altitude plateaux smoothed by the protracted action of long-gone glaciers. The rock is painted in delicate pale hues that take on romantic shades of orange and pink at sunset. This is the least that can be expected from the superb Alta Via 2. But there is so much more! On more than one occasion up there I have felt as though I were undergoing sensory overdose!

The rock giants are in the company of vast cool forests and lush alpine meadows, home to a wealth of divine wild flowers, all personal favourites of mine. It will never cease to amaze

Moretti's bellflower, just one of the endemic blooms in the southern Dolomites

me that such beauty can be concentrated in fragile minuscule plants. Following bitter winter months, through sheer determination they emerge for a mere fraction of the year to stand out bright against the pale stone like Christmas lights, every one unique. Gentians, pasque flowers, edelweiss, mountain avens ... not forgetting the perfumed black vanilla orchid or delicate yellow poppies.

In addition, as is the nature of long-distance treks, Alta Via 2's unhurried progress witnesses transformations in its surrounds. One fascinating change is the language: the German that dominates in South Tyrol during the opening stages gradually gives way to Ladin, an ancient Rhaeto-Romanic tongue still alive and kicking in the central Dolomite valleys. Then comes Italian in Trentino, followed by an assortment of dialects spoken in the Veneto region where the trek concludes.

Bressanone to the Plose

A lovely place to start out, the stately Tyrolean market town of **Bressanone** has tree-filled squares and plenty of train and bus links for travellers arriving from all directions. The pleasant, traffic-free streets are lined with porticoed houses in elegant Baroque style. The ground floor level hosts shops

The magnificent Odle di Eores from Plose

such as family-run bakeries whose fragrant crusty bread rolls and luscious pastries draw in hungry customers, as do the well-stocked delicatessens with mouth-watering displays of local sausages and cheeses. With rucksacks bulging, the majority of walkers then opt for the bus and cable-car runs that take the sting out of the exacting 1900m ascent that opens proceedings. Looming over the town is the Plose mountain and **Rifugio Città di Bressanone**. Here are exciting vistas to the first outposts of the Dolomites – namely the magnificently rugged Odle di Eores, where world-famous mountaineer Reinhold Messner spent his Alpine teething years before heading over to the Himalaya.

After a leisurely wander over pasture slopes towards these mountains, Alta Via 2 heads up a rather steep ravine strewn with broken rock, the path swinging this way and that to ease the climb. The arrival at **Forcella di Putia** comes as quite a surprise as the path emerges on rolling green pasture upland. Anyone reaching this spot with a couple of hours to spare is warmly encouraged to embark on the path to the adjacent walkers' peak, 2875m Sass de Putia. Exceptionally fine 360° views can be enjoyed from either of

the twin points – embracing the snow-spattered Austrian Alps and a vast spread of the westernmost Dolomites, not to mention a good taste of the Alta Via 2 route ahead.

Close at hand is **Rifugio Genova**, for a good night's rest.

The Puez-Odle Plateau

A delightful, well-trodden path sets out to wander along flowered slopes via summer farms. This is the approach to **Forcella della Roa**, gained by way of a tightly zigzagging path up an abrupt gully of blinding white scree. Thus does the Alta Via 2 enter the Puez-Odle group, its heart a curious landscape comprising a broad *altopiano* edged on the southeast by sharp rock spikes that soar skywards as the Odle, which is Ladin for 'needle'. To be honest, these are actually admired better at close quarters from the variant route: branching downhill at Rifugio Genova it takes the divine Sentiero delle Odle, a path also known as the Adolf Munkelweg after its 1904 German ideator. Meandering jauntily through woodland and rivers of gravel, shattered stone flows from giants Sass Rigais and Mesdì, it wanders into one of those perfect summer farms. Malga Brogles is a traditional family affair – no

Dolomites Alta Via 2

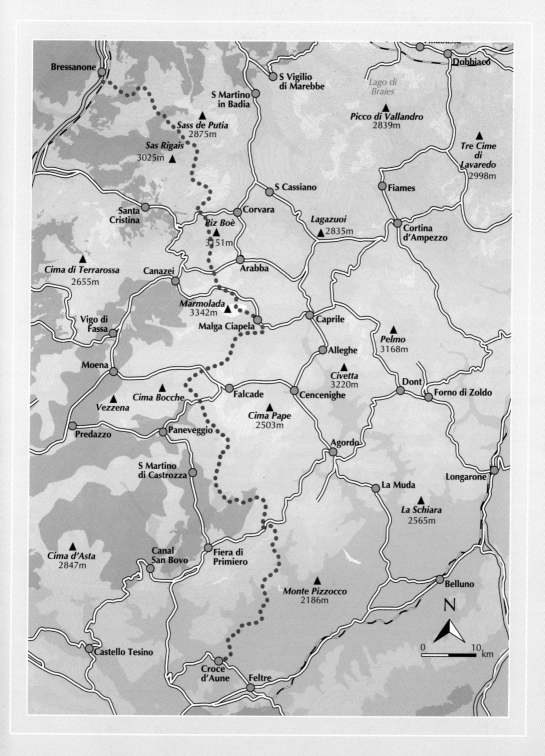

electricity, candle-lit dinners out on the meadow, and snug rooms for weary walkers. Afterwards, the main Alta Via 2 is rejoined amidst flocks of sheep on the Puez plateau itself for an inspiring traverse high over superb Vallelunga, a textbook U-shaped glacial valley. **Rifugio Puez** is the night's stopover in a unique landscape dotted with weird, eroded, cone-shaped mountainous bumps, not to mention the odd lake.

Over the Sella

Soon Alta Via 2 dips over the road at **Passo Gardena** to face a daunting sight, the immense Sella massif. Precipitous walls rear up, apparently impossible geography for trekkers! However, closer inspection reveals a gaping cleft in the block – awesome Val Setus. Up this unworldly corridor of shattered rock and scree creeps a steep zigzagging path that morphs into an aided scramble to a first vast terrace that hosts a spectacularly placed hut, Rifugio Pisciadù. This is the 2585m mark, but the climb is nowhere near over.

Despite immeasurably vast surrounds of this massif, walkers are brought back to earth with the discovery that they are rarely alone. Cheeky coral-beaked alpine choughs glide down on jet black, shiny wings, curious comical creatures

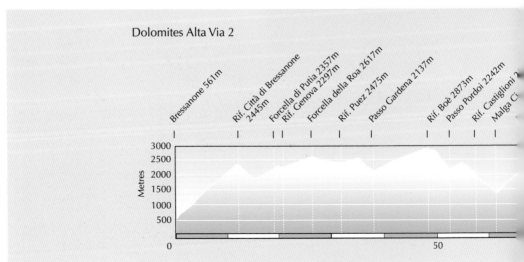

Dolomites Alta Via 2

Bressanone 561m
Rif. Città di Bressanone 2445m
Forcella di Putia 2357m
Rif. Genova 2297m
Forcella della Roa 2617m
Rif. Puez 2475m
Passo Gardena 2137m
Rif. Boè 2873m
Passo Pordoi 2242m
Rif. Castiglioni 2
Malga Ci

Metres

3000
2500
2000
1500
1000
500

0   50

AV2 approaches the Puez-Odle

ever on the lookout for picnic scraps. Then, up on the Altopiano delle Meisules plateau are surprisingly numerous herds of ibex, elegant stocky mountain goats with showy horns. I once spent ages painstakingly creeping up on a female to take her picture surreptitiously so as not to disturb her young. My friends had strict instructions to wait behind so I could capture that 'Wildlife Photographer of the Year' shot. Closer and closer I got, hardly breathing for fear of losing her. She was apparently watching over her offspring, yet as it turned out she was actually keeping an eye on me. And without even a look in my direction, she stretched and toddled off as though to say, 'Not another AV2er.' Needless to say my friends got the good shots – of me stalking the ibex.

A veritable oasis up here is **Rifugio Boè**, a rambling, comfortable hut not far from the culminating point of the Sella, namely Piz Boè, a pyramidal 3152m outcrop easily reachable with a bit of a scramble.

Of course once you're so high up, the only way out is down. In this case there are two feasible choices, both with superb outlooks. Either descend on foot all the knee-crunching way to 2293m **Passo Pordoi**, by no means unpleasant as it gives you time to survey the terrain ahead,

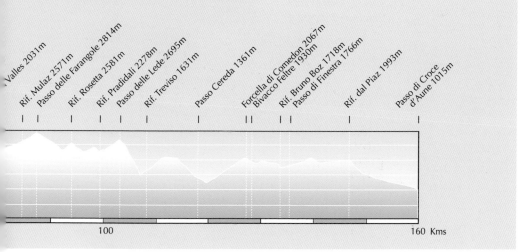

including the Marmolada with its glittering glacier. The alternative offers views that are marginally better – and the going undeniably more relaxing – from the marvellous cable-car that descends from Sass Pordoi, the castle-like extension on the southwestern brink of the Sella.

Around the Marmolada

Unforgettable and delightfully undemanding Viel del Pan cuts across the grassy slopes of a volcanic ridge draped with a bright shawl of myriad colourful wild blooms, from black vanilla orchids to yellow pasque flowers. Little by little the sprawl of the majestic Marmolada and its blanket glacier come into full view. At its foot is Lago di Fedaia, dammed for the purposes of hydroelectricity. There, perched on its banks is cosy, old-style **Rifugio Castiglioni**, a hive of activity for mountaineers bound for the string of rocky points atop the 3342m Queen of the Dolomites, the Marmolada. However, the experience of the high

reaches can also be enjoyed by non-climbers as a little further on, at **Malga Ciapela** (1384m), a spectacular three-stage cable-car ride is an excellent excuse to take half a day out from the trek to marvel at the breathtaking views on the mountain. There's also a small museum up there with poignant images and stories, not far from trenches and man-made tunnels through the rock where Italian and Austrian troops confronted each other during the terrible years of the First World War.

Glimpses of the queen's sheer northern wall are afforded as the route moves off on old military mule tracks. It's a drawn-out climb to the 2490m **Forca Rossa**, amidst layers of colourful soil carpeted with flowers. A whole new set of scenery is at hand here, as the rock spires of the Pale di San Martino rise beyond the next valley, beckoning AV2ers into their magical realms. However, in the meantime a glorious way snakes through Fuchiade with picture-perfect alpine pasture, dotted with time-worn timber huts and picnicking families.

Alpine meadows, Fuchiade

From Rifugio Mulaz looking towards the Civetta

Two road passes are touched on in quick succession, both with comfortable accommodation.

Across the Pale di San Martino

It takes a good few days to traverse the extraordinary Pale di San Martino. Snowfields, slender campanile and majestic peaks that soar to the 3000m mark cluster around an immense undulating plateau whose unworldly landscapes can only be described as lunar. In comparison, the vast Puez-Odle altopiano traversed earlier almost shrinks. Spreading over an area of more than 50 square km, San Martino is composed mainly of limestone rock, though there are also a handful of glacier pockets. It was back in 1864 that the group was 'opened' to mountaineering through pioneering exploration by a British team, including Freshfield and Tuckett. And only years later came the ascent of the 'Matterhorn of the Dolomites', Cimon della Pala, a solid 3184m mountain of majestic proportions, soon to be admired on the trail.

From **Passo di Valles** the trek gains a magnificent panoramic ridge looking to Cimon della Pala.

As the next few stages entail long aided stretches and exposure, many walkers prefer the excellent variant route that branches off here, embarking on a roller coaster of paths that skirt the eastern edge. It also takes in the Crode Rosse ridge. It was here many years ago that my geologist brother stopped abruptly in his tracks, and came to his knees on a smooth slab of rock. OK, the inspirational Dolomites have been known to trigger religious apparitions...but in fact Andy had spotted fossilised ripple marks on the ground. Even though I'd walked that route before, I'd never noticed them but was quickly infected by his enthusiasm. What a wondrous sight – sand that was once beneath the sea, a tropical one at that, washed into rippled ridges and somehow frozen in action.

In the meantime the principal route takes narrow aided stretches leading around the stark hidden inner valley housing **Rifugio Mulaz**, a magical spot of deep silence dominated by the elegant Focobon spires. Clutches of rock pinnacles flank the way up a zigzagging path and the first of many rock scrambles and aided climbs on the dizzy and spectacular Sentiero delle Farangole, a never-ending narrow path clinging to steep slopes high above a deep natural chasm. It finally dips across Pian dei Cantoni, plunging into a veritable 'perfume trap' as, heightened by the warmth of the sun the fragrance from Rhaetian poppies is all-pervasive. They form a veritable sea of delicate papery petals, yellow and orange.

Further uphill is the vast altopiano itself and **Rifugio Rosetta**, a comfortable place to enjoy a good meal and sneak under a duvet for a snooze after all that effort. But before indulging, a stroll is de rigueur. Close at hand rears La Rosetta, a 2743m incline that acts as a brilliant lookout, directly over the resort town of San Martino di Castrozza, and horizons spacing to the neighbouring wild Lagorai, and beyond to the glaciated Ortles-Cevedale ranges.

Moving off towards the western edge of the plateau, an especially gentle descent takes a curious trail with incalculable, tight switchbacks. It dates back to the early 1900s and was constructed by a baron from Leipzig as a gentle way to bring his disabled daughter up here on horseback without her suffering discomfort from steep ramps and bumps. To wander along this broad track today is utter delight. The gradient verges on horizontal in places and obliges walkers to go at an uncommonly slow pace, all the better for admiring the soaring shapes of La Rosetta and Croda di Roda on either side. Moreover, all round the flanks host gorgeous exemplars of the vivid blue bloom, Moretti's bellflower. Surviving on minuscule amounts of soil, this delightful endemic flower bursts miraculously straight out of the rock face.

Further along come dramatic contrasts with an awesome gully negotiated by fixed cable and ledges flanked by the soaring needles of Cima Pradidali and Cime di Ball, which stand astride Passo di Ball. The col affords a breathtaking view of Cima Canali shooting skywards into elegant, smooth towers. And once you shift your glance a tad earthwards, a short descent below is **Rifugio Pradidali**. The brand-new, spick-and-span

building stands on the spot occupied by an earlier hut that had the honour of hosting the King of Belgium in person in the early 1900s. He loved to come on exploratory climbs in these glorious mountains – how understandable!

After batteries have been recharged and stomachs satisfied, the way continues in ascent to cross airy **Passo delle Lede**, a magical spot. Walkers find themselves perched on high enjoying a spectacular outlook dominated by the grandiose twosome of Cima Immink and Pala di San Martino.

A long plunge down a desolate gully brings Alta Via 2 into Val Canali. Here the cover of conifer forest provides a welcome, cool change after days of open, sun-blasted terrain. And nestling in the wood is **Rifugio Treviso**, the last stopover before a long traverse with recurrent airy exposed stretches en route to **Passo Cereda**, a rural road pass. The taxing paths of the past days leave many walkers at the end of their energy reserves, so it is quite acceptable to retire from Alta Via 2 with dignity at this point and catch a bus. However, for those who continue, adventures are in store. It's one of those situations when what the eye doesn't see, the heart doesn't miss ...

The Vette Feltrine

The concluding three days of this trek are both exciting and enormously demanding due to long, tricky, exposed passages and the overall rugged nature of the Vette Feltrine. These interconnected peaks and crests provide the dramatic backdrop for the delightful Renaissance town of Feltre. They are the southernmost outpost of the Dolomites, and their lowest edge is marked by the broad valley where the River Piave swerves southwest to cross the spread of the Veneto plain. Moreover, these mountains are the first barrier encountered by rising warm air from the lowlands, often producing mist that swirls around the ridges, cloaking paths and walkers in swathes of damp. While this means that visibility is often compromised across the range, in contrast it's great news for the high-altitude plants which drink in the cloud-borne moisture. This translates into heaven for wild-flower lovers who can expect floral rarities – endemic columbines and exquisite delphiniums to name but a few.

The scene for the coming days is set immediately as the route embarks on a progressively narrow path that hugs the sheer cliffs of Piz Sagron and its giant neighbours. To offset the fatigue of the stiff climb, the best advice is to simply stop in admiration – breathless in all likelihood – of the inspiring views to Monte Agner and the upper Agordo valley. Finally reached after considerable effort, **Forcella di Comedon** is a belvedere for deep-green Lago della Stua squashed between steep, forested mountain flanks well below. It is also the gateway to a beautiful amphitheatre, home to **Bivacco Feltre-Bodo** on the edge of a glacially formed rock platform. A wonderful place to stay the night, though you need to be appropriately kitted out. You can always take a shower at the waterfalls nearby.

Alta Via 2 moves off in the steps of long-gone shepherds and their flocks who forged a dizzy route over more ridges past breathtaking Sass de Mura. The day concludes at pastoral haven

Rifugio Boz, where a good night's sleep is desirable in view of the rigours ahead.

Old military tracks snake their way along ledges both natural and man-made, in the company of felty clumps of unusually large edelweiss that sprout from apparently bare rock. Some acrobatic ability and steadiness of foot comes in handy as the path narrows to a goat track with a series of dizzy, exposed passages on the approach to Sasso di Scarnia. Thereafter it's an exhilarating roller-coaster route sticking tight to the crest line amidst jumbles of fallen boulders and sweeping views back to the Pale di San Martino group. One memorable landmark is the gently sloping pasture basin Busa delle Vette, where flocks of sheep and cows graze beneath stark Monte Pietena. Just around the corner stands **Rifugio dal Piaz**. Then it's only a matter of an hour and a half to the trek's conclusion at **Croce d'Aune**, a short bus trip away from beautiful walled Renaissance town of Feltre.

The tricky climb to Forcella di Comedon

Trek 20

Julian Alps Traverse

by Roy Clark and Justi Carey

To many the Julian Alps mean Triglav. Not surprisingly this, the highest of all Julian peaks, is very much a totem for the Slovene people and the focus of what has become almost a pilgrimage. But Triglav, for all its outstanding limestone architecture and symbolism, is only part of the range described by the great mountain explorer Tom Longstaff as 'a dreamworld, sundered from time, full of unbelievable hidden nooks, of unsuspected passages, of sudden visions of cliffs which cannot be real. Surely there is no other mountain land like this.' With a two-week traverse of the Julian Alps, which begins with the ascent of Triglav, trekkers have an opportunity to explore Longstaff's 'dreamworld' for themselves along a route which day after day reveals scenes of exotic beauty: not just mountains, ridges and summits, but glorious valleys with the clearest of streams and meadows full of flowers.

Looking west from the summit of Triglav

The Julian Alps, a unique harmonious bonding of sheer limestone peaks and pretty mountain pastures

Route summary

Location	Julian Alps, Slovenia
Start	Mojstrana in the Sava valley
Finish	Bohinjska Bistrica
Distance	122km
Duration	14–15 days
Maximum altitude	2864m
Accommodation	Mountain huts and/or occasional B&B, camping etc.
Grade	First part (8 days): Demanding; Second part (6–7 days): Moderate
Guidebook	*Trekking in Slovenia* and *The Julian Alps of Slovenia* by Justi Carey and Roy Clark (Cicerone Press, 2009 and 2010)

We first became interested in the Julian Alps in 2002 – our previous two years in the Scottish Highlands had involved wetter-than-average summers and we sought to redress the balance by a trip to the Alps with hopefully some sunshine thrown in. Browsing the web, a slogan caught our attention: 'Slovenia, the sunny side of the Alps.' Almost before we knew it, things had developed from a two-week holiday to something more long term. We were on our way to Slovenia to live, work and explore a country where 90% of the land is over 300m high, and where the glorious Julian Alps are just one part of an apparently unending mountain landscape.

This trek through the highlights of the Julian Alps is part of a much longer route, the Slovene High-Level Route, or Transverzala, which winds its way across the country, finishing at the Adriatic coast and taking around seven weeks to complete. We had heard of the route long before we began to think about walking it ourselves; coming across waymarks with a number 1 beside them we asked around to find out what it meant. Since there was nothing written about it in English, we would have to find out on our own. The Transverzala: the first way-marked long-distance Alpine route in Europe was declared open in 1954.

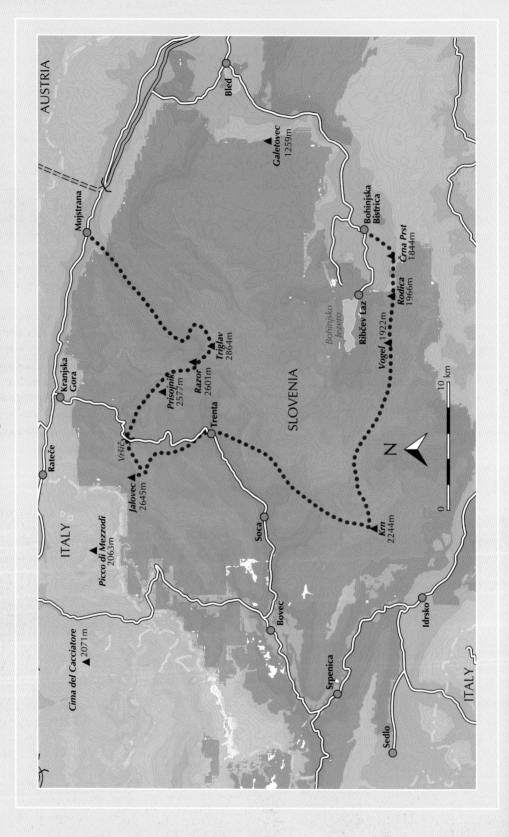

Julian Alps Traverse

AUSTRIA

Bled

Galetovec
1259m

Bohinjska
Bistrica

Mojstrana

Črna Prst
1844m

Rodica
1966m

Ribčev Laz

Bohinjsko
Jezero

Kranjska
Gora

Triglav
2864m

Prisojnik
2577m

Razor
2601m

Trenta

Vogel 1922m

SLOVENIA

Rateče

Vršič

Jalovec
2645m

Soča

Krn
2244m

ITALY

Picco di Mezzodi
2063m

Cima del Cacciatore
2071m

Bovec

Srpenica

Idrsko

ITALY

Sedlo

N

10 km

0

Covering almost a third of the Transverzala, our trek falls naturally into two parts – the first part, eight days in all, tackles the ridges of the main Julian Alps massif, including Slovenia's highest mountain, Triglav (2864m). It continues over steep high ridges for the next few days before crossing the summit of the Vršič pass to ascend Jalovec – one of the country's most beautiful mountains – then descends into the picturesque Trenta valley. The second part, taking six or seven days, regains the higher ground of the Triglav Lakes valley and Krn, and ends by following the gentler, flower-strewn Lower Bohinj Ridge.

A word on equipment needed: the first part involves demanding scrambling with sections of considerable exposure. Pegs, rungs and cables protect the way, but we strongly recommend that you take via ferrata type belay equipment and a climbing helmet. A high level of fitness is essential, and some moderate rock climbing experience would be an advantage – even a necessity if the 'Jubilee' route on Prisojnik is followed.

Mojstrana to Tržaška koča via Triglav

The walk starts gently, from the bus stop on the main road above the village of **Mojstrana** on the road between Jesenice and Kranjska Gora, and follows the river Bistrica through sun-dappled mixed woods to the Aljažev dom (dom means 'mountain hut') at the head of the Vrata valley. Vrata means 'door' or 'gateway', and the valley gives access to Triglav's northern side. This part of the walk has been laid out with information boards relating to the local geography, history and wildlife – don't be tempted to miss it by walking or hitching up the gravel road.

The view of Triglav's north wall from the hut is truly majestic but also somewhat daunting, because the route makes a rising traverse below this great Alpine face before climbing close to its left-hand edge. But these endeavours will follow; first, a short distance along the path brings you to a huge piton and karabiner, a war memorial dedicated to Alpinist Partisan soldiers.

Triglav's north face and the Luknja pass

The Staničev dom

Follow signs for the 'Prag' route, with Triglav's foreboding face rising to your left and the striking Luknja col dominating the view ahead (we will visit this col later on our tour). For now, the way crosses boulders in the river to reach the rocky toes of the great wall. A scramble up a series of

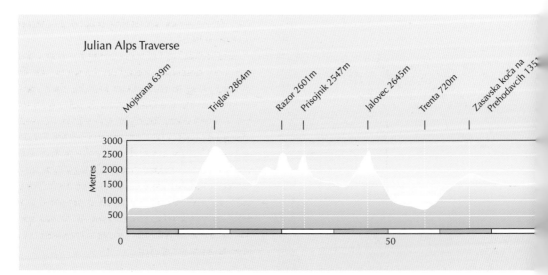

grooves and steps leads to a long traverse, after which height is gained more quickly over steep, broken ground to reach Medvedova skala, the 'bear's crag' – the exciting 25m crux of the Prag route. Two more hours pass as the valley drops away; rests can be taken on airy promontories and boulders where you can drink in the atmosphere of this precipitous landscape, the silence punctuated by the call of choughs. The huge crag of Begunski vrh finally marks a slight easing of steep ground as the route reaches the start of a karst limestone pavement area (Kotel), riven with deep fissures. Ibex are often seen here.

There is a choice for tonight's accommodation: a path leads left to the Dom Valentina Staniča, which stands on the northern edge of this stark mountain kingdom, and another heads right to the big Triglavski dom on Kredarica. The latter is a little further but is closer to tomorrow's goal. If you choose to stay at the Staničev hut, a rising traverse leading to the ridge between Rž and Kredarica will bring you to the Triglavski dom from where most folk tackle the summit. This hut can sleep 200 – it is the highest in Slovenia and equipped with facilities that include a large satellite TV! Cold beer (pivo) or shandy (radler) may help to restore equilibrium after what has been an

exhausting but exhilarating day – but moderation and an early night might be wise, for the morning will bring many of the same rigours and rewards as **Triglav** beckons.

It is difficult to exaggerate the place Triglav has in the hearts of the Slovenes – in many ways it is the soul of the country, and many Slovenes consider it a duty to climb it at least once in their lives. From the dom, the summit is signed one hour, although on a normal summer's day this can easily become two hours as you negotiate crocodiles of people or nervous individuals. The route first ascends the imposing buttress of Mali Triglav, with its delicate traverse along lines of metal pegs and rungs, before continuing along the main ridge, which is wonderfully airy though not too difficult. A final steep scramble brings you to the Aljažev stolp, a metal turret that marks the summit. As Triglav is at least 120m higher than any of the surrounding peaks, the whole of Slovenia now lies at your feet, and what a beautiful land it is! Even the usual noisy bustle from groups of walkers seems muted, touched by a sense of awe and humility instilled by the startlingly powerful vista opening below. However, the aura is often broken by nervous giggles as a unique Slovene initiation ceremony is enacted – a light-hearted spanking of first-time Triglav summiteers – not something usually witnessed on British hills!

After retracing the route along the ridge, the way now descends steeply on the south side of the mountain to reach Dom Planika, then continues towards the Dolič sedlo (saddle) with its hut, where we stay the night. Marvellous views of Miselj vrh's north face emerge to your left, while at its foot lies the tranquil Velo polje pastureland with its typical wooden shepherds' huts. Reaching the rocky saddle below Kanjavec with the Tržaška koča (koča also means hut) beyond can come as a relief, as the route has passed through a landscape which can seem wild and remote if the weather is poor or a storm brewing.

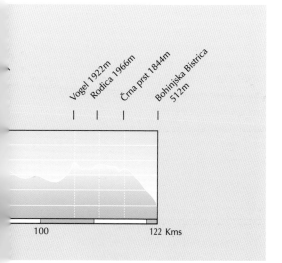

An engineering marvel, the old military track leading from the Dolič sedlo

Tržaška koča to Vršič

Leave the hut on a track that once served as an old military road, carved out of the steep hillside – a spectacular display of engineering. Fierce fighting in both World Wars meant the borders between Slovenia, Italy and Austria were realigned several times, and many old military roads and defensive installations are still strikingly evident in the mountains. A balcony traverse of outstanding beauty above steep slopes of grass and rock, where the shrill call of marmots pierces the warm Alpine air, is followed by steeply descending zigzags to a track that leads left down to the Trenta valley. But we turn right here instead, and ascend to reach the impressive Luknja col at the head of the Vrata valley.

A decision now has to be made: turn left and make a steep ascent to reach the summit of Bavški Gamsovec (2392m) before an even more demanding descent to reach the Pogačnikov dom; or descend a short distance on the Vrata side before turning up the somewhat easier ground of the hanging Sovatna valley. Either way brings you to the Dovška vrata saddle and then on across the karst pavement of the Kriški podi. Take care while crossing this karst wonderland; it would be easy for tired legs to misplace a step between the grikes and fissures. Alpine flowers spring from the rocks and fill inhospitable crevices with abundant colour and radiance, while ibex can be seen wandering between three sparkling mountain tarns. The hut lies within a cirque of mountain ridges in an incredibly beautiful location.

An early start in the cool morning air helps with the steep haul over limestone slabs and scree to reach the Planja sedlo, where you turn right if you wish to include the 2601m summit of **Razor**, one of the peaks that form a majestic

Looking into the deep Trenta valley from the Pogačnikov dom

backdrop to the town of Kranjska Gora. Return to, or continue from, the sedlo on its west side below the massive cliffs of Planja and Razor, to reach a parting of ways. Another decision must now be made according to your abilities or time: left to take a balcony path traversing the southern slopes of the mighty 2547m **Prisojnik** (also known as Prisank), with the option of climbing a series of steep, rocky grooves and runnels that collectively form the mountain's huge south gully leading to the summit; or continue straight ahead for an extremely demanding waymarked route known as the 'Jubilee'. If you do not wish to include the summit in your trek, you can also take the first option but continue past the southern ascent route to reach the Vršič pass.

The Jubilee involves difficult protected scrambling with occasional vertical sections of rock, and traverses paths and ledges high on the mountain's north wall, eventually leading to the summit of Prisojnik. The mountain has two immense natural rock windows; you climb through the eastern one on the Jubilee route. As you descend the western ridge you pass the other window and peer into its dizzying depths from a rocky perch. Your eye will also be drawn to another alluring jewel that lies further west – Jalovec, an outlier of the Julian Alps massif. When seen from the north, this is a mountain of superlative form and beauty, its appearance not unlike a vast crystal that cuts cleanly through the impossibly blue Alpine skies. From the south, as climbed on this trek, it is still a very tempting proposition.

Vršič to Trenta

Accommodation can be found at two huts on the Vršič pass; however, if you feel the need for showers and home comforts, the bus can be taken north to Kranjska Gora with all its shops and tour-ist amenities, or south to Trenta for camping and limited B&B accommodation. Alternatively, stay on the bus to Bovec (about 14km south of Trenta), a much larger village with most of its trade based on outdoor activities like canoeing, rafting, para-penting and skiing. Either way involves a spec-tacular ride down tight hairpins with stunningly beautiful views.

From Vršič, another superb balcony path traverses high above the Zadnja Trenta valley towards Zavetišče pod Špičkom. This small hut occupies a delightful position below the pyramid rock pillar of Spiček and can be reached in four hours. Although this is a short day, after the pre-vious day's efforts we would recommend a halt here, saving Jalovec for the next day. So, take your time as you walk along the flower-strewn path and savour the amazing views that unfold through breaks in the treeline, looking back southeast towards Triglav standing proudly above vast, forested hillsides, and straight ahead to the imposing peak of Bavški Grintavec, dominating the skyline. Jalovec rises high above to your right, but it does not look quite so precipitous from here as it does from the north.

The next morning, cross a boulder field and scree slope to reach a soaring ridge line where the ascent proper begins. Height gain is dramatic and vast depths open up as you gaze down to the hanging valley of Griva, but you should have long since found your rhythm and will soon find your-self on the rocky col between Veliki Ozebnik and **Jalovec**. Rock steps and grooves gain the ridge crest that leads to the 2645m summit of Jalovec. You become aware of the colossal void below you on the peak's north side, as you spy the toy-like hut in the darkly forested Tamar valley. Jalovec deservedly earns the fond place it has in the minds and hearts of Slovenian mountaineers.

On the path that leads from Vršič to Jalovec

Descend to the Trenta valley, where accommodation can be found at the small Koča by the source of the incredibly clear luminous waters of the Soča river, gushing from the limestone and wending past delightful shingle-roofed farmsteads with small fields of myriad flowers.

The next day can be considered a delightful stroll, a chance to recuperate after a week in the high mountains. Follow the Soča trail, a signed path that leads to the small village of **Trenta** passing many points of interest, which include the monument to Julius Kugy (a great botanist and pioneer explorer of the Julian Alps) and the Mlinarica gorge and waterfall, carved by the river of the same name. Trenta marks the end of the first part of the trek, where you can call a halt, stay overnight, or, if you are feeling fit, simply continue on to the next koča.

Trenta to Krn

A short walk up the Vršič road takes you to bend No. 50, where a track heads east signed for the Pogačnikov dom. Follow this before winding your way up the picturesque Zadnjica valley, passing more rustic farmsteads where the locals scythe the meadows, the air filled with the sweet scent of freshly cut grass and flowers. As the valley steepens and a more mountainous scene unfolds, chamois can be seen drinking from the clear waters of a spring that trickles down the upper slopes. Rest awhile at a small saddle called Čez dol, before a well-constructed military road leads you to the **Zasavska koča na Prehodavcih**. This is another hut in an outrageously scenic location. As the evening air begins to cool and house lights flicker below in the Trenta valley, you can relax and contemplate another wholly satisfying day spent in the Julian Alps and eagerly imagine splendours yet to come.

The next day is another highlight as the route makes a descent of the Triglav Lakes valley. Alpine lakes shimmer in the sunlight like emeralds, a backdrop of Yosemite-style peaks and crags tower above bright green larches, all to be enjoyed on a day that involves relatively easy walking compared to the previous high mountain toils – what more could you wish for!

A night spent at either Koča pod Bogatinom or Dom na Komni coincides with a feeling that you are entering a different world. Having left the main massif of the Julian Alps you are heading towards a slightly lower, gentler range of peaks – the lower Bohinj ridge – though there is one notable exception to this, the next peak, **Krn** at 2244m.

Although Krn is distant from the main massif, it has all the attributes of the Julian Alps – wild rocky corries, steep scree slopes and bare limestone crags. However, its ascent is relatively straightforward. It should be mentioned that Koča pod Bogatinom was once a First World War field hospital, and during the next section of this trek reminders of the warfare that once raged in these mountains become more starkly evident in the form of rusted weaponry, tangled barbed wire, dugouts and trench defences.

The way to Krn passes Slovenia's largest high mountain lake – Krnsko jezero – an idyllic place to while away some time before starting the upward pull that leads to boulder fields and steep screes below the grassy summit shoulder of Krn. Just metres below the summit on the south side, the little hut with the big name – Gomiščkovo zavetišče na Krnu – is tonight's accommodation. This little haven appears suspended in the air above the steepest grass slopes imaginable that drop like a green curtain on the south side of Krn.

Krn to Bohinjska Bistrica

Make sure you replenish your water supply, as tomorrow involves a long route on sunny southern slopes. From Krn, the trail traverses below the steep crags of Batognica to reach the lonely Prag col at 2068m – alternatively, ascend a series of stone and concrete steps, made by soldiers during the hellish mountain battles of the First World War, that lead over Batognica's summit to arrive at the col. Beautiful peaks like Vrh nad Peski fix the eye as the trail ahead sweeps across sunny

Looking back along the flower-strewn Bohinj ridge from Črna prst

screes in a level contour, and Triglav and the Julian Alps float in the blue skies to your left, looking strangely detached and distant. You've crossed the very best of Slovenia's highest range and will now be rewarded with superb walking over the gentler tops of the Bohinj mountains – but needless to say, your guard mustn't be lowered too soon, as these are still high hills giving long days. This is one such day, eight hours from Krn to the next koča at Planina Razor, but the route is stunning. There is a feeling of remoteness to this section, but flowers dazzle the eye and human activity proclaims itself in the form of picturesque pasture buildings at Planina Dobrenjščica and Planina na Kalu.

Koča Planina Razor rests in the shade of pine trees and is a most welcome sight after the distance covered today. A time to try the delicious sweet Slovene dumplings (štruklji) and restore your energy, for the next day involves an equal effort. A steep haul up to the summit of **Vogel** (1922m) is accomplished in the fresh morning air

and the Bohinj ridge now stretches before you to the east. An escape from the ridge can be made from Šija (1800m) down ski slopes to reach the Vogel Ski Hotel, where a gondola can be taken to reach the valley floor and scenic Lake Bohinj.

The rounded bulk of **Rodica** (1966m) is added to the tally and for a while the ridge narrows to a rocky crest. This is a natural botanical garden of exceptional worth, and as the final top, **Črna prst**, is approached, flowers become even more abundant and lush, with larger, more exotic varieties carpeting the grassy ridge. *Črna prst* means 'black soil' which gives a clue to the mountain's exceptional flora. At the summit the dom awaits tired travellers and, apart from the descent, our journey is complete. A final night is spent high on the ridge in the warm comforts of a Slovene dom where you may reflect on your experiences of a tour of indescribable beauty in a landscape of dreams.

Next day make your descent to Bohinjska Bistrica, where buses and trains link to major stations.

Crossing a grassy meadow on the way to Krn

APPENDIX A
Useful contacts

Alpine Clubs & Mountaineering Organisations based in the UK

Alpine Club
55 Charlotte Road
London EC2A 3QF
☎ 020 7613 0755
www.alpine-club.org.uk
The Alpine Club is the world's oldest mountaineering club, catering mainly for those who climb in the Alps and Greater Ranges.

Austrian Alpine Club (UK Branch)
12a North Street
Wareham
Dorset BH20 4AG
☎ 01929 556 870
www.aacuk.org.uk
Benefits of AAC membership include reduced accommodation costs in alpine huts in most European countries, and annual rescue and repatriation insurance cover.

British Mountaineering Council
177–179 Burton Road
West Didsbury
Manchester M20 7ZA
☎ 0161 445 6111
www.thebmc.co.uk
The BMC represents the mountain interests of British activists, arranges insurance cover and can offer reciprocal rights for members in alpine huts.

British Association of International Mountain Leaders (BAIML)
Siabod Cottage
Capel Curig
Conwy LL24 0ES
☎ 01690 720272
www.baiml.org
The BAIML represents qualified trekking guides working abroad.

Map Suppliers

Cordee
11 Jacknell Road
Didswell Bridge Industrial Estate
Hinckley LE10 3BS
☎ 01455 611185
www.cordee.co.uk

Stanfords
12–14 Long Acre
London WC2W 9LP
☎ 020 7836 1321
www.stanfords.co.uk

The Map Shop
15 High Street
Upton-upon-Severn
WR8 0HJ
www.themapshop.co.uk

Tourist information

Austrian National Tourist Office
9–11 Richmond Buildings
London W1D 3HF
☎ 020 7629 0461
www.austria.info/uk

French Government Tourist Office
178 Piccadilly
London W1J 9AL
☎ 0090 6824 4123
www.franceguide.com

Italian State Tourist Board
1 Princes Street
London W1B 2AY
☎ 020 7408 1254
www.italiantouristboard.co.uk
www.enit.it

Slovenian Tourist Office
10 Little College Street
London SW1P 3SH
☎ 0870 225 5305
www.slovenia.info

Switzerland Travel Centre
30 Bedford Street
London WC2E 9ED
☎ 00800 100 200 30
www.stc.co.uk

APPENDIX B
Glossary for trekkers

alp/alpe/alm	a summer farm, usually above the treeline
col	mountain pass, or saddle
combe	mountain basin, similar to a cirque but usually more gently formed
trek	a multi-day journey on foot

French

aiguille	needle-like peak
arête	ridge – see also crête
carte de randonnées	walking map
couloir	gully
cirque	steep, three-sided valley headwall
crête	ridge – see also arête
dortoir	dormitory
gardien(ne)	hut warden – male/female
gîte d'étape	walkers' hostel
mauvais pas	bad step, or difficult place
plan	plateau or plain
sentier	path
télépherique	cableway
télésiège	chairlift

German

alpenverein	alpine club
aussichtspunkt	viewpoint
bergweg	mountain path
fels	rock
firn	snowfield
grat	ridge
höhenweg	high path
hüttenwirt	hut warden
joch	mountain pass, or saddle
klettersteig	via ferrata, or protected way; literally climbing path
kopf	peak
lawine	avalanche
massenlager	dormitory – also matratzenlager, literally 'mattress room'

materialseilbahn	mountain hut's goods lift
moräne	moraine
nur für Geübte	only for the experienced
scharte	narrow pass
schlucht	gorge
stausee	reservoir
steinschlag	rockfall
trockenraum	drying room
wanderweg	footpath
wanderkarte	walking map
zeltplatz	campsite

Italian

alta via	high route
altopiano	high-altitude plateau
bivacco	unmanned mountain hut
bocca	mountain pass – also bocchetta
campeggio	campsite
carta dei sentieri	walking map
cima	summit, or peak
conca	see cirque
forcella	mountain pass
funivia	cable-car
passo	mountain pass – see also porta
porta	mountain pass – see also passo
posto tappa	a walkers' hostel
sentiero	path
via ferrata	protected path, or 'iron way'

Slovene

dolina	valley
dom/koča	mountain hut
góra	mountain
grebén	ridge
jézero	lake
planina	alp pasture
sedlo	saddle, or pass
sneg	snow
stezá	path

INDEX

CICERONE GUIDES TO TREKS IN THIS BOOK

Through the Italian Alps
ISBN 9781852844172

Tour of the Queyras
ISBN 9781852845100

Tour of the Oisans
ISBN 9781852845506

Tour of the Vanoise
ISBN 9781852845902

The Gran Paradiso
ISBN 9781852844998

Tour of Mont Blanc
ISBN 9781852845322

The GR5 Trail
ISBN 9781852845339

Chamonix to Zermatt
ISBN 9781852845131

Tour of the Jungfrau Region
ISBN 9781852845964

Alpine Pass Route
ISBN 9781852844059

Tour of the Matterhorn
ISBN 9781852844721

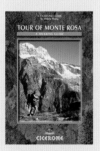

Tour of Monte Rosa
ISBN 9781852844547

Trekking in the Stubai Alps
ISBN 9781852846237

Trekking in the Zillertal Alps
ISBN 9781852843700

Walking in Austria
ISBN 9781852845384

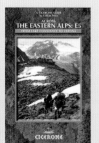

Across the Eastern Alps: E5
ISBN 9781852844929

Trekking in the Dolomites
ISBN 9781852845636

Julian Alps of Slovenia
ISBN 9781852844387

These are just some of many guides to walking, mountaineering, climbing and cycling in the Alps published by Cicerone. For a full list of our current titles, please visit our website: www.cicerone.co.uk.

CICERONE

LISTING OF CICERONE GUIDES

Cycle Touring in Switzerland
Cycling in the French Alps
Cycling the Canal du Midi
Cycling the River Loire
The Danube Cycleway
The Grand Traverse of the Massif Central
The Way of St James

AFRICA

Climbing in the Moroccan Anti-Atlas
Kilimanjaro: A Complete Trekker's Guide
Mountaineering in the Moroccan High Atlas
Trekking in the Atlas Mountains
Walking in the Drakensberg

ALPS – CROSS-BORDER ROUTES

100 Hut Walks in the Alps
Across the Eastern Alps: E5
Alpine Ski Mountaineering
  1 Western Alps
  2 Central and Eastern Alps
Chamonix to Zermatt
Snowshoeing
Tour of Mont Blanc
Tour of Monte Rosa
Tour of the Matterhorn
Trekking in the Alps
Walking in the Alps
Walks and Treks in the Maritime Alps

PYRENEES AND FRANCE/SPAIN CROSS-BORDER ROUTES

Rock Climbs In The Pyrenees
The GR10 Trail
The Mountains of Andorra
The Pyrenean Haute Route
The Pyrenees
The Way of St James
  France
  Spain
Through the Spanish Pyrenees: GR11
Walks and Climbs in the Pyrenees

AUSTRIA

Trekking in Austria's Hohe Tauern
Trekking in the Stubai Alps
Trekking in the Zillertal Alps
Walking in Austria

EASTERN EUROPE

The High Tatras
The Mountains of Romania
Walking in Bulgaria's National Parks
Walking in Hungary

FRANCE

Ecrins National Park
GR20: Corsica
Mont Blanc Walks
The Cathar Way
The GR5 Trail
The Robert Louis Stevenson Trail
Tour of the Oisans: The GR54
Tour of the Queyras
Tour of the Vanoise
Trekking in the Vosges and Jura

Vanoise Ski Touring
Walking in Provence
Walking in the Cathar Region
Walking in the Cevennes
Walking in the Dordogne
Walking in the Haute Savoie
  North & South
Walking in the Languedoc
Walking in the Tarentaise and Beaufortain Alps
Walking on Corsica

GERMANY

Germany's Romantic Road
Walking in the Bavarian Alps
Walking in the Harz Mountains
Walking the River Rhine Trail

HIMALAYA

Annapurna: A Trekker's Guide
Bhutan
Everest: A Trekker's Guide
Garhwal and Kumaon: A Trekker's and Visitor's
  Guide
Kangchenjunga: A Trekker's Guide
Langtang with Gosainkund and Helambu: A
  Trekker's Guide
Manaslu: A Trekker's Guide
The Mount Kailash Trek

IRELAND

Irish Coastal Walks
The Irish Coast to Coast Walk
The Mountains of Ireland

ITALY

Gran Paradiso
Italy's Sibillini National Park
Shorter Walks in the Dolomites
Through the Italian Alps
Trekking in the Apennines
Trekking in the Dolomites
Via Ferratas of the Italian Dolomites: Vols 1 & 2
Walking in Sicily
Walking in the Central Italian Alps
Walking in the Dolomites
Walking in Tuscany
Walking on the Amalfi Coast

MEDITERRANEAN

Jordan – Walks, Treks, Caves, Climbs and
  Canyons
The Ala Dag
The High Mountains of Crete
The Mountains of Greece
Treks and Climbs in Wadi Rum, Jordan
Walking in Malta
Western Crete

NORTH AMERICA

British Columbia
The Grand Canyon
The John Muir Trail
The Pacific Crest Trail

SOUTH AMERICA

Aconcagua and the Southern Andes
Torres del Paine

SCANDINAVIA

Trekking in Greenland
Walking in Norway

SLOVENIA, CROATIA AND MONTENEGRO

The Julian Alps of Slovenia
The Mountains of Montenegro
Trekking in Slovenia
Walking in Croatia

SPAIN AND PORTUGAL

Costa Blanca Walks
  1 West
  2 East
Mountain Walking in Southern Catalunya
The Mountains of Central Spain
Trekking through Mallorca
Via de la Plata
Walking in Madeira
Walking in Mallorca
Walking in the Algarve
Walking in the Canary Islands
  2 East
Walking in the Cordillera Cantabrica
Walking in the Sierra Nevada
Walking on La Gomera and El Hierro
Walking on La Palma
Walking the GR7 in Andalucia
Walks and Climbs in the Picos de Europa

SWITZERLAND

Alpine Pass Route
Central Switzerland
The Bernese Alps
Tour of the Jungfrau Region
Walking in the Valais
Walking in Ticino
Walks in the Engadine

TECHNIQUES

Geocaching in the UK
Indoor Climbing
Lightweight Camping
Map and Compass
Mountain Weather
Moveable Feasts
Rock Climbing
Sport Climbing
The Book of the Bivvy
The Hillwalker's Guide to Mountaineering
The Hillwalker's Manual

MINI GUIDES

Avalanche!
Navigating with a GPS
Navigation
Pocket First Aid and Wilderness Medicine
Snow

For full and up-to-date information on our
ever-expanding list of guides,
visit our website:
www.cicerone.co.uk.

Cicerone's mission is to inform and inspire by
providing the best guides to exploring the world

Since its foundation 40 years ago, Cicerone has specialised in
publishing guidebooks and has built a reputation for quality
and reliability. It now publishes nearly 300 guides to the major
destinations for outdoor enthusiasts, including Europe, UK and the
rest of the world.

Written by leading and committed specialists, Cicerone guides are
recognised as the most authoritative. They are full of information,
maps and illustrations so that the user can plan and complete a
successful and safe trip or expedition – be it a long face climb, a
walk over Lakeland fells, an alpine cycling tour, a Himalayan trek
or a ramble in the countryside.

With a thorough introduction to assist planning, clear diagrams,
maps and colour photographs to illustrate the terrain and route,
and accurate and detailed text, Cicerone guides are designed for
ease of use and access to the information.

If the facts on the ground change, or there is any aspect of a guide
that you think we can improve, we are always delighted to hear
from you.

Cicerone Press
2 Police Square Milnthorpe Cumbria LA7 7PY
Tel: 015395 62069 Fax: 015395 63417
info@cicerone.co.uk www.cicerone.co.uk

CICERONE